*Nicole
Kidman*

Nicole Kidman

THE BIOGRAPHY

Lucy Ellis & Bryony Sutherland

AURUM PRESS

First published in Great Britain 2002 by Aurum Press Ltd
25 Bedford Avenue, London WC1B 3AT

A catalogue record for this book is available from the British Library.

ISBN 1 85410 859 X

10 9 8 7 6 5 4 3 2 1
2006   2005   2004   2003   2002

Designed and typeset by M Rules
Printed and bound in Great Britain by MPG Books Ltd, Bodmin

For
AE, HF, JH, PM, BN, PN

Contents

Acknowledgements

Our first thanks must go to Nicole Kidman for being an inspiration. This book has been an absolute pleasure to write.

We would like to thank the following for their assistance with research and interviews:

Australian Children's Television Foundation (Laura Treglown), Australian Film, Television & Radio School (Elisabeth McDonald), Australian Screen Directors Association (Sylvia Mulaahmetovics), Australian Theatre for Young People (Michael, Jessica Read-Brain), North Sydney Girls' High School (Carol Conomos, Margaret FitzGerald, Janet Grace, Jackie Stevenson), ScreenSound Australia (Elizabeth Taggart-Speers), Sydney Theatre Company (Matt Andrews, Rachel Speers).

Felicity Blake, Wanda Blanch, Jillian Bowen, Charlotte Broughton, Tam Dean Burn and Marcia, Ken Cameron, John Cann, Tanya Carswell, Fred Chate, Neil Clugston, Guillaume Colboc, Philippa Dennis, Clare Ellis, Norma Farnes, John Flaus, Kathryn Fleming, Nanette Fox, Guy Hazell, Jodi Heaston, Anita Heiss, John Ingrassia, Michael Jenkins, Rita Kew-Moss, Ramona Koval, Peter Lathan, Denny Lawrence, George Lee, Rebecca Lewis, Wendy Millyard, Nicole Pearl, Kath Perry, John Prater,

Tim Richards, Stan Rosenfield, Pat and Howard Rubie, Gwen Rudman, Bernadette Ryan, Dee Dee Sadler, Bryon Schreckengost, Jo Smith, Pete Sumner, Richard Taylor, Barbara Thrussell, Michael Tighe, Bob Weis and Lou, Francis Yeoh.

Some interviewees have requested anonymity, so we have respected their wishes.

Sincere thanks must go to our fabulous Australian team of researchers: Michael Bodey, Roger and Alison Foyle, Melissa Whitelaw.

Special thanks to Karen Ings for being human and Bill McCreadie for his dedication to this book. Thanks also to Gabrielle Allen for the pictures and everyone at Aurum Press and Trafalgar Square.

We salute the following for changing (or saving!) our lives in their own special ways: Kevin Ashcroft, Elizabeth Haylett, Natalia Marshall.

Mention should be made of The Singing Budgie, Johnson & Johnson, Pizza Express, Mickey's ears, Nobby, Ivy and Violet from the office (whatcha forkin' doin', woman?). Also to the two seagulls who died during the making of *Days Of Thunder*.

We send our love and appreciation to our long-suffering husbands and families. What an incredible year!

Lucy Ellis & Bryony Sutherland
May 2002

Picture Credits

All Action: page 14 *bottom*.
Big Pictures: page 8 *top right*; page 9 *bottom right*; page 10 *top, centre left, centre right* and *bottom right*; page 12 *bottom right*; page 13 *bottom*; page 15 *top right*; page 16 *top left*.
Benainous-Duclos/Gamma/Katz: page 13 *centre left*.
Camera Press: page 4 *bottom left & right*; page 5 *centre*; page 7 *top left*.
Columbia/courtesy Kobal: page 5 *bottom* (photographer: Merrick Morton).
Columbia/Gamma/Katz: page 6 *bottom*.
Gamma/Katz: page 4 *top right*.
Getty Images/Paul Harris/OnLine: page 10 *bottom left*.
Getty Images/Joan Marcus/Liaison: page 11 *bottom right*.
Jones/Gamma/Katz: page 15 *centre left*.
King/Gamma/Katz: page 4 *top left*.
Lafargue-Lenhof/Gamma/Katz: page 12 *second from bottom, right*.
Lenhof/Gamma/Katz: page 11 *bottom left*.
Limelight Productions/courtesy Kobal: page 3 *bottom left*.

PROLOGUE

Who Is Nicole Kidman?

I'm someone who likes to put her cards on the table. I like to be able to talk to people about who I am, what I am, what I experience. I like to be very open and free about all parts of my life.

When Nicole Kidman permits interviews, she is surprisingly accessible. She captures the public's imagination with her warm, down-to-earth nature. And that laugh — an all-encompassing guffaw which never fails to infect those present.

On the surface, she's a beautiful woman in the prime of life with a slender figure, delicate features, porcelain complexion and volatile hair. She never hides behind her height, instead drawing on her nigh-on 6-foot frame to devastating effect. But underneath, her amiable personality hides a complex woman of intelligence, independence, ambition, romance, *joie de vivre*.

'I think you have to live life to the full, otherwise you have nothing to draw on,' she said at twenty-two, poised on the brink of leaving behind everything she held dear for the great unknown. She has liberally applied this motto to every aspect of her being.

Nicole's unconventional upbringing undoubtedly forged her open-minded perspective on life. Her Australian parents were both liberal and unorthodox. Discipline and control came from her biochemist father, and independence and feminism from her mother. As a teenager, Nicole forfeited a crucial year of her blossoming career to nurse her mother through breast cancer.

A restless traveller, she has visited much of the world. Aged just seventeen, she backpacked around Europe with a Dutchman twice her age, whom she'd only known for a month.

Relationships are of vital importance to Nicole. Many potted biographies overlook the fact that she engaged in two major high-profile love affairs prior to her ten-year marriage to Hollywood's most bankable heart-throb.

Nicole's heart ruled her head when she fell hopelessly in love with Tom Cruise. He left his wife: she left her boyfriend, beloved family and an established career to move halfway around the world to be with him. At the start of her reign as Mrs Tom Cruise, twenty-three-year-old Nicole was totally overshadowed by his status, but eventually her individuality and immense talent shone through.

Plagued by rumours of infertility, Nicole discovered a formidable maternal urge when she and Tom adopted a girl and a boy of differing races. Although forcing her children to conform to her nomadic lifestyle, she is a devoted mother and fiercely protective of her family.

Being a working mum only makes her more determined to prove her ability as an actress; as *Vanity Fair* aptly commented, 'She has pursued her career with the relentlessness of a heat-seeking missile.'

A professional artiste for the last two decades, Nicole started young. Precocious nativity appearances had nothing on her startling stage debut in *Spring Awakening*: at just fourteen, Nicole played a fifty-year-old woman begging for sex. Then, with ten films and television series under her belt, she tackled the award-winning transformation of Megan Goddard in *Vietnam*. Hooking up with Kennedy Miller Productions at nineteen provided her first major break – her immortal portrayal of thirtysomething Rae Ingram in the groundbreaking thriller *Dead Calm*.

Career then gave way to personal life for a while, but Nicole fought back. Appearing as the malicious Suzanne Stone in *To Die For* kickstarted her comeback, and from then on Nicole started to select her films because of the director rather than the script. She worked with Jane Campion in the highbrow *The Portrait Of A Lady* and Stanley Kubrick in the exploratory *Eyes Wide Shut*. Retreading the boards, she bared all in the provocative *The Blue Room*. Since then, she has glided through the musical *Moulin Rouge!*, chilled audiences in the supernatural *The Others*, paid homage to Virginia

Woolf in *The Hours* and been traumatized in the psychological drama *Dogville*. Although the Oscar remains elusive, Nicole has garnered her fair share of trophies, including Golden Globes, Logies and AFI Awards.

The extensive and extreme research Nicole undertakes for all her roles is not common knowledge. She has worn heavy iron shackles, witnessed drug-free childbirth, watched trashy television for three days, addressed sexual jealousy within her marriage, studied several languages, ridden horses and swung on the trapeze in the name of her craft.

Indeed, pushing back the boundaries is Nicole's forte. Her love of adrenalin sports is unlimited: she has jumped out of planes, performed aerobatics, scaled volcanoes and swum in snake-infested seas – leading to at least four near-death experiences.

Despite having left school at sixteen without qualifications, the actress is no dunce. Her parents may have fought a losing battle in their attempts to send her to university, but Nicole has educated herself by voraciously reading the work of authors including Fyodor Dostoevsky, Emily Dickinson, the Brontë sisters, Henry James and George Eliot. She also speaks Italian and Russian, and has recently applied for a helicopter licence. Her love of the performing arts extends to various singing forays, past and present, and she is also keen to write and direct.

Nicole's self-deprecating candour about 2001, her *annus horribilis*, has endeared her to the world. But that's not to say what happened hasn't affected her deeply. In her typically frank manner she looks to the future: 'I'm an actress and the show must go on.' Still, there's an air of mystery about Nicole Kidman that demands interpretation, inviting closer inspection of her incredible life.

> *To be an actor you have to have a certain amount of madness in you. That's why, when people meet you and you seem very together, they are quite surprised – they don't see you behind the closed doors.*

I

An Outsider

Nicole Kidman is often said to be a descendant of Sidney Kidman, the wealthy Australian cattle baron. But, as he was born in Surrey, England, a decade after her real ancestors moved down under, any direct lineage is impossible. Her roots are, in truth, far humbler.

'My dad is of Irish descent, my mother is English and Scottish, so I cover that whole area,' she explains. 'My great-great grandparents went to Australia in 1839 with ten children to a penal colony. These people had guts.'

At the end of the eighteenth century, transportation of Britain's more violent criminals was deemed preferable to capital punishment – the idea being to send them as far away as possible. The government had been looking for an alternative penal settlement, having lost the North American colonies in the American Revolution. Captain James Cook recommended the newly discovered land of Australia, and the first fleet of 750 convicts was duly dispatched to Sydney in 1788.

Life in the penal colony was tough. The offenders didn't have the skills to tame the arid land and living conditions were basic. Fortunately, Nicole's ancestors were transferred at a time when the system was changing. After

1840, a probation system allowed convicts to apply for a ticket-of-leave before the end of their sentence; early discharge was conditional on good behaviour. A further influx of Britons, together with a successful sheep-farming industry and the gold rush of the 1850s, reinvented Australia. Emancipated criminals were subsequently allowed to buy land and thus become respectable citizens.

Nicole's paternal ancestors followed this migration pattern, and, as she suggests, they were resilient people. Arthur David and Margaret Emily Mary Kidman (née Callachor) were Roman Catholics and produced four children. The youngest, Angela, was born in 1950 when Margaret was forty-eight, and, unconventionally, she ran a business while raising her expanding family. The eldest, Antony, was an intellectual and handsome man who, after years of dedicated medical study, became a respected biochemist and psychologist.

Dr Kidman met Janelle, the daughter of British Methodists Arnold Eric Stuart and Gertrude Joyce Glenny (née Hurst and known as Joyce). Antony and Janelle, by then in their mid-twenties, married in Sydney on 18 December 1963.

Antony's vocation took the newly-weds thousands of miles across the ocean to Hawaii, the collective name for the idyllic string of 132 volcanic islands covering 1600 miles of the Pacific. Becoming the fiftieth state of America in 1959, Hawaii's capital is Honolulu (confusingly, on the island of Oahu, not Hawaii). There Dr Kidman worked long hours on a medical research scholarship at the University of Hawaii, while his wife found employment teaching nursing.

After three years of marriage, Janelle fell pregnant and, although far away from their native country, the couple were thrilled to start a family. A healthy baby girl was born on 20 June 1967 in a Honolulu hospital. They called her Nicole Mary Kidman, her middle name in deference to her paternal grandmother, but to friends and family she soon became simply 'Nic'.

Again Antony's profession prompted a move: now they exchanged the tropics of Hawaii for the cooler climes of Washington. While he immersed himself in more research, this time on a grant from the National Institute of Health, Janelle continued to teach. Nicole's memories of these early years in America are scant but fond. 'I have a vague recollection of it being very cold, with lots of snow,' she says. 'I remember eating snow and my parents throwing snowballs at each other!' Not something she would experience again for many years to come.

When Nicole was three years old, the family expanded with the arrival of a baby sister, Antonia, and the Kidmans were soon travelling once more. In 1971 they returned to their Australian roots, settling in Longueville, a suburb of the Lane Cove municipality in the Greater Sydney region. The upmarket community was a beautiful backdrop for the sisters' childhood, with its tree-lined streets, rolling hills, proximity to the harbour and expanse of nearby beaches. Meanwhile, the bond between the siblings grew strong.

The young girls were now surrounded by their extended family of uncles, aunts, cousins and grandparents. Nicole was especially fond of her maternal grandmother, the unique Scotswoman Joyce Glenny, and her paternal grandfather, Arthur Kidman, whom she intriguingly describes as 'a gambler, who won and lost fortunes'.

But it is her parents who had the greatest influence on her life. Physically, Nicole's features resemble Janelle's, while her pale, freckly skin and curly hair are inherited from Antony. Unfortunately, in the sweltering Australian climate, Nicole's colouring forced her to spend much of her childhood slathered in sun cream and hiding under big hats. With tall parents, she and Antonia were destined to be positively Amazonian. Nicole grew up left-handed, allergic to the common bumble bee and scared of butterflies.

Antony and Janelle were liberated parents, allowing the girls a generous amount of freedom. Yet at the same time they imposed strict standards.

'My mother was a strong feminist and a tough lady,' says Nicole, 'and my father always used the phrase when we were growing up: "With love, but firm". Believe me, I grew up with all the rules and guidelines and boundaries. My sister and I were only allowed to watch half an hour of television a day!'

The doctor and his wife were honest and open, and as much as they loved each other, they inadvertently taught Nicole the reality of life and relationships. 'They came close to divorce many times,' she recalls, 'so yelling and screaming that it's all over – none of that scares me. My mother moved out once, I think, for a couple of weeks, so I don't have a fear of people not coming back.'

Antony would establish the Health Psychology Unit at the local Royal North Shore Hospital in 1973, initially specializing in research about the brain and nervous system. He has since become a well-known psychologist and, as an eminent speaker, hosts seminars and lectures on the relationship between parents and teenagers. He is also the author of a string of books, including the self-help manuals *From Thought To Action*, *Managing Love And Hate* and *Tactics For Change*.

Janelle accommodated her husband's unpredictable career by accepting the role of working mother to help support the family. This loyalty and strength stood out to her impressionable daughters. 'I adore her for her intelligence, her wit and what she gave up to help me and my sister,' says Nicole. 'She worked through our childhood but she was always there for us and gave us a great education and belief in our own power.'

Nicole's enlightened mother fought to instil strong feminist ideologies in her daughters, even going so far as to ban Barbie dolls.

'She thought it was sexist – a male fantasy figure,' smiles Nicole. However, the resourceful tot displayed her own increasingly independent streak and stole one. By her own admission, she had quickly become a rebellious, determined and strong-willed child.

Education did not hold any real interest for Nicole while she was at the nearby Lane Cove Primary School.

'I learned to cross my eyes at school,' she reveals. 'In Australia you all sit on a mat while the teacher writes on the blackboard. We'd get so bored, we'd have eye-crossing competitions. I got quite good at it.'

Nicole's schoolroom behaviour belied a sharp intelligence, but she was yet to be stretched academically. Although she would later prove quite a gifted scholar, she displayed more interest in artistic activities.

Antony and Janelle actively encouraged their children to follow their hearts' desires. Nicole was always entranced by the arts, particularly dance and theatre. 'I was doing ballet classes at four,' she recalls, 'and I have always loved masks.' Her passion for performance grew, and she adored birthday trips to stage shows, falling in love with *The Wizard Of Oz*.

It was no surprise that the little girl yearned for the chance to act, and the school nativity play provided the answer. Her first role, aged five, was as the innkeeper's wife, to which she admits, 'I was one of those terrible kids who said everyone's lines.'

Tempted by her first stab at the stage, Nicole wanted to repeat the experience. 'I auditioned all the time and never got parts,' she remembers, already hindered by her fast-increasing height. Her startling hair colour and precocious nature suggested she would be perfect for the lead in *Annie*. She eagerly waited in line but was turned away at the door where the teachers stood with measuring sticks – Nicole was taller than the child cast as Daddy Warbucks, which simply would not do. Having failed to win any of the traditional lead roles in the following year's Christmas performance, Nicole seized the limelight in an unconventional manner.

'I wanted to be one of the lambs because that was the comedy part,' she says. Her outfit was imaginatively fashioned by Janelle from a sheepskin car-seat cover. 'When Mary was rocking the baby Jesus, I went "Baaaaa,

baaaaa, baaaaa", and of course everyone was in hysterics! This stupid kid trying to upstage Jesus as a sheep!'

Although she got into trouble for turning the show into a farce, Nicole had tasted her first real thrill from acting and realized she wanted more.

'I got a laugh and that was it. I thought, "Wow – this is fun!"'

★

'Even though nobody in my family acted, I think we are all performers in one way or another. We all like to express ourselves,' says Nicole, who began mime classes at the age of eight. Her parents were very enthusiastic; for a start, Antony had appeared in amateur theatricals as a student. 'My father was involved in musical societies and he loves to sing,' she reveals. 'I think he would have loved to be an actor.'

Her mother, too, wanted her daughter to fulfil her dream. Janelle herself had actually hoped to become a doctor, but, as Nicole confirms, Australia was backward in terms of women's liberation. Janelle found her progress hampered and never advanced further than nursing.

'My parents were always extremely supportive,' acknowledges Nicole. 'They allowed me any artistic outlet I wanted.' To that end, when she reached double figures, Nicole started attending drama lessons at Peter Williams's renowned acting school, based in the Phillip Street Theatre in Sydney.

'Each weekend I'd go to the theatre at Phillip Street,' she remembers. 'I used to just lock myself in there for the whole weekend. I thought it was fantastic. I'd be teased a lot though, because I'd be going off to the theatre instead of going to the beach with the boys and all the girls. I felt like an outsider because of that.'

If Nicole felt like an outsider, it only served to make her more independent. At the age of eleven, she described herself as a 'latchkey kid looking after myself and my younger sister'. She was, however, quite bossy when it came to Antonia and tended to rule the roost. 'When I was nine I went to her sister's birthday party,' recalls a schoolfriend. 'Nicole bossed us around and made us play games "properly".'

Moving on in her education, in February 1980 Nicole started at the notoriously selective North Sydney Girls' High School. Founded in 1914, the state-run school was, and still is, committed to providing a stimulating and challenging environment for successful, high-achieving girls. In Nicole's day, their more traditional academic curriculum included Latin, which she found boring but came to regard as a great foundation for languages in later life.

'I went to an all-girls school which was very career-oriented and success-oriented,' she says. 'The atmosphere was competitive – it encouraged us all to be ambitious and I don't think that's a bad thing.' Indeed, many of the pupils went on to greater things over the years, including prominent theatre actress Ruth Cracknell, radio personality Margaret Throsby, and costume and production designer Catherine Martin. 'Nicole was a very striking girl,' recalls Janet Grace, the school librarian, 'but then there were a number of talented young girls at the school at that time.'

In her tartan blazer, navy skirt and white blouse, Nicole not only stood out on account of her unusual height and hair, but also because of her background. She was still heavily influenced (and unwittingly humiliated) by her parents.

Lunchtime, for example, was a source of great embarrassment. As Janelle often worked the night shift, Antony would prepare packed lunches for his daughters.

'All the other mums would make these beautiful little sandwiches,' she says, 'but my daddy would just put a slab of butter on top of the bread and then say, "Whaddaya want – peanut butter?" Wouldn't cut it and wouldn't wrap it properly, so by the time you opened it at school it was all stale, and all the kids would tease us.'

Even Dr Kidman's good intentions of keeping fit caused his eldest daughter to be self-conscious. 'He ran 8 miles at lunchtime,' she recalls, 'and I used to get terribly embarrassed when the kids at school saw him running, as he'd be all sweaty and look like hell.'

Nicole was also ribbed because of her parents' political beliefs.

'My father was involved in the labour movement, and my mother was a feminist, and we lived in a conservative neighbourhood, so I'd get teased at school,' she says. 'Particularly because of the feminist stuff – that was considered really daggy.' Compounding matters, the Kidman girls would often be coerced into distributing their parents' political pamphlets on the streets of Sydney. 'My first memory of dad is handing out how-to-vote cards at elections,' recalls Nicole. 'He has brought me up to believe in certain issues, definite values. He encouraged me to find time off by myself to meditate every day. He swears by that.'

Both girls would be expected to debate a current event each evening, a ritual for which Nicole would later be grateful but probably dreaded at the time. 'There's always been conversation over the dinner table and I have always been encouraged to question. That's great for an actor,' she said a few years later. 'At home I've always been taught to demand a lot of myself, and I think that stands you in good stead.'

Janelle's feminist ideals left the greatest mark on the receptive girl.

'It was about giving us confidence as women to be whatever we wanted to be,' she reflects. 'The main emphasis was sisterhood, because my mother always said it was about helping other women. My mother once said that she wished she had had a boy she could raise as a feminist male!'

Nicole's parents were open-minded on all topics. Sex education proved a prime opportunity to illustrate their liberal attitude – and unintentionally shock their children in the process. Janelle showed the girls her nurse-training films to explain the facts of life. 'We would have to sit there and look at everything, *in detail*,' squirms Nicole. But it was Antony's antics that really made her cringe.

'He would take me to modern dance . . . I'd be sitting next to my dad and fully-grown men would be walking around, totally naked. My parents *over*educated me – my sister and I were so embarrassed.'

While the Kidmans agreed about many aspects of their children's upbringing, they were opposed on the subject of religion. Janelle had tried to adopt Catholicism to appease Antony and appeared committed when they first married. The girls were therefore brought up in the traditional Catholic faith, so while Nicole attended the North Sydney Girls' High School, Antonia was sent to the nearby convent school, Monte St Angelo. However, Janelle never truly converted, eventually admitting in an interview that she was agnostic.

Already feeling ostracized from her peers thanks to her unconventional upbringing, Nicole suddenly became very conscious of her body when she turned thirteen in June 1980. She had previously accepted her boyish figure and was resigned to her father's stringent exercise regime. 'Every morning he made me do star jumps and push-ups,' she says, proud of the fact that she could do a gruelling fifty of the latter. But with the onset of puberty, Nicole became acutely aware of her extraordinary features and wished she could fit in rather than stand out.

'When I was growing up in Australia, the "beautiful" look was straight blonde hair, blue eyes and olive skin,' she remembers. 'I was a fair-skinned redhead. I used to pray for God to give me tanned skin but if I tried to tan, I'd go red and peel. So I had to put zinc oxide on my nose, wear sun hats and cover up.

'My curly hair embarrassed me. I'd spend ages trying to blow-dry it straight.' It would be a few more years before she was able to manage her unruly mane – in the meantime she tried everything to flatten it down. 'She used to wash her hair in this rosewater stuff,' recalls one childhood friend, 'and when she came to class it stank the whole room out. It smelt like rose toilet freshener, it was so strong.'

Furthermore, Nicole found her looming height, 5 feet 9 inches as she entered her teens, increasingly awkward and she acquired the nicknames 'Stork', 'Storky', or alternatively 'Stalky'. 'I even had a bit of a stutter as a kid,' she says, and although she slowly overcame her speech impediment, it only served to exacerbate her distress during adolescence.

Cursed, as she saw it, with an abundance of freckles, Nicole believed she was 'the ugliest person alive on earth' and confided her anguish to her mother. Janelle reassured her that she was beautiful and that men liked tall women. Nicole recognizes that, 'If you have a mother who adores you, that can offset a lot of the other things that may happen.'

She vividly remembers the torment of being the last girl asked to dance at her first school disco – eventually a boy had to be dragged across the floor, kicking and screaming, to be her partner. Trying to protect her gauche daughter, Janelle would march down to the schoolyard to tackle her tormentors. This could have been the final straw for the mortified teenager, but Nicole is remarkably forgiving and says, 'The great thing my mother did was that she was always on my side.' In time she conceded, 'It's character-building not to be a pretty child. You can't rely on batting your eyelashes and saying, "Please can I have this?" You develop other strengths.'

Nicole's love of the stage at least offered a way of coping with her bleak self-image. 'Theatre was a place where I could go and just be somebody else,' she says. 'I was like, "I hate who I am, I hate how I look, I hate how I feel with all these hormones racing through my body."

'It was natural for me to want to disappear into a dark theatre. I am really very shy. That's something people never seem to fully grasp because, when you're an actor, you're meant be an exhibitionist.'

2

Protect Your Talent

A permanent fixture at the Phillip Street Theatre throughout the evenings of 1981, Nicole was excited to be cast in their amateur production of Frank Wedekind's *Spring Awakening*. The drama, which centred on the juicy theme of carnal repression in the late 1800s, no doubt called Nicole's sexually liberated parents' bluff. Soon they witnessed the astonishing sight of their daughter, barely in her teens, making a reappearance onstage in a rather different manner to her sweet school nativity plays.

'At fourteen, I was playing a fifty-year-old American woman in petticoats, talking about sex,' the actress recalls. 'I had my first kiss onstage; I had to yell, "Beat me! Harder! Harder! Harder!" every night.'

Backstage, Nicole was enjoying herself almost as much as under the spotlight. It was during rehearsals for the play that she first became interested in boys, especially since her acting tutor had unknowingly cast her opposite a sixteen-year-old on whom she had a 'major crush'. As the theatre facilities were limited, the girls and boys in the production were forced to share a dressing room, changing in front of each other. 'It was thrilling!' says Nicole. 'All of us girls would peek at them, laughing.'

Another scene, alongside Nicole's pleas for a beating from her youthful object of desire, involved a group of naked boys whipping each other with towels. While the actors would exit the stage red-faced after this spectacle, the actresses would spy from behind the curtains with their jaws hitting the floor. Nicole was no exception.

'Every night, I looked forward to going to work,' she says, recalling that this was the first time she saw a naked teenage boy, having previously been subjected to somewhat older specimens on those modern-dance excursions with her father. 'It was amazing for me to be dealing with all that stuff at that age.'

Regardless of what her parents may or may not have thought of their daughter's fast-developing sensibilities, Nicole's appearance in *Spring Awakening* was striking enough to attract the attention of some bright young things in the business.

'I first met her at an audition,' says John Duigan, then a television casting director. 'She was several inches taller than the other girls and had this great shock of red hair. But she was remarkably poised and very smart. She got to the kernel of things without pussyfooting around.' Duigan requested that Nicole perform a screen test – a terrifying prospect for the novice actress, but she willingly obliged.

Propitiously, the interest of Jane Campion, a gifted student director from New Zealand, was also piqued. 'She stood out as having an incredible passion and facility for making things seem immediate and real,' recalls Campion of Nicole's early appearances onstage. At that time, the budding director was on the verge of completing a degree at the Australian Film and Television School, and had been searching for an unknown to star in her graduation project, a film entitled *A Girl's Own Story*. She approached Nicole, who in turn approached her headmistress at North Sydney High to request time off school. Unfortunately, the headmistress refused, insisting that the teenager turn down the exciting opportunity in favour of studying for her upcoming exams.

Disappointed, Nicole was then faced with telling Campion that she would be unable to contribute to the film. She was perhaps surprised by her elder's reaction. Before abandoning her young charge to search for a new face, Campion graciously wrote her a postcard, saying: 'I think you made the right decision and I hope one day we will work together. Be careful with what you do, because you have real potential.' Campion signed off by very specifically – and perhaps a little ominously – advising the young actress to 'protect your talent'.

Thwarted by the practical necessities of education, Nicole began to wonder if she was on the right track. 'I saw acting as a fantasy career: light, fluffy and not quite possible. I was going to be a journalist or a lawyer,' she recalls. Alongside these ambitions she had always harboured a love of the written word, and considered broadening this into a profession.

'My parents thought it was nice to develop my imagination, but they never seriously thought that anything would ever come of it,' she continues. 'They said that I couldn't be an actress because I'd be taller than all my leading men, so I thought I'd be a writer instead!

'By the time I was a teenager, I had developed skills as a writer, and my father encouraged me to think about a career in journalism. I began keeping a diary, which I maintain to this day. I used to fill whole notebooks with my writings.'

Nicole took her inspiration from the classics. Tales of teenage hi-jinx were clearly not for the erudite scholar as she immersed herself in tomes such as Fyodor Dostoevsky's heavyweight *Crime And Punishment*; she also adored the poetry of Emily Dickinson and the novels of the Brontë sisters, Henry James and George Eliot. 'The first book that really influenced me was *Middlemarch*,' says Nicole of the latter author. 'Eliot was so perceptive about human nature. I could understand it at an early age. Whereas I read James's *The Portrait Of A Lady* and didn't understand it, and needed to read it again after I'd been through certain life experiences.'

Although, in her own words, Nicole would continue to 'dabble' in writing for a while, much heartened by Jane Campion's stimulating letter she made the conscious decision to dedicate herself to acting and see what transpired. By and large, her family supported her resolution and even her grandmother Joyce would regularly appear in the audience at the Phillip Street Theatre. 'She'd always turn up to watch me and encourage me,' recalls Nicole fondly.

✳

After the success of *Spring Awakening* and three happy years at the Phillip Street Theatre, Nicole moved on to the Australian Theatre For Young People, which offered good exposure to the industry.

A non-profit organization, the ATYP was founded in 1962 by five theatre devotees as a part-time alternative to full-time professional drama schools such as the National Institute of Dramatic Art. 'Our students don't learn anything that they might have to unlearn if they go to NIDA,' said Colette Rayment, the ATYP's artistic director and company administrator, a little defiantly.

During Nicole's time, the ATYP was based in Myrtle Street, Chippendale, in a historic building dating from 1860 that had once been an old sailors' home. No auditions were necessary to enrol and some 600 students attended classes there, ranging in age from eight to twenty-five. Nicole avidly learnt more about acting as a trade, improving her vocal abilities and knowledge of behind-the-scenes production and theatre history.

'All students walk in the door equal no matter where they come from,' said Rayment. 'They just phone and say they want to come. Everything happens after school on afternoons, nights and weekends. We also have classes every school holiday.'

The ATYP staged four productions annually, each showcasing thirty-four students, under the supervision of fourteen part-time tutors, a workshop co-ordinator and Colette Rayment. 'We try to teach them the hardships of the profession,' said Rayment of the company's aims. 'It gives confidence to those who don't have it and teaches the extroverts to be patient and bide their time.' Nicole was devoted to her studies at the ATYP – which in time also yielded the fine actors Mark Ferguson, Angelo d'Angelo, Victoria Longley and Naomi Starr – and many years later would donate $100,000 to their worthy cause.

It wasn't just her love of challenging literature and the fact that she went to 'drama school rather than Bondi Beach' that set Nicole apart from her peers. Inspired by her mother, the gangly teenager initiated an enduring passion for antique attire that conflicted with her normally shy and retiring nature.

'My mum used to always take me to flea markets because she loves vintage clothes, she'd always dress me in vintage clothing,' says Nicole. Neither did Antonia escape her mother's fashion preferences. 'We'd look like these weird, old-fashioned children walking around in dresses that were from the 1920s.' When Nicole ventured out alone shopping, she proved to be her mother's daughter. 'I always looked for fifties pieces. I had this white tulle skirt that I used to wear with fishnets and little black ankle boots. It was a very eighties look.'

Her hormones raging, Nicole initially 'had no confidence. All I could see was this tall, gawky girl who towered above every boy in the class. Boys didn't want to go out with me. They didn't even particularly want to be seen with me!'

It was only now that the self-assurance bestowed by her acting came into effect. 'As the years passed, my work gave me confidence. At about fourteen, I really started to like boys. It's wonderful when that happens.

Those tingles are priceless.' However, with the theatre already demanding much of her precious time, Nicole didn't pursue her adolescent love life with much vigour and instead relegated it to the realms of an amusing sideline. 'By the time I started dating, I knew that I didn't want to be with somebody too serious. I always wanted to go out with the class clown more than the stud. They're more fun,' she smiles.

In her quest for 'fun' Nicole proved herself quite the regular teenager – Dostoevsky aside, that is. 'I was pretty naughty when I was growing up,' she says. 'I went through my rebellious teenager, turn-my-mother's-hair-grey stage. I remember drinking and smoking at school. To this day, I can't touch port. I made myself so sick . . .' But it didn't stop there.

'I've been working in the film industry since I was fourteen, so I've been in contact with every drug imaginable. I've never done LSD, but yeah, I've done my share of drugs,' she admitted in articles for *Newsweek* and *Movieline* magazine in 1998. 'I had a lot of friends that did a lot of drugs.' Showing a maturity in advance of her years (and simultaneously acknowledging the close bond encouraged by her parents), Nicole chose not to hide the truth from her nearest and dearest.

'I told my mother everything. She explained the effect drugs would have on my body, how many brain cells I was destroying. She knows me, so that had an effect . . . but I never was addicted to them. I get a huge depression after drugs. I was lucky.'

Nicole's sister Antonia agrees wholeheartedly with Janelle's impartial approach. 'One of the most valuable lessons our parents taught us was to not always follow popular opinion,' she says.

Under the benevolent guidance of their parents, the Kidman girls continued to enjoy a thoroughly exemplary upbringing. When Janelle worked the night shift, Nicole would babysit her younger sister and the two became inseparable. They also treasured the quality time they spent with their mother when she wasn't working, during which Janelle would share with them her love of art and nature. 'Mum would take us to the theatre and museums, and when we got older we were always going on bush walks,' recalls Antonia.

However, when Nicole wasn't being 'cultured' by her mother or led astray by her acting associates, she was just a teenager at heart, with a taste for pop music – Abba to be specific. Her youthful adulation was to be cruelly squashed when her parents drove her and Antonia to the airport to welcome the Scandinavian group to the country.

'I remember being at the airport when Abba came to Australia, and they didn't stop, they just drove right past! I thought, "Aw . . . I've been waiting here for ages!"' The adult Nicole suggests it was this defining moment that would shape her own attitude to fans many years later. 'It's nice to get out and talk and sign some autographs. People are very warm. I enjoy getting out there and saying hello and remembering what it was like for me when I was fourteen.'

When Nicole was still only fourteen, she landed her first-ever onscreen role, as Helen in the children's TV movie *Bush Christmas*. She had been talent-spotted while still attending the Phillip Street Theatre by Howard Rubie, the much-loved director of the seventies series *Spy Force*, who was initially in charge of the project.

'I wanted to do a remake of a classic 1947 Australian film called *Bush Christmas* that involved a group of children – including a little aborigine kid – lost in the bush, chasing horse thieves,' recalls Rubie today. 'We did a big search Australia-wide to cast the kids and eventually arrived at Peter Williams's acting school. We went into the auditorium and the students were all lined up and did a scene.

'And then, striding on to the stage, came this very tall, red-headed kid. She was taller than everybody else and she just *shone* – she left everyone else for dead! So I cast her in that, but then the money fell through, which so often happens in these things, and I ended up not doing the film.' Although Howard Rubie was replaced by Henri Safran (*Storm Boy*, *Norman Loves Rose*) as director, Nicole kept her part and filming of Paul Barron's first feature commenced in December 1981.

'We were all flown up to a lovely part of Queensland, inland from the Gold Coast where there are a lot of studios in the beautiful bush,' recalls Peter Sumner, who played Nicole's father, Ben Thompson, in the movie. 'The shoot was about four to six weeks, all on location. There was a nearby resort with accommodation, which was very pleasant.'

The cast and crew busied themselves with the task of lovingly updating an old favourite. '*Bush Christmas* is a legendary Australian film with one of our great stars, Chips Rafferty,' says Sumner, 'and I remember as a kid I liked this tall, lanky, drawling bushie that Chips was. When Barron Productions asked me if I could play the father in the remake, I jumped at it. So I found myself up there with the gang, galloping around on horses!

'The film is based on the dad, my character – the mortgage is due and we're going to lose the farm if we can't pay,' he continues, outlining the plot of the entertaining equestrian adventure. 'The bank have said they won't extend the overdraft, so what are we going to do?' The Thompsons own a thoroughbred racehorse, which is then 'borrowed' by two bumbling and broke musicians in the hope that they can recoup their losses. Enter Helen, her younger brother, an English cousin and an aboriginal ranch hand, Manalpuy — Australia's answer to the *Famous Five* (substituting Prince the racehorse for Timmy the dog).

'The kids realize in the middle of the night that the horse has been stolen and so they take off after it, with the help of Manalpuy as a tracker.' In the process of hunting down the thieves, the children brave many dangers, such as falling into an abandoned mineshaft in which they nearly drown, and staving off hunger pains by eating witchety grubs (insects indigenous to the bush). 'Then mum and dad find out the kids are gone and call the police and get a tracking party together. The tracker manages to catch up with them and somehow the kids have got the baddies who are all tied up.'

The film concludes with the Thompson family entering their recaptured horse in a cross-country race on New Year's Day. Prince predictably saves the day by winning the race and the farm's mortgage is paid off with the prize money. 'The film ends with a bush dance and everybody lives happily ever after,' concludes Sumner.

Clearly, the youngsters who played the children were integral to the wholesome movie's success, and Nicole soon made a name for herself as an enthusiastic, if a little serious, actress.

'I remember Nicole as being a wonderful person to work with — she was so open,' Sumner recalls. 'I distinctly remember she was deeply involved and utterly committed. I loved working with her. She listened very carefully and seemed very natural in her acting. I'm sure like all of us she would have been a little nervous underneath at times, but she was an intelligent, interested and involved teenager who delivered the goods with great panache.'

Despite such accolades from her co-star, Nicole herself would later adopt a cavalier attitude to her time on the set. 'I thought filming was boring when I did *Bush Christmas*,' she said years later, before revealing there *were* some bonus points. 'I was a fourteen-year-old kid living away from home, being treated like an adult. I was having a good time and I was blown away with that.'

Nicole and her youthful colleagues were in fact cared for by an on-set chaperone, who supervised their 5 a.m. starts and concomitant publicity for the film, such as posing for photographers and giving interviews.

During the shoot the hard-working actors were afforded a few breaks, socializing after hours in the resort restaurants and visiting the coast *en masse* on Sundays. The end of filming was celebrated with a big party, where even the littlest actor (Nicole's screen brother, eleven-year-old Mark Spain) stayed up well past his bedtime.

Bush Christmas was an excellent debut for Nicole, who gained a tremendous amount from her adventure. 'I would suggest that at the end of the film she had grown enormously in confidence in her own ability to act in front of the camera,' says Sumner. 'For Nicole's sake it was a lovely start, a really nice film to be in to begin with and I'm sure she took so much away from that production in terms of new knowledge and experience.'

Sadly, when Nicole finally viewed the fruits of her labour for the first time, her reaction was totally unforeseen. 'I was shocked,' she grimaces. 'I couldn't believe it was me walking about in that stupid way, and speaking in a voice that I would never have imagined . . .' Regardless of the heroine's unexpected chagrin, *Bush Christmas* (aka *Prince And The Great Race*) became a national favourite and is still shown in Australia every festive season.

For Nicole, the film meant a decisive move into professional acting. Pushing any lingering doubts about on-set boredom to the back of her mind, she called every agent listed in the phone book. After some minor disappointments, June Cann of June Cann Management agreed to represent her interests. 'It made me realize that I had different priorities from the other girls at school,' said the actress.

Bush Christmas was filmed during the long summer holidays and so did not interfere with Nicole's schooling. Now, with the aid of an agent, more projects started to come through and her education became a consideration. That she was intelligent enough to attend such an academically prestigious school benefited her, as her history teacher Margaret FitzGerald explains: 'It's a selective school, full of bright young girls, so we saw things like that as opportunities for them and, being bright, they were able to catch up easily.

'She would have needed the principal's permission and it would have only been on the understanding that she caught up with the work.' As the headmistress had already blocked Nicole's initial request of absence for Jane Campion's graduation project, the student would have to work hard to earn the privilege of being excused from school during term time.

'I used to get dragged off the set in between shoots and piled into the back of a van with my tutor to do schoolwork,' Nicole recalls of what transpired when she was finally given the go-ahead. FitzGerald's classes covered Australia's place in the world over the last century and her student now understood the importance of keeping up with her studies. 'I remember one time when she came back from filming,' says FitzGerald, 'she sat on the chair with her long legs all folded up underneath her, because the chair was too small, listening intently to the work I was setting her.'

The only real drawback to her acting dedication was that Nicole lacked a social circle at school. 'She wasn't a loner as such,' says FitzGerald, 'but she probably had fewer friends than most girls and that was because of her commitments elsewhere. Being away from school a lot of the time, she wasn't able to make friendships or bond as the normal girls would.' One of her few friends was another aspiring young actress, Rebecca Rigg, who would go on to achieve a degree of fame on Australian television and in films including *Doctors And Nurses*, *Spotswood* and *Tunnel Vision*.

Attending auditions in her school uniform did not impede Nicole's chances. *Bush Christmas* was presently followed by a role in another children's action film, entitled *BMX Bandits*. The story was essentially the same – Nicole as the solitary female opposite three bike-riding boys who pursue, and are pursued by, thieves (this time the loot is hi-tech walkie-talkie radios) across the picturesque Australian landscape.

Nicole plays Judy, a fellow BMX-er who becomes embroiled in the saga when the youths wreak havoc at her local shopping mall. After the endless fast and furious chase scenes, legions of helpful BMX-ers stop the robbers in their tracks by pelting them with flour. For added feel-good factor, in the end the local community gives in to the obvious demand for a suitable biking venue and builds a BMX track on which the courageous kids can ride to their hearts' content.

With zero extra plot development, *BMX Bandits* (aka *Shortwave*) is saved by the sheer splendour of the backdrop and expertly shot action scenes, with high-speed pursuits and biking stunts aplenty. Denim-clad, with her wild hair trailing behind like an angry red cloud, fifteen-year-old Nicole Kidman holds her own on a BMX.

After *BMX Bandits*, Nicole's interests were further served by Howard Rubie, the director who had first cast her in *Bush Christmas*. 'After that audition, we talked and she was just a very nice, lovely teenager,' recalls Rubie. 'And then, about a year later, I did a mini-series called *Chase Through The Night*. It was a six-episode children's show; an action-adventure based on the book of the same name by Max Fatchen. I remembered Nicole and she became the star of that show.'

Chase Through The Night turned out to be a crime drama in which a motley crew of bank robbers seeking a safe haven arrives in a small country town, taking the residents hostage. The prisoners eventually triumph by reversing the situation to their advantage and trapping the criminals. Nicole was cast as Petra, a brave and beautiful teenager, opposite the slightly older heart-throb Brett Climo, who played Ray.

Filming took place over two months on a fairly minimal budget in Kankillenbun, in the outback of Queensland. Everyone stayed in a country motel, and Rubie describes the underage actress as 'quite capable, being on her own'.

Even if she didn't realize it, Nicole stood out from the very beginning, as the director recalls. 'She was stunning to look at – all the young fellows' jaws dropped when she was about. But there was an amazing degree of sensibility there. When it came to the crunch, she had a job to do and she could jump in and out of character very easily. As a director you appreciate that.

'She would ask the right questions. She would say, "I'm not sure about this, can you help me here?" or, "Why am I doing this?", which were pretty sensible questions and the sort that a fully-fledged actress would ask.'

Despite Nicole's obvious screen presence and quiet dedication apparent is all her films thus far, Rubie felt she still had a lot to learn. 'When she started to go for these roles in children's films, things started to open up for her. By the time we did *Chase Through The Night*, she had expanded a fair bit and she was very confident. She understood what she had to do to a certain extent. But her life skills at that stage were pretty sheltered.'

Rubie recalls a pivotal scene set on a rickety old railway track with a single cart train travelling back and forth between communities. The robbers hijack this train and the titular chase through the night begins, shot in extreme and challenging conditions. 'Nicole had to work through the night a couple of times, in the freezing cold, and she just hung in there,' he says. 'I remember looking at her at 3 o'clock one morning, there was ice on the ground and her teeth were chattering. I said, "We have to go again," and so she did – no complaints.'

Chase Through The Night was also memorable for Nicole's first-ever screen kiss, with Brett Climo. 'We shot it by the side of the railway line, between a couple of hydrangea bushes. It wasn't the most romantic place! They had a couple of lines of dialogue and then they kissed down behind the bushes. When I yelled "Cut!" their heads popped up, looking quite startled. They were a little bit awkward and we all ended up laughing about it.

'"Anyway," I thought, "now they've relaxed a little, we'll change a couple of things and go again." It was interesting; at the end of it they were both still unsure, but it looked good. It only took a few takes, but it's pretty tough for two young kids to have to do that.'

Nicole's new role as 'love interest' initiated her metamorphosis to more adult actor. She was surrounded by grown-ups, as Rubie noted: 'She got on with the other members of the cast and crew. It was interesting, because she was unnaturally tall for her age, so she would stand around with the adults and I think she felt at home in their company. She was a very good team player.

'But on top of that, she had to go to school of course. We had a schoolroom and a tutor, and when she wasn't on the set she was going to classes.' It seemed that Nicole's tender age would dog her for a while yet.

Nicole's experiences on *Chase Through The Night* were essentially pleasant, and she bid farewell to her new friends at a party held at the end of the eight-week shoot in a Chinese restaurant. 'I think on this particular production she was just having a great time, in the outback in the middle of Australia with about thirty or forty happy people making a film,' summarizes Rubie. 'It was a bit of a dream come true.'

Proud that he had been the one to 'discover' her, so to speak, the year before, the director was most impressed with Nicole's evolving abilities and wished to keep the lines of communication open for forthcoming projects. He recalls, 'At about the same time I was trying to get a film off the ground about mermaids, and I sent Nicole my script. When she returned it, she had written, "Dear Howard, I will be your mermaid any time." But the production company folded, and then Daryl Hannah came along and did a mermaid film [*Splash!* in 1984] – and that kind of put a damper on it.'

In 1983 Nicole was keen to take on any part, no matter how small, for the exposure – and the pocket money. Under June Cann's watchful eye, the enthusiastic fifteen-year-old turned up as one of the extras in a music video. 'Bop Girl' was recorded by Pat Wilson and produced by her husband, the veteran Aussie rocker Ross Wilson, and its accompanying promotional film was directed by Gillian Armstrong. It was the now-respected director's first foray into the world of music video, and Nicole can be easily spotted in the background, showing off her red hair and long legs.

Although the brief appearance in 'Bop Girl' was far from a starring role, the young actress was happy enough to go along for a giggle, for she had just landed the lead in an episode of *Winners*, an eight-part television drama series focusing on social issues affecting teenagers. As well as regular television broadcasts, videos of each programme were (and still are) available to schools and interested parents, accompanied by a book and helpful information pack dealing with the relevant topic.

Winners provided Nicole's first opportunity to work with the director John Duigan, who had screen-tested her after *Spring Awakening*. Nicole was struck by his passion for the screen and it was mainly thanks to his encouragement on *Winners* that she knew she had made the right decision to stick with acting. 'He has the ability to draw things out of people and I suddenly thought, "Oh, I love doing this,"' she recalls.

Playing Carol Trig in the sixth instalment of *Winners*, entitled 'Room To Move', Nicole was called on to hone her natural athleticism to portray a 1500-metre runner. Her character is dedicated to her training under the strict supervision of her father. When one day Carol encounters Angie, the new girl at school who is ostracized for her punkish looks and peculiar attitude, she realizes there might be more to life and starts to let her training slip, much to the exasperation of her dad. This leads to her coming second in the most important race of her sporting life.

Although Carol disappoints her family, the moral of the tale is that she develops respect for someone at odds with society and the norm, and discovers that in addition to being a talented sportswoman, she is a person in her own right.

Appearing alongside television veterans Terence Donovan and Veronica Lang, who play her parents, baby-faced Nicole turns in a perfectly plausible performance as the fifteen-year-old athlete, and she charms the cameras with her trademark playful grins, red cheeks and pouting teenage sulks. On watching her competitive teasing across the family dining table with her onscreen younger sister, it is easy to imagine a similar real-life Kidman scene with Nicole and Antonia's familiar banter being brought into line by Antony and Janelle.

However, the one aspect that undeniably leaps out at today's viewer on watching the young Nicole Kidman in action has to be her hair.

'I remember when I first worked with John Duigan, I had this mass of frizzy red curls,' she recalls. 'John said, "Listen, I find that your hair is distracting from your face and from the performance." But there was nothing you could do with it, it was just *wild*. He *hated* my hair.' Duigan's feelings are understandable – while Nicole's elevated height is nothing new (viewers are now well used to seeing her a good head taller than her peers), her hair *is* truly awful. Totally uncontrollable with a huge fringe and stealing every scene for all the wrong reasons, Nicole's brightly coloured mop adds almost a foot to her height and prevents anyone from seeing her face, surely a hindrance for any actress.

Frizz aside, while the subject matter of 'Room To Move' is thought-provoking for its teenage audience, Nicole's performance interestingly shows a slight hesitance, unlike her recent film roles. Even so, Nicole was lucky enough to forge an ongoing friendship with the director. They spoke on the phone once a week and he kept an eye out for suitable roles for her. Duigan quite rightly looked on the teenager as his protégée, and Nicole was grateful for his support.

'It is inevitable that you get a relationship if you work very closely together,' she says. 'I think it's important that [directors] get to know you and your moods so they can really direct you.' It seems Duigan's views on her acting were clouded only by her looks, but that was about to change.

3

The Cinderella Transformation

Notably the teenage Nicole Kidman was always cast in physical, sporty roles – ranging from dangerous pursuits to bike-riding and running – and to a certain extent this reflected reality. After her sixteenth birthday in June 1983, she was furious when her mother refused to sign a consent form allowing her daring daughter to skydive.

The actress was left to make the most of her tall, slim figure by taking on the odd modelling job, such as advertising Clairol Glints hair products. It certainly helped with pocket money, as she only had one other source of income: 'I used to work as a theatre usherette.'

During an audition for advertising swimwear (which she failed), Nicole met Naomi Watts, another model, who was to become one of her closest friends. Naomi originally hailed from England, where her father had been the sound engineer for Pink Floyd. After his untimely death, Naomi and her mother moved to Australia when Naomi was fourteen. A year or so later, she encountered Nicole.

'It might only have been for some trashy swimwear, but we both needed the job!' laughs Naomi. 'We hadn't got the bodies for it. We got chatting and shared a taxi home because we lived in the same area. We've been friends ever since.' The pair became thick as thieves and attended various modelling assignments together.*

It was during one of these modelling jobs that a hairdresser attacked Nicole's unruly and badly blow-dried mane with some tongs and a bottle of dye. The actress was suddenly transformed into a vision of loveliness. Returning to school the following Monday with her fine features framed by romantic red ringlets, Nicole amazed her fellow classmates. It was as if Cinderella had arrived at the ball.

'It was the swan thing,' remembers Rebecca Rigg. 'It just went around the school like wildfire. Nic had found her essence just simply through allowing her hair to be what it is naturally. And that was definitely a turning point for her as a teenager.'

Equally, Nicole found that disappearing from school for a couple of weeks filming created a buzz around the building, and she acquired some much-needed street credibility. 'I remember that what she was doing was quite exciting at the time,' says Margaret FitzGerald. Janet Grace witnessed Nicole enjoying her first taste of fame: 'Nicole would spend a lot of time in the library talking to a rapt audience.'

Scholastically she began to suffer a little, and Grace admits, 'She didn't shine academically, but then it's all relative as these girls were in the top 2 per cent of the state. I understand from her science teacher, Karl Hall, that her mother often wrote notes to excuse her uncompleted work.'

The biggest indication that school came a poor second to acting was in February 1984, when Nicole was absent from an important class trip.

'When the girls enter Year 11 it's seen as a big transition. They are treated like adults and the work becomes more serious,' explains Grace. 'Back then they would go on an acclimatizing week away to a resort in the country called Vision Valley, which is about an hour and a half away by bus. The week was filled with communal activities and the girls were there to bond and support each other.

'However, Nicole didn't attend this – which was quite unusual – and she missed out on the start of Year 11.'

This time, Nicole's absence was due to a couple of stints filming for television programmes. First came *Matthew & Son*, a short Aussie drama directed by Gary Conway and written by Marcus Cole and Bert Deling. Nicole's fleeting and fairly unmemorable role was as the character Bridget Elliot. She then made a brief appearance as Simone Jenkins, an aerosol- and glue-sniffing teenager in an episode of *A Country Practice* called

---

* Naomi would later famously decline a date with one Tom Cruise in favour of a lamb roast in a well-known advertisement.

'Repairing The Damage'. The actor Patrick Phillips worked with Nicole in the latter and later recalled: 'Even then, I thought she was incredible. She just had this naturalness and loved the camera. A good personality, Nicole; she's something really special.'

With her more mature appearance came meatier roles, and Nicole next became involved in the controversial *Wills & Burke*. 'It's a film about two Australian heroes, Burke in particular, who were two of the early explorers chosen to lead an expedition across the country in the nineteenth century,' explains Bob Weis, director of this historical marathon. 'The difficulty was that Burke was an Irish policeman from Castlemaine who used to get lost in Castlemaine, let alone having any skills as an explorer.

'On his expedition all but one of them died in the desert, in an area where aboriginal people were living quite happily, because they had no bush craft and didn't know how to survive – they wouldn't accept the help of aboriginal people because they saw them as savages. So while he became an great figure in Australian history, we took an iconoclastic approach to the film. Instead of making a heroic epic, we made a comedy about a guy who was without a clue.'

In casting this unusual film, Weis secured Kim Gyngell as William John Wills and Garry McDonald as Robert O'Hara Burke. 'I hadn't worked with Garry before,' says the director, 'but he had a television character called Norman Gunston, an in-your-face, nerdish character. Garry was an incredibly good actor in his forties, and he had a nervy quality which was good for Burke.'

But Weis still needed a beautiful lady to play the alluring Julia Matthews, with whom Burke was obsessed. 'I wanted somebody who was entirely inappropriate – Burke was fixated on somebody who was supremely unaware of him, and who wouldn't have been interested in him even if she was aware. The whole point to me was that Burke *was* a berk.

'I had seen some tapes of Nicole Kidman,' Weis continues. 'I remember looking at a piece where she was playing a young athlete who was in training for competitive races [*Winners*]. My casting agent said, "This is a very talented young actress and you ought to consider her." It was really on the basis of that – she didn't have any star status or market value at the time.'

Weis was impressed with Nicole's audition and was eager to cast her in the adult role. He encountered some problems, though, as she was still at school. 'She had done other television work, but her agent June Cann was very protective of her,' explains Weis. 'She didn't want to overexpose her or put pressure on her home and school life, which I agreed with.

'So I said, "Look, this is an issue for you guys, but I'm very keen and if you would pass it on I would appreciate it." I'm pretty sure June said to Nicole, "I don't think it's a good idea that you do this", but Nicole said, "No, no – I really like this project, I really want to do it." I don't think it was a big fight, but she was very much her own person and made her own decisions.'

Although relatively small compared to her earlier excursions, Nicole was intrigued by the curious part. 'In Australia, a lot of films have been focused on our history which, as they say, is mainly *history*,' she says. 'A lot of films and plays are very male-oriented – I think it's hard for actresses anywhere. Roles for young actresses are rare, and then they're mostly stereotypes.'

Nicole was determined to play Julia – quite a departure for someone who usually portrayed do-gooders of her own age. 'Nicole's character was a singer and a bit of a temptress, although more of an unwitting one,' says Weis. 'We only ever see her in the context of the theatre and a couple of scenes backstage. There's one particular scene where she's singing as he's dying in the desert. She's singing a song that suggests she doesn't care – the two had a relationship in his mind, but I'm not sure she was even aware who he was.'

Weis recalls that this young *femme fatale* showed great promise as a serious, up-and-coming actress. 'I thought that she was incredibly receptive to direction, but also had a good sense of how to read text, which is unusual of somebody at that age. She was very good at immediately being able to understand the tone of the piece and what was required.

'Nicole's role was comedic in intent, although she wasn't required to play it with broad comedy – I wanted her to do it as straight as she could.' Describing her as a 'very attractive young woman', Weis observed that she had a real passion for what she was doing, rather than merely surviving off raw ambition. She was in good company.

'It was a very experienced cast, drawn from both film and theatre backgrounds – people who had done an enormous amount of work. She was by far the youngest, the only actor in that age group.' That said, the director recalls that Nicole mixed well with her colleagues even though they were not her peers.

With his unique objective on a piece of native history, Weis was destined to upset traditionalists. 'When the film came out, people were appalled with this treatment of an Australian hero, and some people thought that it was unAustralian,' he says. 'But when an academic book came out on the history of Burke and Wills, it alluded to our film as one of the more accurate portrayals.'

Weis's real difficulty, however, lay in the fact that another film on the heroic duo came out at the same time. This was a Hollywood-style production called *Burke And Wills*, as the pair are traditionally known, and was a sympathetic tale of their incredible deeds achieved in the face of adversity. Weis admits that this film damaged his because, 'People started saying that we had made our film as an attempt to cash in on what they were doing and that we were just some sort of pathetic spoiling exercise.' Sadly, this view is still held by some critics today, who fail to understand the black comedy of the project.

To counteract the negative publicity, Weis and the cast were obliged to perform the usual rounds of promotion. Of this Weis comments, 'The thing that struck me about Nicole was the poise and professionalism she had. It's quite an accomplishment for a young actor to be able to deal with that whole world.'

To complete Year 11 at North Sydney High, Nicole would have been obligated to attend classes until the end of December 1984. But the actress had no intention of finishing her schooling: after all, what was the point of a few extra months and a piece of paper? Her vocation as a performer was blindingly obvious to teachers and casting directors alike; and she already had some four films, three television series, a music video and at least one highbrow theatre production to her name.

To her credit, the ambitious yet sensible teenager waited for some guaranteed work before making any rash decisions. 'I wasn't prepared to leave school until I was assured of another job to go to,' she affirms. 'My parents had mixed feelings.'

But when Disney came calling, asking if Nicole would like to appear in a children's series called *Five Mile Creek*, Dr and Mrs Kidman knew better than to stand in their daughter's way. Nicole left school without ceremony shortly before her seventeenth birthday – and nine months before she was due to take her Higher School Certificate. 'I was lucky because my parents were extremely encouraging and I don't think I could have made the decision without their support,' she says today.

In truth, for a long time Nicole's lack of academic qualifications privately worried her parents, both of whom were deeply involved in teaching. Antony, in particular, having himself spent ten years at university, felt his intelligent daughter should not rule out the possibilities of further education. Luckily for Nicole, the Kidmans respected her serious attitude towards her craft and bit their tongues – at least most of the time.

'There was definite tension about my not going on to college – with my father especially,' says Nicole. 'My parents always thought I would go to university and become a barrister. They are very level-headed people and have nothing to do with the film industry. They're very supportive, *very*; the best parents you could hope for. They have pushed me, yes, but have never forced their attitudes on to me.

'My parents have always thought acting was a great way of developing the imagination and as a person. But when anything went wrong, they'd say to me, "Well, you *can* always go to university . . ."'

'If we had aspirations for her then, it was to do something at university,' admitted Janelle much later in her daughter's career. 'Acting is such a wretched business – it is so insecure. It was a profession Nic forged for herself, but I have to say we were always supportive.'

In the years to come, Nicole would frequently depend on her parents whenever she was away on a film shoot, and the familiar gentle reminders about university would always be there in the background.

'As an actor you tend to be at either acute heights of happiness or the depths of depression,' says Nicole, 'and I'd ring in a panic from, say, London about something and my parents' stock answer would be, "Oh well, you can always go to university." Then you think, yeah, there *are* other options. But acting is what I want to do, so I am willing to work hard at it.' Nearly twenty years on, Nicole remains adamant that leaving school at sixteen was the right decision.

Nicole had not taken such life-changing steps while only being offered mainly lightweight Australian children's parts. Landing a role with Hollywood giants Disney was quite a different matter.

Five Mile Creek started life as a pilot called *The Cherokee Trail* in 1981 and was based on Colorado's gold rush in the 1860s. When producer Doug Netter transformed it into an American television series, he shifted the location to Australia, which had also witnessed an influx of prospectors and booming mining communities in the late nineteenth century.

The adventure series is based at Five Mile Creek, an isolated inn on a stagecoach route. Nicole joined the cast as the impish Annie for eleven episodes (numbers 28 to 39). She discovers romance when she sets out to win the heart of love-shy Jack, but her home-making skills threaten to let her down. She also causes more than her fair share of mayhem, not least when she mischievously generates an epic confrontation between the two lads, Jack and Con, to find out who is the better coach driver.

During this exciting time, Nicole spent several months living alone in Melbourne. Although she had been away on location before, this was the first time she was given complete freedom to make her own decisions. More importantly, a role in an American production ensured much greater exposure and Nicole was soon courted by eager agencies.

One offer came from the agency which had rising star Eric Stoltz (*Mask*) on their books. In order to woo the Australian actress, they flew her to America, hoping that she would be dazzled by the bright lights. Displaying a maturity in advance of her years, Nicole resisted. 'I went to L.A., had lunches and talks, but I decided it would be better to stay here, to gain experience and recognition,' she said.

'I like Australia, the way they operate . . . you don't have to have a big caravan and you're just part of the crew. There's too much pressure with the star system – Los Angeles is the mecca if you want to be a big star. Australia is where my family and friends are. I can still work in America – but I don't have to live there.' This attitude is one the actress retained throughout her career, and to this day she feels more comfortable in her home country.

Nicole's striking looks were noticed by royal photographer Lord Patrick Lichfield around this time. He was so enticed by her ethereal elegance that he included her in his latest assignment. Lichfield captured her youthful charm as part of his portrait of Australia's ten most beautiful women, which he produced for *Harper's Bazaar*. Not bad for a seventeen-year-old.

Stunned and self-conscious at receiving such an honour, Nicole modestly demurred.

'I wouldn't say I was beautiful or glamorous. I would say I have a versatile face. It's almost a hindrance as an actress to have a beautiful face. But I have the sort of face that can change. That might be flattering myself, but it is one of my greatest assets.'

Without the worry of schoolwork and exams nagging in the background, Nicole now had the time to concentrate on her personal, as well as her professional, life. Mixing frequently with adults in her industry and with experience beyond her years thanks to her trade, it was fairly predictable that she would attract the attentions of older men. Soon she became romantically involved with a Dutch actor some seventeen years her senior, whose name has been lost in the annals of time.

Surprisingly, Dr and Mrs Kidman were not worried by this relationship. 'My parents were quite open,' says Nicole. 'My mother would always say, "It's not age, it's people."' In fact, Janelle in particular had always been quite amenable about her elder daughter's blossoming love life – she preferred to let Nicole's boyfriends stay at the family home overnight rather than drive back having drunk alcohol during the evening.

Still, nothing could have prepared the doctor and his wife for Nicole's shock announcement just one month into her romance: that she would be leaving the country with $3000 of her hard-earned acting money and a man twice her age.

'At seventeen, I announced to my poor parents that I had met this Dutch guy and was going to live in Amsterdam,' she recalls. 'I travelled over there and we were together, on and off, for about six months. We travelled all around Europe – I think being an actor you have this voracious appetite for life.

'We went to Paris, stayed in a tiny attic room, could barely afford bread and cheese. But boy, it was so romantic. We went to Italy, to Florence, and it snowed, which it hadn't done in eighteen years . . .'

Before the couple left Amsterdam for Paris, they visited a flea market one day, where Nicole purchased a 'very simple but very beautiful' thirties brocaded gown. It was the dress that she would eventually get married in – but not, as it turned out, to her lover.

'I *thought* I was going to marry the guy I was with. And I didn't. Thank God! I'm sure he says, "Thank God!" too. But I knew it was the dress for me,' she smiles.

Eventually, Nicole's money ran out. And the romance hadn't really worked out the way she had anticipated. 'When I got over there I said, "I really think we should just be friends." I naïvely did not understand male sexuality at that age . . . But, because he was so much older, he realized that I probably wasn't going to stay with him. Most men that age would have been insecure and controlling.'

Fortunately, Nicole's Dutchman let her go and she returned, more worldly-wise, to her native Australia. 'It was a huge mistake,' she later admitted of her rather rash decision to throw caution to the wind and run off with a man she barely knew, 'but I did it, and I survived, and since then I've just kept travelling.'

★

The timing of Nicole Kidman's return to Sydney was more opportune than she could possibly have imagined. As the teenager reacquainted herself with all things Aussie in early 1985, her world fell apart with the news that her mother had been diagnosed with breast cancer.

'I suppose it was the first time in my life that I was hit by the possibility that somebody very close to me could die,' she says. 'I didn't think anything could go wrong. It shocked me to such an extent and led to a different way of thinking.' Immediately Nicole, who had been staying with a friend, moved back home.

There, surrounded by her bewildered family, Nicole witnessed Janelle battling with painful chemotherapy and radiotherapy, and coming to terms with the possibility that she might not survive the treatment. 'Suddenly the person you love most in the world is losing her hair and sobbing every night,' Nicole continues. 'It was so difficult to see her go through such pain.

'It opened my eyes to mortality and from that point on I was determined to support her, be a part of it and in some way help.'

Nicole withdrew from all acting jobs and enrolled on a massage course so that she could relieve her mother's suffering with physical therapy. As a fully qualified masseuse she was able to soothe her mother's frozen muscles every day.

Janelle's eventual recovery was in no small part due to the loving care of her daughter. As Dr Kidman later explained, in such times of crisis, 'social support is crucial – from friends, partners, parents and family. They should be listening and empathetic, and not trying to jolly them along. It's about accepting their mood swings, and having someone listen and not to get upset themselves.' The Kidman unit emerged all the stronger from their ordeal, and Nicole was left with the distinct impression that Janelle had beaten the illness with immense dignity.

The brush with cancer changed the entire family profoundly. Nicole had always been close to her mother, but now the bond strengthened tenfold. Today she recalls of the harrowing experience, 'It was very hard on me and it still remains a big thing in my life.' Her sister Antonia was fifteen and still at school at the time, but she too remembers the agony of dealing with a potential loss: 'This was the first bad thing to happen to our family,' she says. 'The prospect of her dying changed me and I became more thoughtful and less self-indulgent.' Antonia also observed the deepening of her sister's relationship with Janelle, later revealing, 'She tells mum everything.'

As a direct result of his wife's illness, Dr Kidman altered the entire focus of his career. Having helped establish the Health Psychology Unit at the Royal North Shore Hospital a decade earlier, he now oversaw the shift of the unit's direction into research about drugs and therapy for cancer patients. Where possible he specialized in breast cancer and psychoncology (helping patients and their families cope better with the psychological effects of the illness and its treatment). Of the latter, he says, 'People get very anxious, depressed, angry and fearful and they worry about dying and pain. Of course people can live for a considerable time and do quite well. It is quality of life that is important. Our work at the unit helps them improve this no matter how long they have left.'

One of the Kidmans' primary thoughts once they overcame the trauma of Janelle's illness must have been the implications for the two girls, as to a certain extent breast cancer is thought to be a hereditary disease. Since Janelle was the only member of her family to have suffered, Nicole and Antonia were not considered to be at high risk, especially as their mother has not experienced a recurrence.

Nevertheless, the possibility heightened Nicole's awareness and she admits to being 'completely paranoid' about the various theoretical environmental causes of cancer. She vastly lessened her consumption of red meat and chicken, and introduced tofu to her diet because, 'They think Japanese women have a much lower degree of breast cancer because of the soy protein.' Later in life she would take on an official role as the Advisory Council Chair of UCLA's Women's Reproductive Cancer Treatment and Research Program, becoming directly involved in the finances of the facility and the assembly of the advisory board.

'When you see someone with cancer, it gives you compassion for any suffering,' she says today. 'It shows you it's how you deal with the hard times that defines you. It takes such courage to get through that. I do a lot of fund-raising for women with ovarian cancer.'

4
Bit Parts

With Janelle on the road to recovery at the end of 1984, Nicole felt free to start socializing again. Encouraged from an early age, she had always loved music. 'My mother is a very good pianist,' she says, 'and I have wonderful memories of the two of us singing Christmas carols and hymns.' Such classical tunes were a healthy introduction, but now she branched out into teen pop.

'I actually sang in a band on weekends for a few months when I was seventeen, with some girlfriends. We were called Divine Madness. We'd sing at parties but we never received money, we just did it for fun.' Primarily a sixties and seventies covers band, Nicole imitated Debbie Harry while her friends strutted around mimicking other female icons like Tina Turner. Divine Madness lasted three months over the hot summer and the girls excelled in their efforts at choreography and theatrics, but little else. 'We didn't do so well,' admits Nicole. 'We didn't become world famous – we didn't even become famous in Sydney!'

Although this was fun, she still needed to earn a living and so eased back into filming in a familiar formula. She was reunited with the man behind her first screen kiss, Brett Climo, for another all-action children's movie, *Archer's Adventure* (aka *Archer*). The period drama is still shown on satellite channels today, particularly in France and Germany.

'I hadn't seen Nicole's work until late 1984,' says director Denny Lawrence, 'when a colleague, Brian Trenchard-Smith, showed me *BMX Bandits*. We both agreed that her presence, in what was a modest little children's film, was really powerful. I determined to see if she'd be interested in what was a small but pivotal role in a family picture I was due to direct.

'I contacted Nicole through the Australian Theatre for Young People. I needed to make the meeting fairly early, and meeting in my hotel room seemed wrong, so I suggested the coffee shop, but it turned out to be closed. We sat there anyway and talked in the semi-gloom, or at least I talked.

'Nicole seemed incredibly shy. When the interview was over I suddenly wondered whether the girl I had barely seen or heard was the right one.' Sticking with his initial conviction, Lawrence hired the uncharacteristically meek teenager he'd just met and was thankfully proved wrong. 'Nicole really comes alive when she's in character. Not that she is a colourless person, but, like many actors, she is more comfortable, it seems, when invisible, or in character. At least, in the early days she was.'

Based on the true story of the horse that won the first Melbourne Cup, Nicole portrays Catherine in this film about courage, strength and endurance. Brett Climo is the hero, Dave Power, who embarks upon a 600-mile excursion across the outback to deliver the horse, Archer, to Melbourne. Naturally, his journey becomes fraught with danger at every turn.

'Nicole plays a girl of about sixteen who proves most precocious – even suggesting Dave kiss her . . . nothing more, of course, in this family movie,' Lawrence explains.

'Despite Nicole's natural shyness, she was suddenly even more flirtatious than I could have hoped when we came to the "first kiss" moment – and she did it in a way that made it slightly humorous and also quite innocent.

'She always looked great on camera, no matter what: even up close on a wide-angle, which I needed to do for a particularly tricky shot.'

Nicole was keen to research her character and was spotted on the set reading about the era. 'I always make the most of my free time,' she said. 'There's so much hanging around, waiting for things like lighting changes, that it's hard to keep your energy levels up, so now I am always occupied and can overcome that problem.' The director recalls, 'She also had to learn to ride sidesaddle, which is not easy. But she mastered it quite quickly.'

Lawrence was pleased with her performance and concurs with Bob Weis's comments on Nicole's consummate professionalism throughout. His only regret was that he didn't increase her involvement as the test screening proved her scenes were the most popular. Although the role of Catherine was not overly demanding, Nicole was lucky to be able to step straight back into work after her extended hiatus.

After celebrating her eighteenth birthday, Nicole's next role was as Jade in another Paul Barron production, *Windrider*, a romantic drama based in the world of surfing competitions. She would be starring opposite handsome Tom Burlinson of *The Man From Snowy River* fame, and alongside some of Australia's most respected character actors: Jill Perryman, Charles 'Bud' Tingwell and Simon Chilvers. Under the working title *Making Waves*, the film was directed by Vincent Monton during the months of October and November 1985.

Nicole was attracted to the part of Jade mainly because the character was older, allowing her to move firmly out of the realm of children's films. Also, as Jade was a struggling rock singer, Nicole was able to draw on her recent real-life experiences with Divine Madness.

Jade's primary objective was to provide an attractive 'love interest' for wealthy sailboard champion P.C. Simpson (Burlinson). *Windrider* would see Nicole appearing in her first-ever steamy love scenes and the passionate clinches with Burlinson caused much excitable press about her 'growing up' on screen. Nicole hated being patronized.

'It's inevitable that I will "grow up",' she shrugged. 'People do still remember me as being fifteen, but it's slowly changing. It's hard for a casting director to know where I fit in – I can play twenty-two, twenty-three, twenty-four, if not physically, then mentally. I'm making the transition.' Soon enough, Nicole would indeed be called upon to do just that, but unfortunately *Windrider* was not about to launch her as a 'serious actress', and Jade proved a less than memorable role.

The film itself was passable but veritably riddled with clichés: first there was the tried-and-tested boy-meets-girl, boy-loses-girl plot line. The lack of understanding between father and son was an equally familiar theme. Then both Jade and P.C. are committed to their respective careers and are determined to win by any means, another fall back into B-movie territory.

One critic even pointed out *Windrider*'s unintentional nod to *Jaws*, in the form of a sailboard-munching shark.

'There's a lot of wind in *Windrider*,' scoffed Australian newspaper *The Sun*. 'Far too much to give the film any box-office appeal. The producers have mixed too many elements into a film which should have been just a beachside romance.'

Around the time of the movie's release, Nicole admitted in interviews that she wasn't thrilled with her performance in this, or anything else thus far. 'I haven't really done anything that I think is good,' she said in December 1986. 'If you keep patting yourself on the back you'll never get anywhere. I know what's good and bad and so far I don't think anything's *that* good.

'I can't look at myself objectively. Everything I do, I find something wrong – I guess most actors do the same thing.'

For Nicole, the main lasting consequence of *Windrider* was that it kick-started her love life once more, as she embarked on a real-life affair with her leading man, Tom Burlinson.

'I accepted roles when I was younger, which I don't regret, because in everything I've done I've learnt something or I've met someone who's been quite instrumental in moulding my career,' she later reminisced. 'On *Windrider* I met someone who I had a relationship with for three years, which was really important to me and helped me to grow. So you've got to look at things positively. I *did* do some things that weren't of really high quality, but I learnt a lot.'

When Tom Burlinson swept into Nicole's life, he was one of Australia's hottest actors. Born on Valentine's Day 1956 to English parents, he had moved around considerably during his youth, living in Canada, America, England and eventually Australia. Shortly after his tenth birthday, his parents divorced and his mother and two younger sisters returned to England, leaving his father to bring up him and his elder sister Susan alone.

At the age of eighteen Burlinson was accepted into NIDA, going against the wishes of his father, who wanted him to be a lawyer; ironically, Nicole had a similar experience with her own parents. Burlinson's big break came in 1981 when he was cast as Jim Craig in *The Man From Snowy River* alongside Kirk Douglas, Jack Thompson and Sigrid Thornton. The film was a huge ratings success and, coupled with his dark-haired good looks, led to a succession of lead roles in a variety of films and television series.

In the beginning Nicole remained tight-lipped about her new beau, pointedly refusing to be known in media circles as 'Tom Burlinson's girl-friend', but soon it was obvious to all who knew her that things were hotting up. At eleven years her senior, her boyfriend was again considerably older, but Nicole's last few years had given her the benefit of life's richest experiences and she felt ready to commit to a long-term relationship. She was practically living with him in time to see the premiere of *Windrider* at Christmas 1986.

Of Burlinson Nicole says, 'He was the one who gave me a great belief in men. He was kind and open, he gave me a lot of freedom. I was really lucky to have had him.' She continued to be discreet about any intimate details in interviews, but Burlinson remained a steady feature in her life for some time to come.

✷

During one of their weekly phone conversations, Nicole's good friend, director John Duigan, found himself counselling her on her future direction. Like Colette Rayment at the Australian Theatre For Young People, he advocated against attending the country's foremost acting school, the National Institute of Dramatic Art (NIDA), which had been the common path for successful Australian actors including Mel Gibson, Judy Davis – and Nicole's new boyfriend.

'Don't you dare go – they will destroy you!' ordered Duigan.

Nicole took his advice to heart.

'I always think I would have loved to have gone because I love being around actors and I love talking about acting. But he said don't go and so I chose the other route which was to work, work, work.'

Echoing Rayment's earlier words, she continues, 'I didn't have three years at NIDA, or at drama school making my mistakes there. I grew up making my mistakes on film, but learning something every time.'

The reason behind Duigan's effective advice remains unknown, but the result is abundantly clear. Nicole had thrown herself wholeheartedly into building up her CV, and while some moves were questionable, other opportunities showed her Australian fans and, more importantly, those in the business her true ability. One such proficient performance was in her next project with Duigan, a ten-part television mini-series called *Vietnam*.

Duigan had kept a beady eye on Nicole since *Winners*, always on the lookout for a suitable vehicle for her – now he mentioned her name at the casting meeting for *Vietnam*. Co-writer Terry Hayes was unaware of her back catalogue and relied on Duigan's word that there was 'something special' about her. That Nicole had worked with the director previously did not guarantee her the role – perhaps he still fostered concerns about her frizzy mane – and she was required to endure a six-and-a-half-hour improvisational audition. Her hair was now under some control and her acting vastly improved, so Duigan was glad to offer Nicole the part.

But it wasn't his decision alone. Kennedy Miller (the powerful production company who memorably introduced Mel Gibson to Hollywood in *Mad Max*) wanted their say. Director Denny Lawrence, who had been so impressed with her work in *Archer's Adventure*, lent a helping hand. 'I strongly recommended her when she was being considered for a role in one of George Miller's productions,' he says. 'Once the Kennedy Miller people saw what she could do, they wanted her in everything they did.'

Nicole was equally excited about the new partnership. 'I knew that *Vietnam* was going to be great. I'd worked with John before and it was a Kennedy Miller production. I remember when they rang and said, "It's yours", I screamed – I was so excited!'

The depiction of Megan Goddard was a far cry from her usual lightweight parts. 'It really made a big difference to me to work with a three-dimensional character and flesh out the comic and dramatic aspects of the role,' she recalls.

Nicole delved deep into Megan's psyche, impressively portraying her transformation from a naughty teenage schoolgirl, through rebellious independence, to an idealistic peace protester in her early twenties. 'In a mini-series you've got time to let the audience get to know you and to take them on a real journey. We had ten hours to set up a character – in a movie you have only ninety minutes.'

Vietnam is an ambitious series, tackling head-on the numerous ramifications of Australia's entry into the Vietnam War. Revolving around the Goddard family, it follows the son Phil (Nicholas Eadie), who is among the first conscripts; his sister Megan, opposed to Australian interference; their father (Barry Otto), the prime minister's aide; and their mother (Veronica Lang), a slowly blossoming feminist who eventually leaves her husband of over twenty years. To complicate matters further, Phil's story also includes two Vietnamese characters, one who joins the Viet Cong, and the other who escapes with Phil's friend, a seriously wounded Australian soldier, while Megan's tale involves her boyfriend Serge (John Polson), who runs from the law to avoid conscription.

The series is hard-hitting, covering graphic scenes of rape and murder alongside heavyweight political theories and adult themes. 'I want to make films that could possibly shed new light on world situations,' the actress stated. 'The works can still be entertaining, yet thought-provoking.'

For her part, Nicole pours her all into an excellent performance. She effortlessly plays the loveable, mischievous kid sister at the start, with spotty skin and a frizzy fringe sprouting at the top of her long plait. Art

mimics life as Megan is affectionately teased about being 'flat as an iron-
ing board' and nicknamed 'Lofty' due to her excessive height. Nicole has
a good command of comedy and throws many cheeky grins, winks and
funny faces at her family.

'It's good to have a director who listens to you, and actually sees you as
a thinking person and not something to push around,' said Nicole, who
enjoyed improvising. 'They wrote the part after I was cast so things like
my height were written in.'

Megan morphs into an adult, retaining certain characteristics of her
younger self, and Nicole's looks mature accordingly with the aid of a
clever stylist, trendier clothes and careful make-up. Formerly enjoying
discos with her friends, she grows up and develops a political conscience,
joining protests against Australian involvement in the war. She then has to
deal with a rapid personal wake-up call – she loses her virginity to the
man she loves and, within hours, finds him to be unfaithful. Nicole shines
as Megan discovers the sexual revolution.

The series as a whole is littered with period references and original
black-and-white film footage to authentically set the scene. Nicole took
her background investigations seriously – this was about more than just
reading a book or riding a horse.

'I became obsessive about acting,' she says. 'I did all sorts of research
about the culture of the 1960s. I wasn't even born when the Beatles
became popular, so I had to sit down and study life in the 1960s, as if for
a term paper.' Since Megan was required to show off some appropriate
moves at the local disco, Nicole undertook a crash course in dances like
the locomotion, the turkey trot, the hitchhiker, the jerk and the mashed
potato, absorbing the fashions and feelings of the era. 'What I learnt
about the 1960s from *Vietnam* was the immense strength and determination the youth had, to band together to change the world. In the
1980s people are individually trying to achieve success, it's a different
thing.'

Although the Goddards are generally shown as being close, they display
a surprising lack of emotion when Phil's letters cease. The piece loses
some of its direction at this stage and many actions are confusingly left
unexplained.

Meanwhile, Serge refuses conscription and, in protecting him from the
police, Megan becomes a minor celebrity. On election day she is invited
to be a guest on a radio phone-in. Seizing the opportunity to excel in an
emotional scene, Nicole captivated her director and audience as one caller,
a certain Vietnam veteran who has gone AWOL, prompts her to break
down.

'I did that scene in a single take,' says Nicole. 'A six-minute segment, one long facial reaction – not having seen my brother in a long time and finally recognizing his voice.' Although her footage is interspersed with images of her mother's shock and her brother's anger, Nicole amply proves her ability. It is this moving moment that pierced everyone's memory. 'Watching her, there wasn't a dry eye in the whole country,' recalls Duigan.

Interviewed after filming had wrapped in August 1986, Nicole was perceptibly passionate about her work. 'It's been my most challenging role. I got to do more emotions than just being scared or sweet. It was a real female role, bittersweet with different sides. I do tend to get inside my character. She became very real to me. Sometimes it was hard to go home from playing a fourteen-year-old to being nineteen – and then, when I played a twenty-two-year-old, I became calmer, mature. The character has to be real to me, otherwise you're just playing.'

It was clear that she was now completely hooked. 'From then on, there was never the slightest doubt about the path I was going to follow,' she recalls. 'Win or lose, I was going to stick with acting.'

The implications of Nicole's accomplished role in *Vietnam* were far-reaching. On a financial level, she gained her independence and rented a flat in Melbourne. This enabled her to spend some quality time with Tom Burlinson in private, as well as discover the joys of being house-proud. 'During the making of *Vietnam*, I had my own pad and was really on my own for the first time, cooking and housekeeping,' she enthused.

The first thing Nicole had promised herself when filming completed was a well-deserved two-week skiing holiday. But she was never one to rest on her laurels and was always planning two steps ahead. Veronica Lang, who played her mother in both *Vietnam* and *Winners*, remembers how enterprising the actress was: 'She used to say to me, "Veronica, we should start up a business of some kind – you've got to have something else to fall back on." We were talking about setting up a shop selling antique lace and linen – we both like that sort of thing.'

While nothing came of this particular venture, Nicole did not waste her spare time. 'After doing a film I like doing lots of classes; it brings me back down to earth when I see how many other good actors there are,' she said modestly. Alongside brushing up on her acting skills, she wanted to master various accents to broaden her ability and to that end she enrolled in speech classes.

In a move that would greatly please her parents, Nicole also attended Workers Educational Association evening classes in play-reading and international current affairs. She told reporters that she planned to study for her HSC one day and progress to university. Ultimately, she said, she would love to write her own script, but for the time being, she had other projects up her sleeve.

In December 1986 Nicole returned to the action genre, filming the violent martial-arts movie *Nightmaster* (aka *Watch The Shadows Dance*). In it she plays Amy Gabriel, who hangs around with a group of undisciplined students. At midnight the gang congregate in a derelict building and play 'The Game': contestants have to follow a computer-designed course to reach their base before being shot by rivals armed with guns firing coloured dye. Robby Mason (Tom Jennings) is the champion and Amy desires both him and his title.

The students' science teacher, Sonia Spain (Joanne Samuel), is the only responsible adult – but she is a former lover of Steve Beck (Vince Martin), a villainous martial-arts teacher with an unpleasant secret. The kids inadvertently get mixed up in an undercover narcotics ring, which gives rise to a very graphic shot of a drug injection. The bleak scenes were filmed in a disused power plant against a harsh backdrop of industrial pipes and steel machinery.

'Obsession Is The Deadliest Weapon' the promotional literature claimed boldly, but unfortunately the film was too muddled to truly understand. Nicole and Jennings do their best, but this sinister, futuristic TV movie cannot be described as an appropriate follow-up to *Vietnam* for the actress, particularly as there is little dialogue and the gymnasts and stunt performers almost outnumber the actors. A die-hard Nicole Kidman fan must endure endless martial-arts stunts and gratuitous violence to sit through *Nightmaster*. If you're that way inclined, watch her hair colour mysteriously change whenever she jumps on to the trampoline or exercise bar . . .

When filming drew to a close, Nicole hoped to relax as she was aware that she would soon be involved in extensive promotion for both *Windrider* and *Vietnam*. 'When you're constantly at work it's easy to take it all for granted,' said the level-headed actress. 'I see actors who have been out of work for five or six months, and it jolts me. I think if I get away, take a break, it'll bring me back down to earth and make me appreciate it more.'

After spending Christmas with her family, Nicole revisited one of her old haunts, travelling to Rome in February 1987. This was not the break she had promised herself, but more work, although she rightly described it as a dream role. 'Imagine – I was paid to sight-see all over Italy for two weeks before shooting even started,' she told anyone questioning her relentless schedule.

The ABC production, titled *Un'Australiana A Roma* (*An Australian In Rome*), took six weeks to film. Nicole played the part of Jill, an innocent Australian in Italy's capital for the first time, enjoying the attentions of two Latin lovers.

'Jill is twenty-two, and quite naïve,' explained the adventurous nineteen-year-old. 'But by the end of the movie she has learnt about love and becomes rather cynical. I had to scream and cry and endure a lot of mental torture. The movie is very Italian – by that I mean passionate. It's all about a love triangle which develops between Jill and two brothers. My co-stars are delicious and I'm learning a lot about Italian men! They definitely don't like skinny women and have been trying to make me put on weight since I arrived here.'

Nicole was able to overcome her leanness by tucking into pasta, but found the language barrier a little more difficult, particularly with her director, Sergio Martino. 'It was so hard because I was working with an all-Italian crew and an Italian director who couldn't speak English. As I speak very little Italian, I had to have an interpreter to tell me what Sergio was saying.' Granted, it was an excellent experience, but Nicole complained that it was exceptionally hard work and felt a little out of her depth. 'They have a completely different style of work. They dub everything and, much to my dismay, they might use another voice to dub my part.'

5

Making Waves

'*Vietnam* opened so many doors,' acknowledged Nicole of the series, which aired in spring 1987, while she was in Italy. 'Without it, I would've probably just drifted along, maybe done a couple of unmemorable film parts until I lost heart and just faded away.' Having already undertaken some 'unmemorable film parts', Nicole suddenly saw her professional status rocket.

Terry Hayes, who co-wrote *Vietnam*, was so impressed by Nicole's poignant radio scene that he penned a script with the actress at the forefront of his mind. 'I know when I was writing *Dead Calm* I kept saying, "Nicole for the lead role,"' recalls Hayes. 'I think they were all thinking, "Oh, he's fallen in love with her." Well, it's not true, but I did feel very protective towards her.'

Based on Charles Williams's 1963 novel *Dead Calm*, Hayes's gripping screenplay revolves around an Australian couple, John and Rae Ingram, struggling to survive after their cruise is interrupted by psychotic American Hughie Warriner. Orson Welles had previously attempted to film the story, retitled *The Deep*, in 1969, but the project was shelved when actor Laurence Harvey died on location. This time around,

Australian director Phillip Noyce (*Heatwave, Echoes Of Paradise*) was at the helm for the $10 million Kennedy Miller production.

While the relationship between the actress, the writer and the producers had become close, Noyce needed some convincing that Nicole was indeed right for the lead. 'We could have cast anyone in the world to play Rae Ingram,' says Noyce of the decision, which was made in 1986, before *Vietnam* was broadcast. 'We had people like Debra Winger and Sigourney Weaver in mind; money wasn't an issue. But Terry kept drawing my attention to Nicole.

'I saw the [radio station] scene from *Vietnam* by itself, out of context from the rest of the show. I was watching Nicole and she was so convincing – that was it. Once we screen-tested her it was hard to see anyone else for that part. Terry, George Miller and myself all believed so firmly in this woman's ability, we were prepared to suffer the consequences of not having a "name" actor in the role!'

Nicole was actually in Italy finishing *Un'Australiana A Roma* when she read the script for *Dead Calm*. Whether or not she knew the lengths to which Hayes had gone to secure her the role, her first instinct to decline the opportunity must have been galling for him. With only two other actors in the story, she initially felt the project was too demanding. Upon further contemplation, she realized that the best roles would always be a challenge – and this was one to which she would rise.

Aged just nineteen, Nicole was cast as a woman at least a decade older who is mourning the loss of her child with her husband, a distinguished naval officer. 'I knew how lucky I was to land such a dramatic role, because every actress in Australia wanted it as much as I did,' she says. Winger and Weaver aside, this was a much-coveted part and pitted her against 'name' actors Sam Neill (*My Brilliant Career, Plenty*) and Billy Zane (*Back To The Future, Critters*).

Anxious to justify the supreme faith shown in her acting ability by Hayes and Noyce, Nicole left no stone unturned. Not content to just cope with events onscreen, she tried to understand the history of her character. 'She wanted to meet navy wives, mothers, and mothers who've lost children,' explains Noyce.

And so Nicole became deeply entrenched in Rae's emotional state. 'I somehow had to find maternal feelings,' she says. 'About a week before we started shooting I woke up from a dream believing, *really* believing, that I had my own little boy in bed with me – just for those two seconds or so when you're not sure whether it's a dream or reality.

'When I had experienced that amazing maternal feeling, *then* I could work on imagining losing that.' Sadly, as the audience only sees a few flashbacks of the traumatic car crash in which Rae's son dies, much of this research was in vain – the drama at sea quickly supplants any concerns for her recent history.

Before she could begin work on *Dead Calm*, Nicole had to endure some pain of her own. 'I can't smile,' she mumbled at the beginning of May 1987. 'I've just had my wisdom teeth out and my mouth hurts.' She spent a week recuperating in her new home – the independent teenager had just bought a flat in Mosman, New South Wales (just west of Sydney). 'I've been determined to get a place of my own by the time I was twenty,' she proclaimed, 'and I'm twenty on the twentieth of June so I scraped in.' The timing was right for her goal, but wrong for her schedule: the apartment promptly remained empty as she was immediately away filming.

Dead Calm took over four months to film, mainly on location in the Whitsunday Passage, in between the Great Barrier Reef and the eastern coast of Australia. The cast and crew primarily lived on Hamilton Island, but spent weeks at a time on a flotilla, shooting out at sea. 'It was just brutal,' recalls Nicole. 'We filmed from sun-up to sundown. The weather was hot and sticky. We were all drained and exhausted.'

No wonder she was shattered. Nicole had taken it upon herself to arrive on location in advance of the others in the name of research. 'I focused all my energies on this part,' she remembers. 'I learnt how to sail an 80-foot yacht by myself so I could do it convincingly. I had an Italian skipper who trained me for six weeks and was extremely tough. He'd yell at me all the time, but he taught me to love the sea.'

Her studies paid off. When Rae has to take manual control of the boat at the onset of a storm, Nicole's performance is genuine. 'You become very obsessive when you're making the film and you tend to take quite a few risks,' she says. There were some limits, however: the thrill-seeker was forbidden from climbing to the top of the mast. 'That wasn't me in that shot – it was too dangerous. If I'd put a foot wrong I would have been dead.' A stunt double could also have been used for many of the other tough scenes, but the resilient actress always strove for realism.

'One day it was pouring with rain,' she says of the bad times. 'We'd been out sailing and shooting for four or five hours. On the way back a storm came up and I threw up over the side for ten minutes. I couldn't work. I just thought, "Yeah, this is glamour!"' She was not the only one to be severely seasick. 'Sam had that worse than anybody – he'd get off the boat and be positively green!' she sniggers, but Neill had the last laugh as

Nicole's sensitive skin turned lobster-pink from constant exposure to the elements.

Perhaps Nicole's greatest challenge was to convincingly appear ten years her senior. 'She studied posture so that she could carry herself like an older woman,' recalls Noyce. 'And she did a lot of voice training so she'd sound older.' Her height, now a fully-grown 5 feet 11 inches, helped the teenager to seem more mature, and Nicole tried to add to the weight she had gained in Italy, hoping it would lend some authenticity to her role. Sadly, with her features still undefined, the extra layer resembled puppy fat waiting to be shed, and, combined with her strident Aussie accent and strangely masculine good looks, this made the actress seem incongruously young as Rae.

More importantly, she needed to be credible as the wife of John Ingram. Sam Neill was an established actor in his forties with an attractive weathered quality, and Nicole had butterflies before their first meeting. 'Then we went out to dinner and I thought, "You're pretty gorgeous but you're much older than me,"' she said, still content with her own mature leading man. 'We established a fabulous working relationship and understanding of each other.'

Although comfortable as friends, the pairing of a fresh-faced woman with a man obviously twice her age unfortunately left the audience somewhat doubtful about the plausibility of their marriage. 'Originally, the role [of Rae] was a lot older, but they decided to make the age difference between the couple into a positive thing,' Nicole justifies. 'You don't see an older–younger partner relationship presented very often in a way where it isn't being judged.'

Nicole bonded well with Neill, which was picked up by the cameras; they manage to connect through only the most sparse dialogue. At the weekends, after a gruelling week's filming, Nicole let her hair down, had a drink and danced the night away at the local club. 'I used to take Sam out every Saturday night when we were up on the island. And he loved it because they'd play sixties music, and I'd learnt to do all the sixties dancing for *Vietnam* – he was just bowled over,' she says.

Mindful of Rae's disposition, Nicole felt she couldn't be too wild as it would go against her work. Instead, apart from Saturdays, she ensured she slept ten hours each night in preparation for her strenuous day ahead. Conversely, the dark, intense Billy Zane played the role of deranged Warriner with chilling precision and, staying in character, went out every night raising hell.

Nicole believes she could not have built the same relationship with Zane as she had with Neill, because he was supposed to be her antagonist.

'Billy and I were playing characters that were constantly in conflict, and I think there was an unspoken agreement between us that we weren't going to get on. I don't think you can be buddy-buddy with someone you're meant to be struggling with and feeling so much animosity towards.'

Nicole's scenes with Zane were increasingly violent and she found she had inadvertently picked up numerous injuries. 'I've never been so bruised in my life! I was quite proud to be able to pull off my jeans and hear people say, "My God! I've never seen a bruise like that before." It's funny – when you're doing it, you don't feel it. I was so involved and concentrated on the work that I didn't realize a bang here or there is, in two days' time, going to be massively swollen. It keeps you on your toes. It's a great challenge to do your own stunts in your own style.'

A personal distance was undoubtedly required for one of their most difficult scenes together. 'The sex scene was tough acting work – it's rape without one party thinking it's rape,' explains Hayes.

'The real focus is on my face,' says Nicole. 'We see the rape through her reactions, her mind. I did it instinctively. I don't like rehearsing – I want spontaneity.' Using her feminine wiles, Rae agrees to intercourse, buying time to load the ship's shotgun. 'It was very much developed that I wasn't just to be the damsel in distress,' continues the actress. 'Rae grows and finds her inner strength through the course of her ordeal.' Her director was simply in awe of her abilities. 'Only God knows how a teenager could so convincingly play all the complex emotions experienced by that character,' marvels Noyce.

Despite some misgivings about her age, the film has become a classic, largely due to Nicole's insightful portrayal of Rae Ingram. Zane's maniacal appearance and Neill's sterling, primarily solo, performance are complemented by the unsettling direction, featuring numerous extreme close-ups to heighten tension. Graeme Revell's timeless score, heightened with heavy breathing, operatic wailing, ghostly voices and the natural groaning of a sinking ship, helps to create a spooky atmosphere from the outset. As a result of this cinematic minimalism (just three people, two boats and a dog), the film has hardly dated and can still be enjoyed as much today as when it was released.

Although only a modest financial success, *Dead Calm* afforded Nicole her first major breakthrough and showcased her talent to the world.

'It's this ability to be a man's woman and a woman's woman which makes Nicole so extraordinary,' declared Noyce. 'There is a purity about her. She is very beautiful, but she never exudes a sexuality, particularly one that is manipulative. I shudder to think what she will be like in ten years if she continues to develop like this.'

'I think it's a great piece of film-making and I do have a great role,' said Nicole, but she was typically less happy with her own performance. 'I think I could have done it better, or with a different interpretation. But it's up there now and that's that. But *I* wouldn't be raving about it.' Fortunately, the public disagreed when *Dead Calm* was released around the world in the spring of 1989.

✷

'When you're doing a physical film like *Dead Calm*, I think you wish you were doing dialogue and stage more. Then when you're doing stage, you wish like anything that you were outside.

'At the time, though, *Dead Calm* was all-consuming. It was hard to sustain that level of energy through the whole film, and to keep changing. It could have become very boring if the reactions were always the same, so I had to find different levels of fear. I was exhausted,' says Nicole.

Other than the odd visit to the local nightclub, Nicole's only light relief had been the celebrations for her twentieth birthday. She was much mistaken if she thought it would pass unnoticed. As a treat, Terry Hayes flew in Tom Burlinson and sent the couple, along with a handful of friends, for a blow-out party on the neighbouring Hayman Island. With that sole liaison during the entire fourteen-week shoot, Nicole was now looking forward to spending some quality time alone with Burlinson.

After filming wrapped, Nicole settled into her new flat properly and got stuck into some renovations. Proving that she had a domestic core somewhere under that independent feminist exterior, Nicole took pride in baking for a good cause. On 25 October 1987 Australia's favourite actress entered her delicious lemon sponge in the local Great Celebrity Bake-Off at the Wharf Theatre, raising money for the Sydney Theatre Company. Although failing to win a prize, she preserved her culinary integrity. 'I won't be telling anyone the recipe,' she teased coyly. 'A real cook never reveals what goes into the dish.'

With the commercial success of *Vietnam* secured, and *Dead Calm* under her belt, Nicole could have rested. But, verging on 'workaholism', she accepted yet another project. 'I guess I was scared of being out of work and I wanted to learn, so I would do two or three things at one time. It was hard to say no,' she admitted a year later.

In this vein she managed to squeeze in *The Bit Part*. Written by The Comedy Company's Ian McFadyen, the wryly amusing script delivers clever digs at the more pretentious side of showbusiness – the auditions, the agents, the parties and the rivalry. McFadyen's gently cynical touch is obvious throughout as Nicole's character quips, 'I don't object to nudity, just *exploitative* nudity.'

In a meatier role than some of her previous parts, Nicole appears as the aspiring actress Mary McAllister. She befriends Michael Thornton (Chris Haywood) when he ditches his job as career counsellor to pursue fame as an actor. His wife Helen (Katrina Foster) is less enthusiastic and seeks advice from their friend John Bainbridge (John Wood). While *The Bit Part* has a disappointing ending, it is a well-rounded cautionary tale for all wannabes. This low-budget comedy was initially planned for cinema release but instead ended up going straight to television in January 1989.

Finally getting the chance to go on holiday with Tom Burlinson in March 1988, Nicole couldn't have chosen a worse time if she tried. She wasn't around to hear that her portrayal of Megan Goddard in *Vietnam* had just secured her first trophy – the prestigious Australian Film Institute Award (equivalent to the Emmys) for Best Actress – TV Drama. But perhaps her decision to be the other side of the world in rainy Britain during the ceremony wasn't a coincidence. 'I was travelling in Scotland, it was better not to be there,' she said.

'Terry Hayes gave a wonderful speech and left a bit of mystery in the air, and that was it. I think it is better than me getting up and saying, "Oh thank you, thank you." I would do it, certainly, if I had the chance, but rather than sitting around seeing if you've won awards I think it's much better to be working or travelling and getting on with your life.'

Besides relieving her of award-night nerves, the trip served another purpose. Nicole, who had always seemed an atypical Aussie because of her looks, at last discovered why. 'My boyfriend and I drove into this Scottish village one day and I saw all these people who looked like me – the same skin, the same hair – it was amazing!' she exclaimed. 'It was the first time I had seen anyone in the world who looked like me, and I realized I look like my Scottish grandmother. It was nice.'

Nicole's feet had barely touched home soil before she was planning her next trip. 'Whenever I can, I just take off for a couple of weeks,' said the born traveller. 'I have already been to America and Europe this year, and my next stop is Russia. I love Italy and I am learning Italian.'

Equally passionate about her work, Nicole was already embroiled in another film by April 1988. Without pausing for breath she launched into a small role in the misleadingly titled *Emerald City*. It wasn't a *Wizard Of Oz* rehash as one might think; the name instead refers to Sydney, the verdant city of hopes and dreams, and the hub of the back-stabbing Australian film industry – the familiar world on which native author David Williamson based his plot.

'Essentially it's about a screenwriter who aspires to get a waterfront place and generally succeed in the business,' summarizes director Michael Jenkins. 'It's also about the cultural divide between Australia and America. It was the determination of the character Colin not to give up work, trying to write something Australian.' One could be forgiven for thinking this was fundamentally identical to *The Bit Part*.

The central characters are the screenwriter, Colin Rogers (John Hargreaves), his publisher wife Kate (Robyn Nevin) and an ambitious editor, Mike McCord (Chris Haywood). Colin persuades Kate to uproot their family to further his career, but when he meets Mike he is tempted by his unscrupulous, money-grabbing ideals as much as by his sexpot girl-friend, Helen (Nicole).

Although Helen introduces herself to Colin as a fellow writer who adores his work, this is not her true purpose in the story, and it quickly becomes clear that she is simply alluring totty. While the older, more experienced cast are able to develop well-rounded characters, Nicole's remains purely one-dimensional. This is apparently intentional, as during the film she is described as 'a material girl of the 1980s' by Kate and 'a walking male fantasy' by Colin. She is just an object. Middle-aged men drool over her while their wives seethe with jealousy.

'I play a supporting role, but I did it because it's a film with a lot of dialogue in it,' Nicole says, justifying this odd change of direction. 'I play a girl who wears beautiful clothes and is terribly ambitious.'

'I wanted to use Nicole because she was quite high-profile at the time,' explains Jenkins. 'Although she was extremely young, she was known through her television work and *Vietnam*. I had known her for a long time because we shared the same agent, June Cann. She was a good person to have on board.'

With only a dozen fleeting appearances in the film, Nicole's role as temptress was clarified early on. She performs a pseudo-erotic exercise scene, thrusting her pelvis clad in typical eighties attire (skin-tight leggings, leotard and a crop top) while Mike McCord explicitly narrates the details of their sex life, namely her ability and powerful orgasms. It was certainly a step down after *Dead Calm*.

Ultimately, Helen is there to tempt Colin and the two come together in an urgent, breathy tête-à-tête at a party. 'The most interesting thing about the film was the combination between her and John Hargreaves,' recalls Jenkins. 'John was one of Australia's most famous actors and he was clearly much more mature at the time. The age range was meant to be quite extreme and the combination of them was pretty spectacular!

'She had a couple of reasonably outrageous scenes with John. When they end up together in a hotel room, it turned out to be a comical thing rather than a sexual thing.' Indeed, as the two are stripping and ravishing each other, Colin pictures the potential ramifications of this infidelity in dreamlike flashes. His hesitation frustrates Helen, who runs out, leaving the affair unconsummated.

'It was kind of cheeky,' says Jenkins, 'but Nicole didn't have a problem doing that. She had a lot of style and humour. John was publicly gay so the love scenes between the two of them are really hilarious.'

Otherwise, *Emerald City* is unmemorable. The dialogue is extremely fast-paced and with broad Australian accents it can be hard for a foreigner to follow. The music is consistently overbearing and the audience develops little feeling for any of the lead characters. After appearing in such heavyweight roles in *Vietnam* and *Dead Calm*, it seems the only reason Nicole could have wanted to be involved in this project was the opportunity to work with such respected actors on a satirical script, akin to *The Bit Part*.

Jenkins remained pleased with his casting choice: 'Nicole was a complete professional to work with. She hadn't come through the traditional avenue, but had done so much work that she understood what it was all about. She wasn't difficult at all and would have a go at anything.

'I don't think the film had particular commercial success internationally,' he recalls, 'but it did very well locally and within the industry.' Nicole would find out just how well the following year.

6

I Keep Forgetting She Is Only Twenty-One

Nicole was always keen to build up her CV, tackling as many diverse roles as possible and continually striving to prove herself. While still filming *Emerald City* in April 1988, she lined up her next project, but this time it wasn't another film.

Having never been in a professional stage production before, Nicole was elated to land a part in the Jon Ewing-directed play *Steel Magnolias*, due to open in the York Theatre, Seymour Centre, the following month.

Playwright Robert Harling's comedy had been a smash hit in New York the previous year and Ewing now wanted to put on an Australian version. Set in Miss Truvy's Beauty Parlour in small-town Chinquapin, Louisiana, the play eavesdrops on the gossip of a close-knit group of women who go through the emotional wringer while having a cut-and-blow-dry. The chronicle of marriage, childbirth, illness, sacrifice and loss is carried along by quirky humour, warmth and characters whose observations and apprehensions are shrewdly accurate. Harling uses the phrase 'steel magnolias' as a term of endearment for the six stalwart Southern belles.

Nicole's significant role was that of Shelby Eatenton Latcherie, an imperious, spoilt woman who is plagued by illness.

'My character, Shelby, is a tough introduction to the rigours of live performance,' said Nicole apprehensively before the event. 'She is onstage for the duration of the play and is, in effect, a headstrong girl who is accustomed to getting her own way. It is a demanding role that should well and truly tell me whether or not this is the right path for me to take.

'It is an all-female cast – which is why the play appealed to me in the first place. Men are central to the plot, but being in a play about women, I feel some security in submerging myself in a role that could easily be related to. The other girls have all been there to teach me a lot, which is a bonus. I feel they have so much to offer and I have so much to learn that it is a mutually rewarding experience.'

Rehearsals started on 1 May and, with less than three weeks to curtain-up, Nicole clearly had more than her lines to grasp. 'It's exciting to be working with actresses like Nancye Hayes, Maggie Dence and Pat McDonald, because each rehearsal I feel I am learning something new,' she said. The other stars, including Mellissa Jaffer and Genevieve Lemon, were all respected theatre veterans – Nicole's few appearances on the amateur circuit several years earlier hardly compared.

Well aware that this production was her litmus test – could she really cut it as a stage actress? – Nicole saw the nerve-racking experience as the obvious next challenge. 'I know I have done enough in the past to look with reasonable confidence to the future, but making a name for myself on the stage is important to me,' she said. 'These days, it is important for any actor to be able to be equally at home on television, film or theatre. You have to be versatile. Now I have overcome my fear of working in front of cameras, I have to get over the same fear of working in front of a live audience. It is a goal I have set for myself and I won't be happy until I conquer it.'

With advanced group bookings reaching $120,000, she belatedly confided her greatest fears before the opening night on 18 May: 'I suppose I am something of a pessimist. My dearest hope is for *Steel Magnolias* to be a smash hit, but I do wonder whether or not my performance will be up to the standards of those around me . . .'

In the end, audience and critics alike loved the show and Nicole received rave reviews. 'At the centre of the play are the bride of the first scene and her mother, the counsellor. These are played by Nicole Kidman, making an impressive professional stage debut after her success in films, and Nancye Hayes,' wrote the *Sydney Morning Herald*. 'The teaming of vigorous promise with the assurance and judgment of experience, does much to win our goodwill.'

As the doors opened on the York Theatre's version of *Steel Magnolias*, Hollywood planned to produce a film adaptation of the play. Redoubtable screen veterans such as Elizabeth Taylor, Bette Davis and Katharine Hepburn were among the first names considered, but not cast. Julia Roberts eventually took Nicole's part, receiving an Academy Award nomination for her efforts.

While screen legends were being discussed for the roles in the film, Nicole was asked whom she most admired in the business. Initially, she was inspired by Katharine Hepburn's magnificent performance in 1940's *The Philadelphia Story*. 'She shows you how to do it; she was elegant and funny and smart,' explained Nicole. 'She's a survivor, she is independent, a bit of a rebel and she had always stuck to her guns.'

Nicole's cinematic heroines were diverse – Ingrid Bergman, Vanessa Redgrave and Jane Fonda – but possessed a common denominator: 'They all rebelled against what others wanted to slot them into. They were women with a cause. I think what Fonda did in the 1960s was wonderful, how she stood up and defied her country and said how terrible the Vietnam War was.'

In time, she added more contemporary figures, Meryl Streep and Cher, to the list. 'I think Cher was terrific to be able to shed the Sonny and Cher image and establish herself as a serious actress,' said Nicole, acknowledging something with which she could identify in her transition from child to adult actress. Proving that her evening classes in current affairs had not gone to waste, she also cited a handful of international strong women. 'I admire Margaret Thatcher as a woman, not for her politics. And Benazir Bhutto for getting where she has. I admire Australian film producers Pat Lovell and Margaret Fink for making beautiful films at a time when it was very difficult for women to get into the industry.'

Celebrating her twenty-first birthday while still appearing in *Steel Magnolias* prevented excessive partying, but Nicole had a small-scale affair after the show with her co-stars, her family and a few friends. Tom Burlinson was unfortunately in London filming a mini-series about Second World War fighter pilots, but Nicole mysteriously told the press that the couple planned something 'very big' on his return the following month. 'I don't consider myself twenty-one,' said the birthday girl. 'I've been working in the industry for seven years so I feel a little older than that. Emotionally sometimes I feel a little younger.'

In September 1988 Nicole's long-term relationship with Tom Burlinson came to an end. This was significant enough news in media circles to make headlines in all the Aussie gossip columns.

'After a three-year relationship, actors Tom Burlinson and Nicole Kidman have split, according to friends,' said the *Daily Mirror*. 'The popular young thespians who, because of work commitments, have seen little of each other for the past six months, told friends of the split a few weeks ago. "Tom wanted to settle down, but Nicole was reluctant to make that commitment," one friend of the couple said today. "Nicole is still very young and wants to consolidate her acting career."'

The general consensus was that, fresh from his success in the sequel to *The Man From Snowy River*, thirty-two-year-old Burlinson had decided it was time to make an honest woman of his twenty-one-year-old girlfriend. Sadly, his proposal of marriage was apparently rejected by the actress, who felt she was too young to become his wife.

As was her way, Nicole refused to comment on the break-up, although it was always the first topic on any interviewer's lips. Her understandable reticence on the subject meant that she was still being asked whether she and Burlinson were an item as late as February 1989, some five months later. By March, the pressure to comment had become too much, and she finally admitted, 'It's over now. We are still close. We always will be. He was my first love.

'I wanted to establish my own independence first without having to depend on a man. I think it's unhealthy to get too settled early on in life so I like to move around.' When questioned on marriage itself, Nicole answered:

'Marriage is not a big issue with me. It's finding someone who is supporting, loving and concerned that matters and I think that's very hard. Life is short. You don't have much time so you must follow your own star. That may sound selfish but it isn't meant to be. It's just what my mother always said to me: "Whatever you do in life, don't give up your own dreams".'

As luck would have it, Nicole was not alone for long.

'I first met Nic at the end of 1988, when she came to see me in *Heartbreak Kid*,' recalls Marcus Graham, another Australian actor. 'I then met her again in the foyer at the opening of something and I approached her and asked her out.'

At twenty-five, Graham was more of Nicole's generation than either of her previous boyfriends. His dark-haired good looks captivated Nicole, and they began seeing each other. Graham's reluctance to talk about their relationship, which might have heightened his profile in the media, only endeared him to her more.

Graham, who came from Perth, was relatively well-known himself, and not long after meeting Nicole he was being hailed as Australia's latest sex symbol. Like Burlinson, Graham was a child of a broken home, his father, the television actor Ron Graham, having walked out when he was very young. He had graduated from the West Australian Academy of Performing Arts in 1986, going on to star in theatre productions including *Biloxi Blues*, *The Rivers Of China* and the aforementioned *Heartbreak Kid*. Setting his sights on the big screen but by no means restricting himself to a life in front of the camera, he injected Nicole's life with his enthusiastic dedication to her world.

While their romance bloomed, Graham found himself accepting a succession of roles as a television heart-throb, in *Good Guys Bad Guys*, *Halifax FP* and *Blue Murder*. He would continue shooting his best-known part as 'Wheels' in the popular teen soap *E Street* in June 1989, having been called back following a ratings-grabbing stint in March. Wheels was a reclusive character who had been confined to a wheelchair since a motorbike accident. His part really took off over the summer and, compounding Nicole's success, the pair became one of Sydney's most glamorous and talked-about celebrity couples.

Nicole wasn't yet ready to move in with her lover, as personal space was very important to her. Acting work was coming thick and fast, so although she was very much taken with Graham, she kept him at arm's length. 'I got to think of my personal life less and less. There never seemed to be time for romance,' she recalls.

An in-depth interview with the young actress in *Australian Rolling Stone* published at this time gives a good insight into her innermost thoughts and general lifestyle. On the subject of her love life she was, as always, reserved, but she officially acknowledged her link to Marcus Graham. However, she stressed that she was a long way away from settling down.

'I never show my own personal emotions when I'm working, I save it for when I go home and I'm by myself,' she confessed. 'That's why I like living by myself, because you've got to deal with it, and you can't really lean on someone. You can't go home and cry on a shoulder, you've got to go home to an empty house and you've got to be there with you and your mind.'

Nicole continued to divulge the hardships of such an intensely pressurized job. 'I can understand people going off the rails, it's really difficult. One minute you're travelling around the world first-class, staying in the best hotels as though you're a multi-millionaire. The next minute you come back and you're not working and you can't afford to go out to dinner.

'So you've got these incredible extremes in your life, which make it very hard to cope with. If you get too attached to luxury then it's dangerous.' It seemed the awareness of being better off than others was also a consideration. 'It's so strange. People are continually saying, "Anything you want, just tell us." You end up walking around going, "My God, I don't deserve all this," and feeling like you're bluffing it.'

Elsewhere, Nicole hinted at the domestic differences that had emerged between her and her peers. 'Most of my friends have nothing to do with the world of movies,' she said. 'We've all known each other since we were students so we're all more or less the same age, but many of them are now married with children. That's not something that attracts me at the moment. I'm still young and I've got my whole life in front of me if things don't work out.'

When not up to her eyeballs in acting offers, Nicole relaxed in the most regular ways she could. 'I go out and see bands and movies, I play tennis and do aerobics, and I've got friends that I see who are really important in my life,' she said. She visited her family at least once a week, attended her acting classes and listened to jazz.

'You must have as much normality as possible and live and experience things,' she stressed. 'You're portraying real people on stage or screen and if you're living the superficial life, how are you going to be able to tap into the emotions that are required?'

Even her chosen means of transportation was not a flash limousine, but her mother's second-hand car. 'I had an old bomb for a while. I'm not into cars, I'd never ever buy an expensive car, because I like being able to hit a pole and not having to worry. I hit a lot of things,' she laughed, displaying her charmingly self-deprecating sense of humour.

In fact, the only thing that seemed to bother Nicole was the public recognition. She had one particularly disturbing experience after she slipped up and named the location of her property. 'I had this crazy hanging around outside the house,' she said. 'It scared the hell out of me.'

On the whole, though, she was quite tolerant of her devotees. She had a famous face and a famous boyfriend, and her fans always wanted a piece of her, regardless of the circumstances.

'It doesn't *really* bother me, but sometimes, when you're having a relaxing meal in a restaurant and chatting about personal things, it can be an unwelcome invasion of your privacy,' she shrugged. 'But I suppose from the minute you decide to be an actress, you become a public personality and must accept the consequences. After all, it's the public that have brought you fame, and signing an autograph isn't too much to ask.'

Six months prior to its release in early 1989, *Dead Calm* had aroused substantial interest within the industry. As early as July 1988, Nicole was considering new offers from four top American showbusiness agencies.

By October, she was ready to start meeting people and making some decisions. Braving what was an alien world alone, the Aussie actress flew to Los Angeles to find an agent. It was tougher than she expected. Bewildered, she called Dr Kidman one night at 3 a.m. in tears. 'It was weird,' she mused later. 'I suppose it was jet lag, but I said to my father, "I don't know what I'm doing here. This place is so strange and all these people want to do is talk, talk, talk." He told me to order room service, take a warm bath and go to bed and relax. Everything seemed OK after that.' Soon after, she wearily returned home with her tail between her legs. Despite the buzz around her name, Nicole had been overwhelmed. Without some kind of guiding light, she reiterated her decision to remain in the safe haven of Australia.

A month or so later, Nicole again found herself inundated with interest, this time with some direction. 'I got agents calling me, in the middle of the night because of the time difference, saying, "I want to represent you". So Kennedy Miller flew me to Los Angeles,' she said matter-of-factly.

These calls weren't from any two-bit agencies. In November Nicole Kidman was having a breakfast meeting in Los Angeles with none other than Sam Cohn. The co-founder of International Creative Management (ICM) in 1975 along with a group of industry veterans, Cohn specialized in moulding the careers of young actors. He famously took both Meryl Streep and Sigourney Weaver on to his books straight from Yale.

'It is extraordinarily rare that not only do you find beauty and talent, but that it is highly developed in a person of that age,' remarked Terry Hayes of Nicole. 'I keep forgetting she is only twenty-one. That makes her in a group of one at the moment, not just in Australia, but in the world.' It was this potential that appealed to Cohn.

Something of a demigod in Hollywood, Cohn was used to doing business in a no-nonsense fashion. He arrived in Los Angeles on the night flight from New York, met the young actress for breakfast, told her he had seen her work and announced that he wanted to represent her. Nicole signed the contract as Cohn finished his coffee. Then he was gone, back to New York to start work. As simple as that.

Nicole was taken aback at the ease with which she joined the ranks of Oscar-winning actors such as Woody Allen, also represented by Cohn. 'I had a really good response over there,' she explained. 'They're into Australian girls at the moment. They just find us very strange, apparently. I suppose we're a bit rougher round the edges and a lot more laid-back.'

Undoubtedly talented, Nicole also benefited from pure good fortune. 'After *Dead Calm*, what she could do was very obvious, but I didn't think she would be lucky enough to make that leap,' says Howard Rubie frankly. 'There were hundreds of leading ladies in Australia and I think you have to bear in mind her age at that time.'

But Nicole was always brought up to be a realist, something which fortunately kept her grounded during this whirlwind period. 'It's pretty crazy for a girl of her age to have the world's leading agent fly over for breakfast with her in Los Angeles and sign her up,' said Terry Hayes. 'To be paid very, very substantial amounts of money; to be constantly told that she is an extraordinarily beautiful woman and have that made manifest by magazines all over the world – you know, one could go really crazy.'

Returning to Australia jubilant this time, Nicole had to consider her boyfriend's feelings. At that point, Marcus Graham had been unemployed for five months, while it seemed that Nicole kept landing on her feet. 'While I was really happy for Nic, I felt it magnified my own inadequacies,' he openly admitted. 'Nic was ringing me from New York and telling me she had just joined Meryl Streep's agent, Sam Cohn. I thought, that's great, I can't even get a bloody commercial.

'I really felt lousy and small, but instead of feeling envious, I turned the situation into a positive thing. Nic is very supportive and believes in me, so she drove me to succeed in spite of the odds. An actor's most valuable tool is his confidence and Nicole, no matter where she is, has always given me lots of that.'

Having comforted Graham, Nicole wasted no time and in December 1988 was back in America. She visited Cohn and met with film stars including Melanie Griffith and Natasha Richardson. But the person who caused the greatest tabloid sensation was Oscar-winning actor and director Warren Beatty. Hollywood's greatest lothario apparently had both personal and professional interests in mind.

'I saw him about a film,' said Nicole, 'and he asked to see me again, and again and again. And then it became almost like, "I want to take you out to dinner" – you know, the typical Warren Beatty thing . . .' Despite her penchant for older men, Beatty was not her type. She quickly tried to downplay the episode, perhaps for the sake of Graham. 'Sometimes stories get blown out of all proportion. You get to meet a lot of people and sure, I met Warren Beatty and he was very nice and gave me some good advice. It's always important to listen to people in that situation because they've been through it all. And he did have some good advice.'

The beginning of 1989 saw the start of promotion for *Dead Calm*. During a whirlwind trip to America and Britain, journalists wondered how she kept going. 'When I decided to become an actor, I knew there were two ways I could approach it. I could be either very disciplined or more flexible,' she said sensibly. 'I chose to discipline myself. It's not a matter really of what I do, but what I don't do.

'I don't stay out late. I don't smoke, drink or take drugs. It means saying to myself, "No I can't go to that party tonight", or "I've got to stay home to work on this", not turning on the TV or going to bed when there's work to do.

'I try to do weekend workshops if there are some available at the Actors' Centre. I also try to stay fit and go to the gym four or five times a week.' One wonders when the poor girl ever had time to have fun, let alone see her boyfriend, but her hard work was starting to reap rewards.

In January 1989 she was nominated for the Best Newcomer Award by the Sydney Theatre Critics for her role in *Steel Magnolias*. But the Australian Film Institute Awards later in the year caused some consternation. That Nicole would be nominated in the Best Actress category for her work in *Dead Calm* was believed to be a given – but she was not. Terry Hayes had something to say about this perceived snub. 'It's ridiculous that Nicole didn't get a nomination for Best Actress,' he ranted. 'The fact that she didn't is a testament to the bitchiness of the Australian film industry.'

Even more remarkable, then, that when the awards were announced in Melbourne in October, Nicole won Best Actress In A Supporting Role. Amazingly, it was her work in *Emerald City* that earned her the accolade – maybe Hayes had a point. With its pertinent jibes at the industry, *Emerald City* was actually nominated for a handful of awards by the AFI, who perhaps felt they needed to display a sense of humour.

Despite the critical acclaim she was receiving, Nicole remained her harshest critic. 'I'm never pleased with anything,' she complained. 'I don't sit there watching myself and think, "Yeah, I'm fantastic in that role." I pick fault with everything. But you must never tell anyone your faults, because then everyone else will see them! I used to see my height as a fault, and now I see it for what it is. Basically you have to realize there are things you just can't change.'

7

Play To Win

'I've been lucky and part of that luck has been the alliance I have built up with the Kennedy Miller company. I've been taken as a very young actress and given some of the best roles written in Australia,' acknowledged Nicole. 'I have a strong alliance with them. It's like a studio thing. If it had been the 1930s I would have signed to them. They feel like a family to me.'

After the runaway success of *Vietnam*, Kennedy Miller were keen to cast Nicole in future productions. She actually signed up for their next project before it was even written, and while still working on *Dead Calm*.

Terry Hayes was tickled to be commissioned to write a six-hour mini-series especially for Nicole. 'It is the only thing I have ever written for an actor,' he said. 'I was so impressed by her in *Dead Calm*, I said I wanted to work with her again.'

The result was *Bangkok Hilton*, which Hayes described as 'totally fictional, but something that many people will be able to identify with'. With an impressive cast under Ken Cameron's expert direction, filming on the multi-million-dollar drama commenced in March 1989 and lasted twelve weeks.

'It's a story about unrequited love, betrayal, rejection, and a father and daughter who find each other,' elaborates Nicole. *Bangkok Hilton* starts as the story of Hal Stanton (Denholm Elliott, star of *A Room With A View*), an officer court-martialled from the army who rebuilds his life under a pseudonym in Australia. He meets and falls in love with Catherine Faulkner, a wealthy socialite. When Stanton's roots are discovered he is disgraced, and Catherine's disapproving mother, Lady Faulkner, keeps the lovers apart. But her daughter is already pregnant. Lady Faulkner insists that Catherine keeps the unwanted child as a constant reminder and consequently there is little love between Catherine and her daughter Katrina, known as Kat.

Here enters Nicole, an awkward girl with very pale skin, unruly hair harshly pinned back and thick glasses. She is nervous and edgy, and her chronic asthma is treated as a disability. Oppressed by her mother, the twenty-year-old has rarely left the confines of the family mansion and engrosses herself in building dolls' houses, including a replica of her own prison-like home. She also draws, a skill inherited from her father, whom she believes to have died shortly after her birth.

The greatest challenge for Nicole was to act 'introverted and submissive, which is the opposite to my own personality. That was the hardest thing for me to do in *Bangkok Hilton*, but, like anyone else, I can tap into feelings of betrayal and rejection in my experience.'

When her mother dies, Kat discovers her journal and with it the truth about her father. Finally she has a purpose in life and sets off to England to trace the tarnished Hal. Feeling a little lost on arrival, Kat is shunned by her uncle because of her father's disgrace. With a few days left before her flight home, she meets Arki Ragan (Jerome Ehlers), a handsome, confident photographer who bowls her over with his amorous attentions. Her uncle has a change of heart, gives Kat a lead in Bangkok (Hal's lawyer) and introduces her to her cousin Sarah. With Sarah's help, Kat is transformed from an ugly duckling into a beautiful swan.

Arki offers to accompany Kat on her journey, and presents her with a camera in a metal attaché case. *En route* to Thailand a relationship develops, and, not for the first time in her career, we see Nicole in various states of undress. Kat is unaware that Arki is a decidedly dodgy character who has planted several bags of heroin in her camera bag. At Bangkok airport Arki swiftly disappears, leaving Kat alone when the drugs in her bag are exposed by sniffer dogs.

Nicole gives a fine performance as the confused victim interrogated in a foreign language and threatened with the death sentence. 'The role was written especially for me so I felt insecure a lot of the time about how I was doing,' she recalls. 'Kat believes she can't cope, then she finds strength from somewhere. It was very emotionally draining at times and at others very frustrating.' Nicole convincingly displays a range of emotions, from despair and remorse to anger, courage and determination.

With nowhere else to turn, Kat contacts her father's lawyer again and the second half of the series depicts her attempts to escape the death penalty. Nicole looks suitably terrified when Kat is sentenced during an overwhelming courtroom sequence. She then finds out what life is like in the city's most notorious prison, cynically nicknamed the 'Bangkok Hilton'. Graphic scenes show the squalid conditions in the jail, where bribery and corruption are commonplace, as are drugs and disease.

'We did one very emotional scene and there were camera problems so we had to go back and do it again,' remembers Nicole. 'It was very difficult. You couldn't throw a tantrum, you just had to be very disciplined and do it again. People expect feature-film quality from a mini-series but you don't have a feature film's time or budget, so it puts added pressure on every word.'

Bearing in mind her professed wish to shed new light on world situations and produce thought-provoking pieces, Nicole embarked upon the research for her role in earnest. She talked to a woman who had spent six years in a Thai jail, studied books on the subject and wore authentic heavy iron shackles for the jail scenes.

For the first two months of filming, Nicole continued getting into character in a rather unpleasant manner. She spent an hour every day in make-up, where the artists created ugly bruises and mosquito bites on her pale arms. 'It wasn't easy,' she says. 'The minute I would get to work they put dirt under my fingernails, oil in my hair and painted large, black circles under my eyes. It was very hard to work that way, five days a week, twelve hours a day for eight weeks. It was so depressing, but you can make that work for you.'

Originally aired as three two-hour episodes on the ABC network beginning on 5 November 1989, *Bangkok Hilton* was later rebroadcast in six one-hour segments. Nicole would go on to win another AFI award for her performance.

Bangkok Hilton as a whole is less impressive than *Vietnam* and comes across as somewhat stilted and unrealistic in parts. However, Nicole was afforded a series in her own right and was joined by a stellar cast featuring television regulars Norman Kaye and Gerda Nicholson as well as Elliott, Ehlers, Joy Smithers and Noah Taylor.

On another positive note, the big-budget production enabled Nicole to travel extensively as segments were shot all around the world. 'Those location shots in Bangkok and India are the connective tissue,' explains director Ken Cameron. 'They provide the realism and the colour. Also, the adventure of making a film in places you haven't been to before is exciting. It adds to the spontaneity and I think that shows in the series.'

After a gruelling first stint in Sydney, Nicole relaxed when a skeleton crew hit exotic Goa on the west coast of India. 'This is the easy bit,' Nicole said when the press caught up with her. 'Sydney was heavy going. I feel I have been a bit lazy here. Usually when I am acting I feel more concentrated. I don't laugh and carry on between scenes. But here, in this beautiful place, I feel more relaxed.'

In Goa the rising star was spotted ambling through a bustling riverfront market at dusk. Cameron was amused as he watched her haggle with an old woman selling mangoes. 'This is what makes Nicole such a professional and so wonderful to work with,' he said. 'She goes with the flow, staying in character.

'You are continually surprised by the fact that one moment she seems to be a very young woman enjoying herself and being spontaneous. The next minute she's a serious actress, capable of a performance which can move you in a way you don't expect from one so young. She looks wonderful, is enormously appealing onscreen, and has something about her which belongs to the time. To have all those qualities is a rare thing.'

Only four members of the cast were required for the overseas shoots and Nicole spent her rare days off with Ehlers. Together they took in some of the local sights and visited an animal sanctuary to see the enormous pythons. Ehlers politely declined Nicole's daring invitation to join her in a midnight swim in the snake-infested sea.

More down-to-earth were their regular games of tennis, although the woman with boundless energy even managed to turn those into a competition. 'I have always been taught that you play to win,' says Nicole. 'I believe you should have drive and determination in whatever you do. You don't have to be ruthless, but you have to be disciplined. The people who are successful are the ones who know what they want and go for it.' Ehlers conceded defeat one morning and hung a large sign on his hotel room door saying 'No'.

'I really hate hotel rooms,' says Nicole, explaining her incessant need for activity. 'The only thing I do in a hotel room is sleep and I'll go out and do anything rather than stay there after that. It's a pet hate of mine. It doesn't matter if it's the most luxurious hotel room in the world, what do you *do* in there, apart from pick up the telephone?'

The late Denholm Elliott also travelled with them and treated her with paternal politeness. 'I think she's very talented,' said the older British actor. 'She has a very strong personality. She reminds me of Vanessa Redgrave.'

Although she did form friendships with the other members of the cast, Nicole was glad to have her mother's company for some of her journey. 'I've been very lucky,' she said. 'I'm close to my parents and my sister – my mother travels with me whenever she can, which is marvellous. Their support and love make me feel much more secure when I'm far away from home.'

If Nicole was to fulfil her latest goal, she would increasingly require the stabilizing security of her loved ones at home.

'My ambition is to have worked in every country. That's why I like to travel. I think you have to live life to the full. That's my creed both as an actress and a person.' She hoped her quest would include a few other adventures: 'I'd like to have a farmhouse in Tuscany, make a movie in Egypt and play Chekhov in Russian.'

During the filming of *Bangkok Hilton* in March 1989, Nicole was offered two very different projects simultaneously. The first was a major role in a big-budget Hollywood movie, backed by Paramount. She would have appeared opposite a well-known actor in a romantic comedy, and with the American release of *Dead Calm* set for April, it could have set her up immediately as an international lead actress.

However tempting and potentially lucrative this offer must have been, under Sam Cohn's counsel, Nicole made the bold decision to turn it down. 'He understands I want to be based in Australia,' she said. 'Basically he's keeping my options open.' Although America was beckoning, she was happy with her life in Sydney, near her family, friends and boyfriend. There were enough appealing Australian offers pouring in, so any part which might remove her from her home for a substantial amount of time and thrust her under the world's microscope would have to be absolutely perfect.

'I decided it was probably the wrong thing for me at that stage,' says Nicole of the Paramount movie. 'But I felt a bit strange, like, "Oh my God, I should never have turned something like that down!" But you have to make a decision whether you do it for the money and to become famous, or whether you do it because you want to keep working for the rest of your life. I want to do something that's got more substance.'

Instead, Nicole surprised her critics by announcing that she had accepted the second project – the part of Helena in the Sydney Theatre Company's upcoming production of *A Midsummer Night's Dream*. This gave her the opportunity to establish herself as a credible stage actress, building upon her considerable success in *Steel Magnolias* the previous year.

'If I'd accepted Paramount I could buy a wonderful house and drive around in a super car,' she said. 'But I'd be selling myself in something I really hated and I'd be bored to death in a big house, probably yearning to do Shakespeare.'

Nicole neglected to mention the added bonus – that she would be starring opposite Marcus Graham in *A Midsummer Night's Dream* – but relayed that she had not even mentioned her momentary dilemma of choosing between the two options to her parents.

'They wouldn't have a clue! As a joke they used to say, "Take the money and run," but now they realize that I have to be more selective and there's no point doing something my whole heart isn't in.'

There was another benefit – in addition to working with her boyfriend – of having chosen the 'serious actress' route via William Shakespeare: 'My parents have even stopped going on about how I could always go to university,' she grinned.

Towards the end of April 1989, Nicole embarked on a gruelling publicity tour for *Dead Calm*. She headed to America first for a week's visit, then followed the film's progress back to Sydney, in time for its Australian premiere on 8 May.

Although Sam Cohn had no doubt warned her what to expect, the actress was a little surprised to discover that she was already something of a favourite with American audiences. They had lapped up her televised portrayal of Megan in *Vietnam* and taken extremely well to Rae in *Dead Calm* in the film's test screenings across the States some months previously. When *Dead Calm* opened to rave reviews and substantial box-office returns, Nicole made the transition from modest household name to instant superstar almost overnight.

'It's weird,' she said. 'People have different feelings towards you – and it's only happened in the last three months.' Publicity demands were tough in America and Nicole found herself typically doing twenty-five interviews per day, fending off endless questions about when she was going to move to the States, her fellow Aussie actors, Mel Gibson and Paul Hogan, and the vital differences between Australian and American women. 'I have a temper, but it would probably be detrimental to my career to lose it during an interview,' griped Nicole of these junkets after her return. 'You've got to keep yourself in check – you don't want to be like Sean Penn and slam people in the mouth. It's part of the job.'

Many journalists understandably focused on Nicole's age. Still only twenty-one, her fans marvelled at how she could appear so mature while barely a woman. 'I think it was Debra Winger who said acting was a child's game with adult rules, and I agree,' Nicole would say. 'As for growing up too quickly, well, I don't even know what it means. Sometimes you try to be adult and you have to have a certain amount of common sense, if that's what being an adult is. But you've got to keep the child in you alive.'

The novelty of the overwhelming American interest wore thin fairly quickly and Nicole had no trouble keeping reality in check. 'It's crazy,' she later remarked. 'It's not a situation where you feel relaxed. You sort of feel like a fraud. You live like that for a week then you go back to your little unit and you drive your old car. I can't place a lot of emphasis on it. I mean, you can be hot one day and not the next. One moment you're on the "in" list and the next you're "out" . . .'

Nicole gratefully returned to Sydney for *Dead Calm*'s Australian premiere. She arrived on the sturdy arm of Phillip Noyce. 'Yes, I am nervous,' she admitted to the throngs gathered outside. Unfortunately, the promotion in her own country was, if anything, more challenging, as she plunged into another PR treadmill involving television and radio interviews, press conferences and photo shoots.

'I don't know if I like the media attention but I'm prepared for it,' she said, which was just as well considering the coverage that month: six pages, including the cover, of the *Australian* magazine, two pages in *New Idea*, features in all the daily newspapers and a piece on *60 Minutes*. Nicole Kidman was definitely the film world's darling, and there were now rumours that she might start winning awards outside Australia.

'Well, I don't know about winning an Oscar next year!' she responded in her usual down-to-earth manner. 'They say you shouldn't believe your own publicity and this is very true. If the media wants to say things that are nice and complimentary, that's fine. I know what I'm really like. I know I can be a pain in the backside!

'I think there is a lot of pressure on me at the moment, particularly to come up with the goods and do a film in America. But I don't know if I want to do that.

'I like living in Australia. I feel relaxed here. I get very stressed when I'm overseas. I don't sleep very well and I have to watch that. Stress can be very damaging.'

Although she was greatly flattered, the ever-unpretentious Nicole found herself more than a little bewildered by the effects of fame. 'I used to be able to go almost anywhere and no one would bat an eyelid. But I was at Grace Bros the other day buying lingerie, and I got these guys coming up to me and asking for my autograph.' Totally unprepared for the attention, the hottest new actress saw no reason why not to put down the underwear and scribble something appropriate – she was lucky to escape an embarrassing 'Nicole's Knickers'-type tabloid splash.

Nicole's parents initially had the same bemused reaction.

'Mum and dad are baffled,' she said. 'They've never seen anything like it. My father was lecturing in Brisbane the other week and someone put his hand up and asked if he was my father. Imagine! He's spent ten years at university, he's got a PhD and all anyone wants to know is whether I'm his daughter.'

An interview in the *Sun-Herald* a few months later revealed that all the extra attention was beginning to get to Nicole, although she was always at pains to stress that she enjoyed her work and was grateful for the praise: 'It's good, it's fun and I get a lot of encouragement, but when you get there people start pulling you down,' she sighed. 'I have received a lot of criticism from other actors and I used to get very hurt by it when I was younger. Now I don't place so much emphasis on it. I place emphasis on the opinions of about five people. I can't listen to everyone because I'd be an absolute mess.'

The actress went on to confess that she would be 'devastated' if her career was now to sink without trace, but she had a 'Plan B' in reserve if necessary. 'I love what I'm doing but if it all fell through I would take myself off to Italy for a while, go to university there, but it would be very hard.

'I suppose that's what scares me because I feel like it hasn't really been that hard up till now. I spent seven years trying to get good roles and in the last three years I've had some fantastic ones. But you hear of people who have waited forty years for just one good role and I feel strange about that. But I guess someone has to fill the "young actor" role.'

Peer pressure and the ongoing debate over whether she would desert Oz for foreign shores eventually got the better of Nicole. After all the fuss over *Dead Calm* had subsided, in July she returned to America for a couple of months, ironically for some respite. Sam Cohn helped her to find an apartment in New York, and away from all the hyperbole in her native country she spent time finding her feet, reading scripts and attending acting lessons.

Marcus Graham's career was taking off back in Australia, and although the couple kept in touch with hour-long telephone calls, Nicole was on her own. Halfway across the world, Janelle made a concerted effort to keep her daughter's spirits up, sending Nicole 'care packages' containing Australian magazines and jars of Vegemite, but still Nicole was heard to admit, 'The hardest part is the loneliness. It can get very lonely so far from home.'

While the actress buried her head in piles of prospective scripts over in New York, rumours flew thick and fast about roles she might or might not have turned down. *A Midsummer Night's Dream* would not command her attention until much later in the year as it wasn't due to open until December, so she was free to consider other work in the meantime.

Ghostbusters III was, apparently, not of interest, and neither was the much-publicized prospect of starring opposite Dennis Quaid in a $10 million McElroy & McElroy production called *Till There Was You*, a comedy set in New Guinea. 'We think it arose when we said the type of people we were looking for were someone *like* Nicole and Quaid,' squirmed an embarrassed McElroy spokesperson.

Instead, Nicole loyally opted to return to work with her fellow countrymen, and jumped at another opportunity to reconvene with John Duigan and Terry Hayes.

Flirting was a relatively low-budget sequel to Duigan's much-acclaimed *The Year My Voice Broke*, the biggest winner at the 1987 AFI Awards. According to Terry Hayes, Nicole agreed to film a cameo in the movie as 'a favour for John Duigan and me, before she heads off to the U.S.'

Said Nicole: 'I will be playing every schoolboy's fantasy – and the schoolgirl the other girls love to hate.' Much was made of the fact that this was the very last feasible opportunity Nicole – who turned twenty-two before filming commenced in October 1989 – would have of portraying a schoolgirl.

Flirting is a beautifully written coming-of-age story, which maintains a healthy balance between sharp wit and endearing charm and intelligently captures the universal language of insolent teenagers. Alongside its realistic depiction of puberty, it tackles racism and various other cultural, literary and newsworthy issues.

Filmed in Bathurst, Braidwood and Sydney, *Flirting* is set in rural Australia in 1965. The draconian St Alban's Boys' College and Cirencester Ladies' College, a carbon copy of St Trinian's, are boarding schools facing each other in an eternal stand-off across a huge lake. Official meetings between the pupils of the schools entail great sexual tension, and unofficial meetings (of the late-night variety) occur only if a boy is prepared to row across the lake, avoiding detection and a possible caning. Pubescent hormones are rife.

Danny Embling (Noah Taylor), a stuttering misfit known as 'the school dag', falls for the knowing charms of Thandiwe Adjewa (Thandie Newton), the only black pupil at the girls' school. They share a love of existentialist writers and later book into a motel room under the name of Camus.

In her attempts to continue their forbidden relationship, Thandiwe forms an unlikely alliance with the outwardly prim and proper prefect, Nicola Radcliffe (Nicole). 'The part really appealed. I played a head prefect with secrets,' says Nicole of her character's whisky habit.

Nicola is tall, very thin and beautiful: 'Australia's answer to Ursula Andress,' rave the boys, who are in constant competition to spy on her in her underwear. As Nicola, Nicole wore a straight blonde wig and, with little make-up to convince the audience that she is a bona fide teenager, she looks pale, washed-out and otherworldly. Unfortunately, her character is given little depth or screen time and it has to be said that the captivating Thandie Newton steals all the scenes.

Nevertheless, Nicole thoroughly enjoyed herself, not only when in character, but also with her colleagues. Duigan, Hayes and Noah Taylor were old working buddies, and she built an enduring relationship with the teenage Thandie Newton. 'That's the great thing about working with people like this because everyone's in the same boat,' says Nicole. 'You build up strong friendships and when you see the same people again in six months, you feel you've experienced something together. Australia is such a small industry, you tend to run into people again and again, but I suppose in a way that means you sort of drift in and out of their lives.'

Flirting afforded Nicole an opportunity to work with her good friend Naomi Watts, who had the role of Janet Odgers. 'Right from the start, I noticed how focused and dedicated she was,' says Naomi. 'She chats to people, but doesn't go overboard like some do. When you're working on a film, you want to be liked and have a nice atmosphere around, but when you have a difficult scene, you don't want to chat to everyone. You have to get a balance.'

Finally, the set of *Flirting* reunited Nicole with an actor she had first met some ten years earlier on Sydney's amateur theatre circuit: Russell Crowe. It is rumoured that the pair had an affair – they were seen together during filming, though he wasn't in the cast – but there was enough going on in Nicole's life (including her relationship with Marcus Graham) to deter her from getting involved with Crowe, and they became firm friends instead.

8

No Going Back

In September 1989 Tom Cruise, the twenty-seven-year-old star of blockbusters such as *Top Gun, Cocktail, Rain Man* and *Born On The Fourth Of July*, took a friend to see *Dead Calm* at his local cinema. Legend has it that the Hollywood heart-throb leant over to his friend and whispered urgently, 'Who's that girl? I *have* to make a film with her!'

Cruise was bewitched by Nicole Kidman's outstanding performance and immediately set the wheels in motion for her to audition for his latest film, which he was also co-producing – a motor-racing drama with the working title *Daytona*, a reference to Daytona Beach, Florida, where the action would be set. Cruise was already one of the most powerful men in Hollywood by this time and was used to making such things happen, so the fact that the part had yet to be written was by the by.

Nicole was at a film festival in Japan when Sam Cohn called her to tell her that Tom Cruise wanted her to read for him. 'What I didn't know at that stage was that there wasn't even a role for me,' she recalls. 'It was Tom who really pushed hard for me to be taken on. He wanted me to play opposite him – to be the girl who falls for the hero in the storyline.

'I thought, oh yeah, right – I'd been to L.A. before. You go in, you audition, you don't get the job. But hey, free trip!' Nicole left Japan for what she assumed would be a whirlwind excursion. She made plans to meet up with Phillip Noyce in Los Angeles before flying on to England to spend some time with her sister, who had recently moved to London.

The reading for *Daytona* took place in an impersonal conference room with Cruise and five male producers. The film was to be backed by Paramount, the company Nicole had recently turned down in favour of *A Midsummer Night's Dream*. Pulling on her actress's confidence cloak, she strode in, disguising any traces of nerves and jet lag.

'I wanted to meet you,' was the first thing her prospective leading man said. 'I thought you were great in *Dead Calm*.'

'As an actress who's been on the audition circuit, to suddenly have another actor say that to you is . . . well, very nice,' says Nicole. But almost immediately, an unforeseen problem floored all those present.

'When Tom stood up and we shook hands, I found I was looking down at him,' she continues. 'It was terrifically embarrassing to learn I was at least a couple of inches taller. It wasn't that he was so short – it's more that I'm so tall. I knew it simply wouldn't do, having the girlfriend tower over the macho race-car driver.'

Nevertheless, the diminutive actor squared up to Nicole, staring her straight in the eye and giving her a firm handshake. Abruptly, the moment passed and everyone took their seats. Nicole was given a couple of test pages. 'I picked up my script and started reading and everyone in the room fell silent.

'Then Tom started laughing and I started laughing, and we looked at each other as if to say, "Isn't this ridiculous?" He took my breath away. I don't know what it was – chemical reaction? Hard to define. Hard to resist.'

Nicole has since said that she tried her utmost to be nonchalant in this first meeting with Cruise. After all, she was well aware he had a certain advantage over her – she had enjoyed his bittersweet but humorous turn in *Rain Man*, but he had seen her practically naked in *Dead Calm*.

'I thought, "Oh my God, he's this huge movie star",' Nicole recalls. 'He was like this powerhouse. He sort of filled the room . . . He sat down and started talking and got really intense. He started using his hands and his eyes started to sparkle. I couldn't believe the energy coming out of this person. I thought he was an incredible man, totally self-confident about who he was and what he wanted, the kind of person who inspires confidence right off the bat.'

'Yet somehow he seemed so down-to-earth and together. He loved sport, especially baseball. He was just so *normal*. There was something very sweet about him.'

However, Nicole has never been reluctant to get down to basics. 'The moment I laid eyes on Tom I just thought he was the sexiest man I'd ever seen in my life. I was like, "Whoa, this is dangerous!"'

Luckily, Tom felt the same. 'My first reaction to meeting Nic was pure lust,' he says. 'It was totally physical. I thought she was amazingly sexy and stunning.'

After the initial hiccup, the pair seemed oblivious to the problems presented by the difference in their heights. It had been an issue for both throughout their careers: Nicole towered over her co-stars, while Tom had often been considerably shorter than the women playing opposite him. In *Top Gun*, Paramount had been so concerned that his romantic lead, Kelly McGillis, was taller than Tom that they sent her a sticker depicting a pair of high heels crossed through with a red line, akin to a no-smoking sign.*

Nicole once explained, 'I have no inhibitions about my height. I learnt early on to be totally self-assured about it. When I see a guy going out with a taller girl, I immediately like him. It shows he's confident. Most men find it intimidating.' Clearly, it was Cruise's magnetic confidence that drew her to him as much as anything else.

As the meeting drew to a close, it was explained to Nicole that although she had read well, nothing was set in stone. 'I left thinking, "OK, at least I got to visit Los Angeles",' she says. The next morning one of the producers called to tell her the good news: although it was yet to be written, the role was hers.

'But what about my height?' she felt compelled to ask.

'It doesn't bother Tom,' said the producer, 'so it doesn't bother us.'

It was a sad decision to make, but Nicole was forced to confess to the Sydney Theatre Company that, having accepted the unspecified part in *Daytona*, she would be unable to star in their Christmas production of *A Midsummer Night's Dream*. In October 1989 they agreed to sever her contract and the company director, Richard Wherrett, graciously issued a statement wishing her the best of luck.

* Ironically, in *Top Gun* Cruise had played a naval pilot but was actually an inch shy of the minimum height requirement for U.S. navy officers.

'I am extremely grateful for the Sydney Theatre Company's understanding, but disappointed in missing out on working with Richard and playing the role of Helena,' was Nicole's official response. The fact that she had spouted endlessly about how any Hollywood offer would have to be 'perfect' to make her leave Australia behind did not escape the press. And they weren't even aware that Nicole's coveted role hadn't existed a week or so earlier.

After apologizing to Marcus Graham that she wouldn't be working with him in the play, Nicole spent two weeks in Australia publicizing *Bangkok Hilton*, which was screening on Channel Ten. Due to the narcotic element of the plot, many journalists questioned her on drugs and their implications for her younger fans.

'At some stage every child becomes aware of drugs. I always saw it as making a decision on what path you took and I never felt the need for drugs,' she replied (sensibly avoiding any reference to her early teenage experiences, which she would only reveal a decade later). 'Of course, occasionally you say to yourself, "My friends are all doing it" and you wonder about this special mystique drugs have, but I always had this terrible guilt that I'd kill off my brain cells and my brain is too important to me.'

Nicole's role as Kat in *Bangkok Hilton* raised some highly emotive topics, and interviewers seemed to look to the young artiste as a figurehead for her generation.

'I have been brought up to believe in certain issues,' she said hesitantly, 'but I don't believe it's right for me to get up and say this, this and this about things like pollution or nuclear disarmament. I can support certain things by giving my name or money, but I'm a little tentative talking about things I'm not completely knowledgeable in.' Nevertheless, she could always be drawn on the beliefs that her conscientious and forward-looking parents had impressed upon her all her life.

'I have grown up in a decade that didn't promise a great future,' said Nicole. 'But we didn't grow up like some others expecting to get married, have children and everything would be all right. Life just isn't going to be like that.

'We all have to become more politically aware. It's important to read and be informed, not just glance at the newspapers and say: "Oh, well." In the 1990s and into the twenty-first century it is saving our environment that will matter most.

'I also think health issues are important. It is already tough for young women to form relationships because of diseases like AIDS. Health fears mean women don't want to leave boyfriends they have had for some time. We are getting back to a situation where women marry early and have kids — and I think that's dangerous,' she concluded with a frown. There was clearly more to this intense young woman than above-average acting ability and a pretty face, and this was reflected in her plans for the future.

'I can either go along the very serious acting road or along the lighter, more commercial road,' she mused, aware she needed to regain some critical respect after dropping Shakespeare in favour of a lightweight blockbuster. 'I'd like a combination of the two because a film *should* be entertaining, but I'd also like to do films that are controversial, something with more substance than sheer entertainment.' There was that 'substance' word again.

'I mean, it's very hard in America if you go along a very commercial road because it's very hard to break out of . . .' she trailed off thoughtfully.

Nicole's departure for America was then delayed a further week due to a nasty bout of tonsillitis. When the last instalment of *Bangkok Hilton* shot to the top of the ratings, breaking all records on 15 November, she was too ill to celebrate properly. 'It is fantastic that so many people watched *Bangkok Hilton*,' she croaked from the sidelines. 'It has been a great send-off for me and great for all those people who worked so hard on it.'

Finally, Nicole packed her bags for the States. As she had been born in Hawaii, she automatically had dual citizenship, so obtaining a green card to work in America wasn't necessary. Her colleagues were simultaneously sad to see her go and curious to find out what adventures would befall her next.

Phillip Noyce aptly described her as 'an enormous talent but a fragile one in a foreign environment'. Jeff Burton, a director of photography who had worked with her on *Vietnam* and *Bangkok Hilton*, agreed, speaking for them all:

'It is no longer in the hands of agents, managers or publicists. Nicole is off and running and it doesn't matter what anyone does, it's all going to happen. The only thing which could go wrong is if she becomes personally affected in the process. Hopefully she will survive the pressure she'll be under for the next five years.

'Nicole has an extremely strong base behind her: her family. She has extraordinary confidence, beauty, diligence and intelligence and I'd say that, after *Bangkok Hilton* and the success of *Dead Calm*, there's a good chance she will be lost to Australia forever. When you're that good, you just can't stay at home.'

★

The filming of *Days Of Thunder* (the revised name for *Daytona*) started in late November 1989 at various locations, including Charlotte and Florence in North and South Carolina respectively, Daytona Beach, Florida and the famous Paramount Studios. 'I felt like I didn't belong,' said Nicole of the latter. 'I felt like a fish out water and intimidated. It's scary – you see the big studios, they're steeped in history. You think of the people who have made movies there. It's profound and overwhelming.' As for acting alongside *the* Tom Cruise, she admitted, 'When you're working with him you worry a bit. You think you've got to get everything right first time.'

By then, Cruise and screenwriter Robert Towne had fleshed out a specific part for Nicole: as Dr Claire Lewicki, an Australian neurologist at the Daytona Beach Hospital, who falls for the racing driver she has treated for a head injury. The fact that not many twenty-two-year-olds are likely to have qualified in the highly specialized field of brain surgery was beside the point; this testosterone-drenched film featured heroes with the improbable names of Rowdy Burns and Cole Trickle (Cruise).

Nicole was ambivalent about this unforeseen development in her career. On the one hand, she was concerned her talents weren't going to be stretched. 'It was hard for me, because I'd been getting great roles in Australia and suddenly I was cast back as the girlfriend, which I'd done when I was sixteen in Australia,' she says. Yet on the other, she counted her blessings. She was, after all, starring opposite Hollywood's hottest male talent in her first American role. 'I was very excited,' she recalls. 'The opportunity is so rare for an Australian actress to appear in a big American commercial film. I just didn't want to blow it . . .'

When *Top Gun* director Tony Scott attached his name to the movie, the Hollywood gossips really sat up and took notice. One particular point of interest was the rapidly escalating budget. The original approximation of costs had been $30 million, but soon estimates more than doubled that figure. Cruise's fee alone was around the $10 million mark.

Filming was then placed under additional pressure – the weather conditions were foul, with unforeseen rainstorms making the racing scenes nigh-on impossible to shoot. Then Scott was required by Paramount to produce the finished feature in time for a release date of the 4 July weekend the following year; the rescheduling meant he would have to complete the complicated editing process in six weeks, rather than six months. Scenes were still being added and re-shot as late as April 1990.

The harsh truth for Nicole is that her character in *Days Of Thunder* is fairly insignificant; she is there purely to provide eye candy for the men and a semblance of a love story for the women in the audience. Although

she had physically and mentally matured since the days of *Dead Calm*, perhaps being cast as a racing junkie instead of a qualified neurologist might
have seemed more plausible.

The film itself is rather tedious for non-racing aficionados. Extremely
dated in both language and plot development, other than the driving
stunts involved it fails to challenge any of its stars (including Robert
Duvall and Randy Quaid) to emit much more than an oily macho grunt.
The film stoops to its lowest point when Cole (a maverick with anger-
management issues) insists on a wheelchair race with his archrival/best
buddy to prove a soon-forgotten point.

For Nicole, none of this red-blooded nonsense really mattered. 'I did
a lot of hanging around and waiting,' she remembers. 'Tom, of course, was
in practically every scene, and shooting was halfway over before we started
getting to know each other.' And what she got to know, she liked. 'I've
never been affected by somebody to that degree. It was very scary, because
you know that there's almost no going back.'

Despite a dynamic description from its leading man – 'It's modern-day
gladiators. It's war!' – *Days Of Thunder* was a resounding flop, the critics
remarking on its over-familiar story. 'Simply a flashy, noisy star vehicle for
Tom Cruise, one which – like the stock cars he drives – goes around in
circles getting nowhere,' slated *MFB*. 'Nothing more than an exercise in
dollar-sifting movie-making by numbers,' slammed *Today*. And the *Observer*
wasted no time in coming straight to the point: 'By any civilized standards,
Days Of Thunder is a monstrosity.' The film went on to gross more than $80
million at the box office, but with equivalent costs, profits were pitiful.

Viewers, however, homed in on the flirtatious onscreen chemistry
between the protagonist and his new Australian leading lady. After all,
Cruise was a married man.

9

I Needed To Act The Way I Needed Air To Breathe

Thomas Cruise Mapother IV was born on 3 July 1962 in Syracuse, New York. Tom was the third of four children of an electrical engineer, Thomas Cruise Mapother III, and his wife Mary Lee, a teacher with a keen interest in amateur dramatics. With his three sisters, Lee Anne, Marian and Cass, the young Tom led a nomadic early life: the family moved frequently due to his father's job, ultimately settling in Louisville, Kentucky. By the age of eleven he had already been uprooted seven times.

Tom's childhood was an unhappy one – he sometimes bore the brunt of his father's temper.

'He was very, very tough on me,' Tom told *Vanity Fair* in 1994, 'in many ways. I'd get hit, and I didn't understand it. As a kid, I had a lot of hidden anger about that. Inside, I believe he was a really sensitive individual. He just didn't want me to have to go through the kind of pain that he had felt in his life.'

The Mapothers' marriage was suffering due to Thomas's endless succession of failed money-making schemes, and one night it all became too much. Mary Lee bundled Tom and his sisters into the car, heading for the

U.S. border. 'We felt like fugitives,' he says. His parents were divorced soon afterwards in 1974, but Tom's father refused to pay child maintenance. Although he was spared the more unpleasant aspects of his relationship with his father, the sensitive youngster felt hurt and alone.

The broken family endured a depressing period of poverty during which Tom helped out variously as a newspaper boy and neighbourhood gardener, his sisters all took on waitressing work in local restaurants, and his mother juggled three jobs at once.

'Nothing makes you more serious than when your parents get divorced,' he later admitted. 'It leaves a lot of scars on you and you become determined never to let anything like that happen to you again. You see the world differently when you have to watch your mother asking friends for money so you can eat.'

Like his mother and sisters, Tom suffered from dyslexia. Kindergarten teachers had forced the naturally left-handed boy to write with his right hand, and he began to copy letters down backwards. For a long time he was treated shoddily at school through ignorance of his condition, before it was eventually properly diagnosed.

'I was put in remedial reading classes,' he recalls. 'It separated you and singled you out. I didn't know whether a "C" or "D" curved to the right or left. That affects everything you do – how you deal with letters and which way they go, the way you pronounce things, your reading comprehension . . . everything. I felt ashamed.

'A lot of kids would make fun of me. That experience made me very tough on the inside because you learn to quietly accept abuse and constant ridicule . . . I now look on it as a character-building stage, although I hated every moment of my life in those days. I would come home crying so many times because of the misery of not being able to do as well in school as I knew I should.'

Raised a devout Roman Catholic, Tom had always been a spiritual individual, and for a while he even considered life in the priesthood. To this end, he spent his freshman year attending St Francis's Seminary, near Cincinnati. An added motive for attending the seminary was that it provided a solid, free education; 'they even clothed you,' he recalls, which must have been a relief for his poverty-stricken mother.

Tom only spent one year at St Francis's, having decided against the priesthood partly because it involved celibacy, something which definitely didn't appeal. Fortunately, his family's financial situation was about to improve, as Mary Lee announced she was getting married again. Tom's new stepfather was a plastics salesman named Jack South, who moved the family on to Glen Ridge, New Jersey.

There Tom attended Glen Ridge High, where he found that his dyslexia – and having attended some fourteen different schools previously – still held back his scholastic progress. So, instead of academic subjects, Tom obsessively devoted his time to sport, favouring racquetball, ice hockey and wrestling in particular. It was also a guaranteed way of making friends. When one day his training led to a painful knee injury, his attention shifted to acting, and the teenager began to participate in musical theatre.

After a few singing lessons, Tom's teacher encouraged him to try out for a school production of *Guys And Dolls*. Winning the part of Nathan Detroit, as played by Frank Sinatra in the hit film, Tom amazed everyone with his spirited performance.

'I can't describe the feeling that was there,' his mother later remarked. 'It was just an incredible experience to see a lot of talent coming forth all of a sudden. It had been dormant for so many years – not thought of or talked about or discussed in any way. Then to see him on that stage . . .' Backstage, an agent who had been lurking in the audience came forward with some welcome encouragement and the advice that the actor should consider turning professional.

Tom has never minced his words about his passion for his new-found vocation. 'I wanted to be an actor. I wanted it very badly. I was hungry. I felt I needed to act the way I needed air to breathe.'

Ultimately, his success in *Guys And Dolls* led to the seventeen-year-old boldly leaving New Jersey for New York, with just $2000 saved from his various part-time jobs. There he waited tables and attended auditions, finally clinching the role of Herb in a theatre production of *Godspell* after competing against five hundred other young hopefuls. *Godspell* inspired Italian director Franco Zeffirelli to cast him for a fleeting seven-minute appearance in what was Tom's first film, *Endless Love*, which took just one day to shoot. Cruise had fallen on his feet.

Over the next five years, Tom starred in some of the top-grossing movies of the 1980s. Dropping the name Mapother for the more user-friendly Cruise, he became a member of the infamous 'Brat Pack', a modern variation on Frank Sinatra's Rat Pack of the 1960s, comprising other strapping young American actors such as Matt Dillon, Rob Lowe, Emilio Estevez, Patrick Swayze and Sean Penn.

Tom's height (5 feet 9 inches) never really hindered his career, and in some ways it helped to make his conventional dark-haired good looks (rendered more agreeable after some major dentistry) more accessible to his target audience of impressionable female fans. Tom's breakthrough role was as Lieutenant Pete 'Maverick' Mitchell in Tony Scott's *Top Gun*, typecasting him to a certain extent as a muscular action hero living life on the edge.

But Tom also proved he could pull off more serious roles in films like *Rain Man* and *Born On The Fourth Of July*; the latter, about a crippled Vietnam veteran, earned him an Oscar nomination for Best Actor. By the time he started work on his next film, a return to type in *Days Of Thunder*, he was one of the highest-paid actors in the world, earning $10–15 million per film.

Reminiscent of his keen pursuit of sports at school, Tom's obsession with background research swiftly became legendary within Hollywood circles. His tough childhood and the taunts he had received as a dyslexic had ultimately brought out the best in this most intense young man.

'He's a demon,' commented his *Rain Man* co-star, Dustin Hoffman. 'He gets up early, he works out, he goes home early, he studies, he watches his diet like he's an old fart, he doesn't drink and he always wants to rehearse.' It was not unusual for Tom to reshape his entire body for a role, or, in later years, to purposefully make himself less attractive by removing a cap from a tooth, allowing his hair to grow wild or applying a temporary tattoo.

Behind this punctilious work ethic, psychologically Tom was quite a complex character. After his father's desertion, he cut himself off completely from his most important male role model, preferring the company of the fairer sex.

'I've always felt much closer to women than guys because they enjoy talking about how they feel. With men, there's too much competition and ego involved. It takes a lot longer to get into an open friendship with another guy than it does with a woman. That's why I've always had girls as best friends,' says Tom, who remains devoted to his mother.

But when Thomas Cruise Mapother III became terminally ill with cancer towards the end of 1983, the actor agreed to a reconciliation. It was an emotional meeting during which he discovered his father had plastered the walls of his hospital room with posters from Tom's films, although, oddly, he had never actually seen any of them. During those lost years, Thomas had unsuccessfully remarried, wandered the highways of America and even written a book, entitled *Winning Through Intimidation*. Notably, he had refused ever to cash in on the name of his now-famous son, self-publishing under the pseudonym of Thomas May.

Thomas died on 9 January 1984. 'I can't take any credit for Tom's success. I'm the last person who'll ever criticize him. Maybe that's one favour I've done for him,' were among his last words. His death left Tom distraught and unsure he had done the right thing in regaining contact.

Meanwhile, life as a top-ranking heart-throb had secured for Tom a long list of famous actress girlfriends: *Little House On The Prairie*'s Melissa Gilbert; Rebecca de Mornay, his co-star in 1983's *Risky Business*; and Heather Locklear, well known for her parts in *Dynasty* and *T.J. Hooker*. He also dated Cher (he was twenty-three, she was thirty-nine), whom he met in 1985 at a special dyslexia fundraiser at the White House, where he accepted an award for Outstanding Learning Disabled Achievement.

'I like bright, sexy, very sexy women, and strong, someone I'm not going to run over, someone strong enough to stand up to me,' stressed Tom of his ideal partner. 'She's also got to have her own thing going. I don't want someone depending on me for everything, because I do need a lot of time alone.'

Finally, Tom settled down with another actress, Mimi Rogers (just six years his senior this time), whom he wed quietly in a secret ceremony on 9 May 1987. Suiting Tom's requirements perfectly, Mimi was an established name in her own right. With numerous television shows under her belt, she was about to become the next best thing after her appearance in Ridley Scott's *Someone To Watch Over Me*. She was an attractive, self-assured brunette, an inch or two taller than Tom, which did not bother the couple in the least.

Living alternately in a $3 million New York apartment, with rock stars Keith Richards and Phil Collins for neighbours, and in a sizeable house in Brentwood, Los Angeles, Tom and Mimi seemed to represent the epitome of celebrity happiness: understated, glamorous and wealthy. By the time *Days Of Thunder* brought Nicole Kidman into Tom's life, his three-year marriage appeared peaceful and strong, at least on the surface.

It soon became clear to Nicole that Tom Cruise was going to be an important feature in her life. When the tabloid rumour mill linked her romantically to her leading man after paparazzi pictures were published of the two speeding away from her Daytona Beach apartment on Tom's Harley Davidson, she did not help her case by stating coyly, 'I *do* get lonely when I'm on the road, especially when I don't have anyone to get into bed with and watch the telly . . .'

When feeling slightly less mischievous, she denied her co-star was anything more than a friend. 'The very first time we met I discovered what a charming and tender man he is – he must be every woman's dream,' she said. 'Tom is going through a hard time in his personal life and I believe at these moments friends should support one another.'

Apparently, Tom's marriage had been suffering anyway, as the chic and stylish Mimi preferred a very different, much quieter lifestyle to his chosen existence of constant upheaval and dangerous extreme sports. Another reason frequently alluded to in discussions of the collapse of their relationship (other than the arrival of Nicole) is that no children had been forthcoming, although Tom had been outspoken about his desire to become a father. There would later be baseless speculation about Tom's fertility when Mimi went on to have a daughter, Lucy, with film producer Chris Ciaffa four years later.

Tom has always maintained he did the honourable thing and resisted embarking on a full-blown love affair with Nicole until he had informed his wife their marriage had come to an end. 'When I met Nic, I thought she was incredible,' he said. 'My marriage was basically over at that point, but to be very ethical, we couldn't do anything until it *was* over.'

Tom filed for divorce from Mimi on 16 January 1990, citing 'irreconcilable differences'. The news caused an immediate media uproar. The actor had led the press a merry dance over the last month, having given a succession of interviews proclaiming his undying love for his wife.

'The most important thing for me is I want Mimi to be happy,' he said in an interview published in the 25 December edition of *Time*. 'I couldn't imagine being without her or being alone. I care about my wife more than anything in the world. She's my best friend. I love her,' he'd said to *Rolling Stone*, published on 11 January. 'I just really enjoy our marriage,' he was quoted as saying in *U.S.* magazine; this was published on 22 January – embarrassingly, a week after the shock announcement.

A brusque joint statement was rapidly released, explaining little to the numerous people following the story with great interest:

While there have been positive aspects to our marriage, there were some issues which could not be resolved, even after working on them for a period of time.

Evidently that 'period of time' incorporated Tom's interviews with *Time*, *Rolling Stone* and *U.S.* magazine, to whom he later apologized.

Shortly after the separation, Mimi was given the house in Brentwood and a settlement estimated at around $10 million. Tom continued to flatly deny any romantic involvement with his leading lady for the next four months, saying instead that the annulment was 'something that had to be done. It's no different to what other people go through. You've got to take responsibility for it and move on.'

Three years later and sorely in need of a career boost, Mimi posed for *Playboy* magazine, naked bar a sequinned bathing cap and a pair of stilettos. The provocative seven-page spread was accompanied by an exclusive interview in which she famously cast doubt on her ex-husband's sexuality, revealing he had been 'seriously thinking of becoming a monk' and had insisted on celibacy during their marriage because he wanted to 'maintain the purity of his instrument'. She then quipped: 'My instrument needed tuning.'

After Tom's lawyers responded with a stiff letter advising Mimi that she'd breached the conditions of the divorce settlement by speaking publicly about the finer details of their marriage, Mimi quickly retracted her insinuations, suggesting to Jay Leno on the prime-time *Tonight* show that she had only been joking. She even wrote to *Playboy* to inform them that her comments had been 'totally playful and completely in jest', although the magazine resolutely stood by their article.

It was all very embarrassing, and, even though he had been the one to make the break, Tom somehow managed to come out on top. Of his wise decision to keep quiet at this time, he later commented, 'When I was asked direct questions by the press about my marriage, I felt that to compromise my privacy was to compromise a basic trust.'

And so, while Tom Cruise was set free to explore his feelings for Nicole, what of her boyfriend back in Australia, Marcus Graham?

While things were hotting up on the set of *Days Of Thunder*, Marcus spent a lonely Christmas back in Sydney. 'Being separated from Nicole is very difficult,' he said in interviews published in January 1990, ostensibly publicizing *A Midsummer Night's Dream* and his new mini-series *Shadows Of The Heart*. 'She is not just my girl, she is also my best friend and I miss her terribly.' Graham went on to explain how he had kept in touch with Nicole via numerous long-distance calls; his phone bill for the last three months alone exceeded $1300.

His interviews were insightful – a glimpse into a relationship made competitive more by the constant media attention than any personal rivalry. Graham wanted to be seen as 'an actor in my own right', rather than being recognized by the press simply as Nicole Kidman's boyfriend. 'While it doesn't really bother Nicole, who is very well balanced about our relationship, it has definitely been a problem for me.' This admission in particular struck a chord, as this was exactly how Nicole had felt during her time with Tom Burlinson.

'The more I establish myself, the less I mind saying that Nicole and I are together,' he continued. 'It was very hard, though, at the beginning. I felt our private life was being exposed for the whole world to see. I felt like people were stealing something from us and I don't like that. It's easier for Nicole to handle as she is more experienced and has already made it. For me, still on my way out, it is much harder.

'I am hoping that further down the track we can work together on a project. We would have done the play I am currently starring in together if she had not received the offer to star with Tom Cruise in America . . .'

Graham refused to be drawn on the potentially thorny subject of Nicole's leading man. 'It is such an American thing to discuss one's personal life in public. Divorces, weddings are all announced in public to coincide with most movie releases. I really hate that.

'When I finish the mini-series, I want to spend some time with Nic relaxing somewhere. We finish shooting at the same time, so it should be possible,' he concluded hopefully. Considering that the articles came out exactly a week after the announcement of Cruise's divorce, it can only be assumed that Nicole had yet to make the break. As she did not return to Australia over the New Year period, Nicole must have let him down gently over the phone.

10

Throwing Caution
To The Wind

From the very beginning, Nicole found it hard to believe that this most eminent Hollywood figure had fallen in love with *her*, a twenty-two-year-old upstart from darkest Australia. 'I really admired his acting and all I could think of was his talent. Yes, honestly!' she laughed. 'When he did ask me out, I was so surprised, I can tell you. I just couldn't see it.'

After the kerfuffle following the announcement of the divorce died down, shooting continued for *Days Of Thunder*, and Tom's motorbike and white BMW were frequently spotted outside Nicole's apartment. They had dinner several times at the Olive Garden restaurant, and were seen shopping together at Publix market, but still they continued to publicly deny their romance.

In private, Nicole believed she should follow her heart, and so in order to explore this new relationship, she announced she had left Australia for good — a genuine star in her home country with thirteen films to her credit, but a relative unknown in America.

'After *Days Of Thunder* we realized that we wanted to be together,' she said. 'It was a big step for me because I had a place in Australia and I had a lot of friends and, of course, my family there. But I took the plunge . . .'

In a whirl of excitement, Nicole phoned Antonia to tell her she could take over her apartment in Sydney. She hadn't even packed her belongings — just a few clothes and minor personal effects to see her into her new life.

'When I first moved to America I was madly in love, following my heart and willing to throw caution to the wind, which is how I live my life,' she said. 'I'm spontaneous at times, which can be dangerous. There are consequences, but if you fall in love, there's nothing you can do about it. If I hadn't followed through, I'd have denied myself that and regretted it. So off I went.'

'It just seemed right,' Tom later recalled of this exhilarating period. 'I think anyone who has met Nicole would understand. It was like nothing occurred before, and just because you get divorced doesn't mean that's it. I was ready, I was really excited.'

Nicole will never forget her first date with her new boyfriend. 'We went to the movies and he was wearing a T-shirt and I took one look at his arms and I couldn't watch the movie. I mean, he had such great biceps! It was really the biceps that won me over. I was a goner after that.'

In later dates she would reveal an endearing naïvety, almost as if she didn't quite recognize the status of the man she was seeing. 'I was thrown into a situation that was far bigger than I could ever have imagined, but I still had this strange innocence about it, in a weird way,' she confessed. 'Like, I would always insist on paying for dinner and buying my own movie tickets — "My shout," I'd say.' Fortunately, the height difference never even came into it. 'Tom doesn't mind my being taller than him. I could wear 3-inch heels and he would like it,' she said.

Although she had already taken a huge step by moving halfway across the world, initially Nicole sensibly held herself back. At first, the ghost of Mimi was still a little fresh — after all, their paths had literally crossed at the beginning of the romance. 'I had a lot of trouble with that,' she said, seemingly oblivious of her own situation with Marcus Graham. 'That was my biggest thing: "Are you going to hurt me?"'

Inevitably, though, Nicole's feelings for Tom grew more profound. 'I do believe in lust at first sight,' said the actress. 'And then I think you're very lucky when that evolves into something a lot deeper; for us that's what occurred. Lust and love somehow combined, I feel, is the best thing for a relationship.'

'It grew into love and respect,' agreed Tom. 'I knew she was it for me. I thought, *this* is the person to share all of who I am with, and her with me. I just knew I couldn't live without her.' It was Nicole's unpretentious, fun-loving nature that appealed most to Tom, and the notoriously 'intense' actor soon found himself taking life a little less seriously.

Although the budding relationship appeared to develop very quickly, both parties were aware of the implications. 'I think you know it's love when you're making sacrifices,' Nicole reflected. 'When you're willing to say this person is more to me than other things. When it becomes about wanting the other person to have everything that they want.

'A lot of it, though, is about saying, "Hey, I'm going to be committed to this. I'm not going to be constantly looking for where the grass is greener."'

✷

In February 1990 Janelle Kidman visited her daughter at Daytona Beach, flying on from Los Angeles in a private Lear jet courtesy of Tom Cruise.

It was very important to Nicole that her parents should approve of her famous boyfriend. Nicole had kept them abreast of developments in the secret relationship with daily telephone calls. When later asked what her daughter had said about Tom, Janelle relayed Nicole's enthusiastic description as 'intense' and 'energetic', 'with a great sense of humour and a very nice way of throwing back his head when he laughs. He's got that American way of not doing things by halves. He works and plays full on.'

Understandably, Janelle admits to being a little 'disconcerted' when she was first told the identity of her daughter's new beau. Although she was aware of his level of fame, she was at that stage unfamiliar with his work and embarked on what she describes as 'a crash course on Tom Cruise'. One afternoon she went by herself to a local cinema to watch *Born On The Fourth Of July*. She was blown away by the actor's performance and even found herself crying in the scene where Tom's character runs through the rain to see his girlfriend for one last time before leaving for Vietnam. Janelle's admiration for the powerful actor won her round and she welcomed Tom into the family – although he had yet to meet Antony.

Aware of how the American and Australian press might portray the relationship given their respective break-ups with Mimi and Marcus, for the first few months both Tom and Nicole refuted the rumours. They braved the world's gaze when they attended the Oscars together on 26 March, with Nicole taking one of Tom's arms and his mother the other, before proceeding to sit conspicuously in the front row, whispering and giggling. Most spectators took this as a public 'coming-out' of their affair, but as late as April Nicole was still swatting away reporters' probing questions like flies.

'We are *not* having a relationship,' she told the British paper *Today* a fortnight after the Oscars. 'I don't talk about people I work with – I make it a rule.'

Did she have a boyfriend? 'No – I mean, I don't want to talk about it. I want my privacy.'

To Australian magazine *New Idea* the same month, she did her best to deflect the interviewer's attention on to other subjects, namely her career. 'I have been too busy and just don't think about it,' she said, after making the rather surprising comment that she had not yet had a 'serious relationship' – three years with Burlinson and two with Graham notwithstanding. 'I have worked pretty well non-stop and set my sights high and have been independent from the age of fourteen. I have been learning to operate in an adult world – as a child.'

But the Cruise name was simply too high profile for the relationship to remain a secret for long. As April turned into May, the lovers, who were at last no longer required on the set of *Days Of Thunder*, escaped media prying for an idyllic holiday in the Bahamas. 'We slept in hammocks on deserted islands, cooked and went hiking,' Nicole remembered. And just in case those activities became too dull: 'We swam with stingrays and moray eels.'

On their return from the Bahamas, the couple finally went public: Nicole confirmed via her Australian press officer that they were definitely 'an item', as had long been suspected. To celebrate their movie's premiere on 29 June, Tom took Nicole and fifty-year-old Mary Lee skydiving. It was one way for Nicole to bond with his family.

Nicole and Tom shared a fanatical love of sport. Back in Australia the actress had taken part in horse-riding, tennis, windsurfing and kick-boxing, and with the entrance of this charismatic man into her life, the sports became more dangerous and more exciting. 'He's kind of wild, and I love that,' Nicole said, before revealing that their cosy dates in the cinema had rapidly developed into life-or-death encounters where they might, say, jump out of a plane.

'Free-fall parachute jumping – there's nothing like it when you're up there at 14,000 feet with the cold air hitting your face!' she enthused. 'It's an amazing sensation – not as good as sex, but almost! You actually fall for about forty-five seconds.'

Plenty of time, then, for their first kiss, which apparently took place in mid-air, miles above sea level. 'It was during our first parachute jump. He got close to me in the air, and put his lips on mine. It wasn't a long, passionate kiss – more of a peck, really. He thinks it's really cool that I'm willing to jump out of a plane for him.' This was evidently not the kind of pastime that Mimi had ever entertained.

Tom and Nicole also searched for thrills where their feet could at least connect with dry land, albeit briefly. 'Before Tom, I was never a skier, and now I love it!' There was more. 'He taught me how to ride a trail bike, we love to drive go-carts – it's addictive! Sometimes we do it until two in the morning.' In fact, the most normal thing they did together as a couple was to play squash.

After Nicole's twenty-third birthday, the relationship intensified and the couple flew to Sydney in August, ostensibly for Tom to meet Dr Kidman, but more than likely for him to ask for his daughter's hand in marriage. During the trip, Tom was welcomed into the family properly.

'They really like him,' said Nicole. 'Tom wasn't nervous about meeting them. He's confident in his ability to communicate. Dad was more nervous. Now we're just like one big family.' Unfortunately, however much they took to Tom, the Kidmans as a unit initially loathed being flung under the international spotlight – a direct by-product of Nicole's romance.

'When a radio station read out the piece from a newspaper which had Tom Cruise buying Nicole a $50,000 Corvette and a house, mum demanded, and got, a retraction,' recalls Antonia, who also experienced problems herself while out shopping. 'In three different stores, I used my credit card which, naturally, has the Kidman name. Every time I was asked if I was related to Nicole. In the end I denied it, not because I don't love and feel proud of her, but because it's easier to pretend that I'm not her sister rather than face a barrage of questions.'

During their trip Tom and Nicole were spotted out at the opera, dining at a trendy Indian restaurant called the Maharani, and socializing with Terry Hayes. Cruise's biographer, Wensley Clarkson, also records a rather tactless excursion to Marcus Graham's house. It seems that Nicole took Tom along for an impromptu social visit and Marcus pretended to be out, sending a friend to shoo away the unwanted guests.

Back in the States, Tom and Nicole were again seen at several public occasions, including the U.S. Open tennis championships in New York. At one such outing spectators noticed Nicole was wearing a large diamond ring, its worth estimated between £130,000 and £150,000. Their engagement was officially announced in September.

Romance apart, Nicole had also moved to America to further her career. *Days Of Thunder* clearly hadn't provided the answer, either as a challenging role or a box-office hit. The search for the elusive follow-up to *Dead Calm* continued.

Oddly, given that she had complained so bitterly about dropping from leading lady to 'girlfriend' roles, Nicole's part in her next film, *Billy Bathgate*, was just that: a frivolous floozy. Worse still, this time she was required to contribute several scenes of gratuitous nudity that had little or nothing to do with the plot. It is hard to view this as a step up, or even in the right direction, but everyone involved raved about her performance.

Director Robert Benton (*Kramer Versus Kramer*) had initially approached Nicole as *Days Of Thunder* was wrapping up. He had been bowled over by *Dead Calm* and wanted her to appear in his next film. Excited, she flew to New York for an audition, but on discovering her co-star was her pint-sized fiancé's equally diminutive pal, Dustin Hoffman, she was concerned that her towering stature would be a serious disadvantage. 'I was 4 inches taller than Dustin, but he loved it,' said Nicole. However, it was not her height that nearly tripped her up.

'My Australian accent almost did me in,' she admitted. 'Robert Benton said he wanted me, but I had to learn to speak American without even a *hint* of an accent. He gave me the name of a voice coach, and I worked on it day and night for two weeks.' Training to impersonate the upper-class New York inflection for four hours each day apparently paid off. Benton, who had expressed serious doubts about her ability to completely lose the Aussie twang within such a short space of time, praised her unreservedly: 'She was phenomenal – her American accent was perfect!'

When shooting finished for the day and Nicole's natural voice re-appeared, the crew thought she was putting it on. The atmosphere on set was a congenial, family one, with Tom visiting almost every day, not least to appreciate her mimicry. 'I do lots of accents,' boasted Nicole, 'they make Tom laugh. We have a lot of fun together.' Benton concurred, 'It really was a happy experience doing this film, even though the work was long, and at times horribly difficult.'

Billy Bathgate is an adaptation of E. L. Doctorow's acclaimed novel about Bathgate (Loren Dean), an enterprising street kid from the Bronx slums who is quickly enrolled in the gangland ethics of crime, money and loyalty by Dutch Schultz, effortlessly portrayed by Hoffman. Nicole's part is that of socialite Drew Preston, who is fond of a drink or two and dates gangsters for kicks. When boyfriend Bo Weinberg (Bruce Willis) takes a dip in the river with a pair of concrete boots courtesy of Schultz, Preston becomes something of a loose cannon, and it is Bathgate's job to protect her.

Not only is Nicole's role again that of the 'girlfriend', but she is a girl-friend of the particularly ditzy, simpering variety. Noticeably, although she had appeared in skimpy outfits or tastefully topless in previous roles (*Windrider*, *Dead Calm*, *Bangkok Hilton*, *Flirting*), here she exposes herself fully, not once but twice. 'I have no hang-ups about that,' she said of the nudity requirement, but a little more dramatic context might have helped.

Her fiancé is unlikely to have approved. Tom famously caused quite a fuss during the making of *Cocktail* and *Days Of Thunder*, apparently refusing to remove his underpants. It was rumoured that he was frequently present during filming of *Billy Bathgate*, persuading Benton to tone down the raunchier moments, a story which Nicole later dismissed. 'I'm not the kind of person who would allow that, anyway,' she said. 'He showed up on the set, occasionally, and was hanging out with Dustin, but not when we were doing those scenes.'

Much was made in the press a couple of years later when the boot was on the other foot. Tom notably had few love scenes after meeting Nicole, but *The Firm* demanded a passionate encounter with Karina Lombard. The young starlet played a prostitute who seduced Tom, but, rather than swoon at his feet, she was quite derogatory about her heart-throb co-star afterwards. Then, in an astonishing attack on Nicole, Lombard slated her for being there during filming of the saucy scene. 'She was on the set the whole time watching, watching, watching,' claimed Lombard. Nicole took it in her stride and simply retorted that Lombard was 'very rude'.

In *Billy Bathgate*, when Drew Preston isn't slurring due to drink, Nicole adopts a breathy Monroe-style voice which neatly disguises any problems she may have experienced with the accent. This helps make her appear more vulnerable than her almost 6-foot frame would suggest. Preston's ingenuousness is displayed to endearing effect as she makes friends with Bathgate – Nicole puts the eye-crossing talents she picked up at school to good use.

Like *Days Of Thunder*, filming dragged on and the project went vastly over budget. This increased the pressure on all involved to ensure that *Billy Bathgate* was a financial success. 'I was naïve,' admitted Nicole. 'I didn't realize there were any expectations. I didn't think, "This movie has cost a fortune and has to make a lot of money." I just thought, "We've made an interesting movie."'

Even with a big-name cast, the lack of drive and spark meant that *Billy Bathgate* failed to ignite. Although the film flopped, Nicole salvaged a Golden Globe nomination in 1992 for Best Actress In A Supporting Role and received good reviews for her edgy performance. Her colleagues agreed. 'She was just astounding,' said Benton. 'She's an astonishingly gifted actress, even more so when you consider how young she is. Her role was very difficult and challenging, but her performance was utterly flawless.'

Hoffman, too, piled on the praise, 'She fills the character with such compassion that she forces you to care deeply. That kind of talent is not commonplace.'

But Joe Public was unconvinced, and Nicole's image remained predominantly that of an attractive bit of fluff. 'I still get insecure,' said Nicole, perhaps picking up on the audience's apparent apathy. 'There is never a time when I don't think the role I'm playing is going to be the last I'll ever be offered.'

★

Just a few months after their relationship was made public, Tom and Nicole moved out of the Bel-Air Hotel where they had been staying. Tom splashed out on a mansion in the affluent Los Angeles suburb of Pacific Palisades. Secluded in its own acre of land, the property ensured privacy and the couple felt safe. Their neighbours, Sylvester Stallone and Arnold Schwarzenegger, certainly oozed muscular protection.

The colonial-style home, valued at an estimated $4.7 million, consisted of five bedrooms, five bathrooms, a sweeping spiral staircase, wood-panelled library, two-storey guesthouse, carport, swimming pool, spa and immaculate garden. Although the house had been recently refurbished, Tom and Nicole commissioned further work, including extensive redecoration, and added a cinema, billiards room and gymnasium. Rumours of nursery designs began to spread like wildfire.

In October 1990 Nicole's personal life suddenly didn't seem so peachy; she began to experience the nastier side of a Hollywood relationship. The tabloids alleged that Tom was so desperate to have children that he insisted Nicole underwent fertility tests before agreeing to marry her. Furthermore, they claimed that she was so furious with his demands that she had threatened to call off the wedding, later relenting and having the tests, which proved positive.

It is likely that what sparked off this particularly vicious and unfounded rumour was Cruise's unusually candid recent disclosure following his childless marriage to Mimi Rogers: 'I would love to have kids. I would turn down an Oscar to see my boy at a baseball game or my girl at a song recital.'

Tom had always been vocal about his desire to have children and speculation about his fertility had been rife over the last two years. The actor had made it very clear that he was not sterile, and yet various papers suggested throughout 1988 and 1989 that Rogers was trying to get pregnant without success and had been exchanging moral support with close friend Kirstie Alley (who was also hoping to start a family). One unsupported allegation was that Tom's low sperm count was the problem, rather than any complications with Rogers.

If an exclusive in the *National Enquirer* a few years later is to be believed, Nicole subsequently suffered very real heartache in a cruel twist of fate shortly after her supposed fertility tests. According to the article, at the end of 1990 Nicole experienced an ectopic pregnancy, in which the fertilized egg grows in one of the fallopian tubes instead of the womb. This condition requires the expectant mother to undergo an immediate termination, which the story claims was what happened to the actress.

Further reports focused on fertility treatment that Tom and Mimi were said to have undertaken, as well as the theory that, following the recent complications, Nicole was now taking fertility pills. Whether or not this tale contains any truth, Nicole was facing firsthand the lack of privacy that accompanies fame, and her impending nuptials were only to compound media conjecture.

11

Pain Passes, But Love Remains

Happier times were promised when Tom Cruise and Nicole Kidman pledged their undying love for each other in a private ceremony on Christmas Eve 1990.

'It was a lovely wedding,' said Nicole fondly. The candlelit nuptials took place at sunset, in a rented bungalow in the affluent Colorado ski resort of Telluride. Nicole wore the thirties brocade dress she had bought in Amsterdam six years earlier with an extended train, while Tom appeared in a smart black tuxedo. After the couple exchanged personalized vows, the groom presented his bride with a £250,000 diamond-encrusted wedding ring.

With her sister Antonia as bridesmaid, Nicole kept the number of guests to a minimum: only a dozen, including Antony and Janelle Kidman, Mary Lee, Lee Anne, Marian and Cass Mapother, and Dustin and Lisa Hoffman. 'We both wanted a traditional wedding,' she said, 'and it was everything we hoped, really beautiful.'

Despite a month of careful planning, Tom nearly ruined the day. The Clarkson biography claims the groom was almost arrested for speeding *en route*. The law enforcer assumed it was a joke when the guilty party said, 'Hi,

I'm Tom Cruise and I'm getting married.' Without any proof of ID, persuading the cop he was the genuine article took some time, but eventually Tom was free to go.

The ceremony bore a striking resemblance to Tom's previous marriage to Mimi. Although the bride and groom then were in casual gear – jeans and bare feet – they too had a small, private service with just a few family and friends, writing their own vows and keeping the press at bay. Quite a contrast to the grandiose wedding of Tom's Brat Pack buddy Sean Penn to Madonna.

Floating on cloud nine, Nicole was able to enjoy her secret married life for only a few short days. With the delays on *Billy Bathgate*, the newlyweds could not fit in a honeymoon (another similarity to the Cruise–Rogers nuptials), and when they returned to everyday life the press quickly uncovered the news. Gossip spread like wildfire, stories being exaggerated all the more because the union had been shrouded in secrecy, and Nicole found herself undergoing further unwelcome interrogation into her private life.

The first questions revolved around her tender age, particularly given the whirlwind courtship. 'I don't feel I'm too young to get married,' the twenty-three-year-old declared, 'because I know I've met the person I want to spend the rest of my life with. I feel totally certain about that.

'Before I met Tom, I was never going to get married. Never. But he was just the most incredible, unusual man I'd ever met.' She didn't cringe when admitting that she gave up her whole life in Australia for love and bluntly offered, 'When we married, part of our promise to each other was that we'd never be separated for more than two weeks. We'll do whatever it takes to just be together for one night, even if it means flying in. It boils down to commitment.'

That commitment didn't stretch to the tradition of adopting Tom's surname, something of which her feminist mother would be proud. 'I love being a part of Tom's life,' said the independent Nicole Kidman. 'I just don't need to carry his name around.' This flurry of attention was nothing compared to what was around the corner.

The most scandalous story appeared in the women's magazine *McCall's* in March 1991 and became forever lodged in the brains of readers and journalists alike. The unsubstantiated and hurtful article was written by an imaginative freelancer who claimed that the second Cruise marriage was purely one of convenience.

Tom Cruise had been dogged by rumours that he was gay from the beginning of his career. Cashing in on his good looks, the majority of Tom's films promote his virulent heterosexuality. His movies pre-Nicole are littered with sexual references which can be read as either macho or homoerotic, depending on your perspective. He is usually seen bedding women and bonding with men, surrounded by objects of masculine power. The phallicism of his props – gearsticks, guns, pool cues, fighter planes, racing cars, speedboats – is often debated. Compounding matters, he was one of the original Brat Pack pretty boys who needed no encouragement to strip to the waist and show off his finely honed, glistening muscles. Pushed, as they were, to their extremes, Tom's showy macho characters could be misconstrued. And they frequently were.

After the demise of his childless marriage to Mimi Rogers it was insinuated that not only was Tom gay, but he was also infertile. The article in *McCall's* took these theories one step further. It suggested that Creative Artists Agency (CAA) arranged the marriage to Nicole to cover up Cruise's homosexuality – Kidman's payoff being a guaranteed Hollywood career.

Just a few months after their dream wedding, the powerful couple couldn't stand for such a cruel and personal attack. Tom and Nicole threatened to sue. Quickly backing down, *McCall's* agreed to print a retraction in their April edition, written by Pat Kingsley, Tom's publicist:

> McCall's *knows of no evidence indicating that Mr Cruise is sterile or homosexual, or that Ms Kidman is anything other than a highly competent actress, or that they married for any other reason than mutual love and respect.*

The grovelling continued with a personal letter of apology. The Cruise camp seemed satisfied; but of course the damage was already done.

'I take offence if people say I would enter into a marriage of convenience,' said Nicole. 'I think that's very sexist because they're saying, "She married for fame and money." It's bullshit. You marry for love.'

Now, everyone was curious about *all* aspects of the marriage. 'I suppose because I'm married to somebody very famous, our love life is under great speculation by many, many people at their dinner tables every night,' she continued. 'But it gets invasive. Both of us are private people. We don't feel comfortable discussing what we do in bed at midnight – even though it is pretty damn good!'

Then there were the insults about her abilities as an actress. Friends had wisely warned Nicole that her identity might be swallowed up by that of her famous husband. Perhaps she naïvely thought that by keeping her surname she could avoid the problem. But with some of her finest work limited to an Australian audience and her recent American exposure confined to insignificant 'girlfriend' roles, Nicole began to recognize that her friends had a valid point. 'When Tom and I got married I thought, "I'll go on with my work", after all I've been working as an actress since I was fourteen. I didn't quite realize the ramifications of being married to this Hollywood superstar.'

A true daughter of Janelle Kidman, Nicole spoke out about the shocking number of women who were still defined by their husbands. 'You don't see a lot of men being judged in relation to their wives, no matter how famous,' she raged. 'It's easier for men to be individuals. I think it's sexist and I have a strong viewpoint on that. I'm committed to marriage, but I want a career and being married doesn't mean I have to give all that up.'

These were strong words from someone who had so far only been seen in one Hollywood film — as Tom's girlfriend. 'People started calling me Mrs Tom Cruise and I felt hemmed in,' she admitted, her loyalties torn. 'I would have gone back to Australia but I didn't want to be separated from Tom.'

Similarly, Tom's ex-wife, Mimi Rogers, could not wait to be seen in her own right again, as she had been tarnished with the same brush. 'All of a sudden her name is never mentioned without his,' she empathized. 'No matter what the article is, it's, "Tom Cruise's wife, Nicole Kidman". You're never again mentioned without that name and that's hard. I am waiting for the moment when I don't have to talk about that fucking name any more.'

So Nicole had no choice but to ride out the storm and hope that future projects would help redress the balance. But, as one storm died down, another brewed up. This time it was religion. As with the allegations about his sexuality, again it was her husband who attracted the attention.

Tom had made a surprising about-turn and renounced his devout Catholicism during his first marriage in order to embrace the faith to which Rogers had adhered since her teens: L. Ron Hubbard's highly controversial Church of Scientology. The official description of the religion reads: 'Scientology is an applied religious philosophy. Its goal is to bring an individual to an understanding of himself, and his life as a spiritual being and in relationship to the universe as a whole.'

Hubbard's admirable goals included 'a civilization without insanity, without criminals and without war, where the able can prosper and honest beings can have rights, and where man is free to rise to greater heights'.

These objectives seemed regular enough to Tom. These new teachings, he claimed, gave him so much confidence that they had helped him to overcome his debilitating dyslexia. 'I was diagnosed as dyslexic a long time ago,' he said. 'Then I was given *The Basic Study Manual*, written by L. Ron Hubbard. I started applying its principles – I had the ability to learn and read anything that I wanted to. Who knows whether I actually had dyslexia or not? Maybe I had the wrong approach to studying as a kid.' It should be mentioned that the Dyslexia Foundation of America was outraged that anyone could suggest the affliction could be so 'miraculously' and easily cured.

Hubbard's religion had millions of followers around the world, with centres in over seventy countries. It was based on years of extensive research by its leader. So why was this belief system deemed more controversial than any other new-age religion?

Scientology's less conventional practices include exorcizing and healing the everyday psychic scars that interfere with rational thought. This is supposedly achieved via spiritual counselling, or 'auditing', which often employs the 'E-metre' – a mechanical device that measures the subject's mental changes. It was this practice that led to claims that the cult was brainwashing its members. That intergalactic travel was mooted within the sect also raised a few eyebrows.

Tom was not the first celebrity to be enticed by Scientology's principles of self-help. John Travolta's conversion in the 1970s first alerted Hollywood to Hubbard's teachings; he was soon followed by his *Look Who's Talking* co-star Kirstie Alley, Mimi Rogers' best friend. Other notable followers include Priscilla Presley and her daughter Lisa Marie. It was Hubbard's own larger-than-life personality and involvement with the arts that attracted the stars. Unlike any other religion, Scientology offered a magazine called *Celebrity* and a whole church exclusively for famous followers. Known as the Celebrity Center, the plush mock-Gothic chateau, located on Franklin Avenue in Hollywood, further isolates its attendees from everyday folk.

Marriage is sacred to Scientologists, and it was rumoured that Tom and Mimi attended church-run counselling sessions in an attempt to salvage their relationship. But Tom never spoke much about his religion, bar one rare admission. 'Essentially it's enabled me,' he said. 'It's just helped me to become more "me". It gives me certain tools to be the person I want to be and explore the areas I want to explore as an artist.'

What the curious reporters wanted to know was whether Nicole also subscribed to this philosophy; after all, Tom was apparently making regular sizeable donations to the church. The loyal wife did not belittle her husband's faith and instead tried to appreciate his conviction, much in the same manner that Janelle originally adopted Antony's Catholicism. Nicole sweetly but concisely told journalists, 'Tom discusses it; I don't discuss it,' but it was widely believed that she learnt the basics of Dianetics and subscribed to some of Scientology's schools of thought.

Nicole preferred not to theorize on religion as such. 'Scientology deals with communication, a lot of things,' she said. 'But for me, my life is my life and I live it the way I want to. I don't want to be about Scientology, just Scientology. And this Henry James quote, "Pain passes, but love remains", for me, says so much about what I think life is about.' Obviously an independent thinker with her own well-formed opinions, Nicole later divulged, 'I would never have married Tom if he had insisted I become an out-and-out Scientologist.'

As the speculation died down, Nicole was finally allowed to start enjoying her marriage. Having missed out on a honeymoon to finish filming *Billy Bathgate*, she was now able to spend some quality time with her husband and proclaimed, 'Officially we'll be on our honeymoon for the rest of our lives!' She continued to give press interviews and used each opportunity to try and squash any lingering feelings that the marriage was arranged. She spoke freely about their mutual love, sometimes to the extent that she was in danger of nauseating readers.

Nicole's main objective was for the couple to come across as human; to strip away the Hollywood glamour and appear as a normal, down-to-earth husband and wife. She insisted that they didn't indulge in the celebrity lifestyle, she didn't go out to posh restaurants, they weren't followed by an entourage and weren't plagued by intrusive fans. They were so ordinary in fact, Tom and Nicole could be your neighbours.

'We have so much in common that it's almost as if we are the same person,' she said of their compatibility, before going on to emphasize some of the reasons why she believed their marriage was going to work. 'I had a couple of serious relationships back in Australia, and I learned a lot about give and take, and Tom learned a lot from his first marriage – we know what it takes to make each other happy.'

One of the keys to their marriage was laughter and happiness. 'I love the way his nose crinkles up and his teeth sort of come forward,' she said of her husband's laugh. 'He opens up his whole mouth and throws his head back. As soon as he does that, I'm in hysterics because it's so infectious.' An infectious laugh is something that has often been attributed to both Tom and Nicole by friends and journalists alike.

Tom also raved about his wonderful, beautiful, clever, amusing wife. 'Nic just makes me feel fun around her. I have never shared my life so fully with a person before. She takes me out into the garden and makes me literally stop and smell the flowers.

'Nic's friends have become my friends. Her interests have become my interests. Her family has become my family. She has broadened my life and given me a sense of who I am.'

Displaying the sense of independence fostered by her mother, Nicole joked that Tom still had to ask her for a date. 'I don't think you should just assume anything or take the other person for granted. We're dealing with two individuals here.'

Fortunately, as with the adrenalin sports, Tom and Nicole had similar desires and fancies. 'We both have gypsy blood in our veins – just taking off somewhere and having an adventure,' she continued. 'I want to do some serious travelling in Africa and spend a lot more time scuba diving and horse-riding.' It was clear that more than pursuing her career, Nicole wanted to spend time with her new husband. 'We enjoy being alone. Tom's very romantic and we're both very, very much in love.'

Only one thing apparently differed on their agenda: starting a family. Tom had publicly expressed his longing to become a father, but Nicole seemed content with just the two of them. 'I would like to have babies,' she said, 'but I'm twenty-three, just married and everything is starting to happen for me. So there's still plenty of time for that.'

12

They're Separate People With Separate Careers

Director Ron Howard had a well-known face. He'd been widely seen on television in a number of different shows as a child actor, culminating in his most popular role as amiable teenager Ritchie Cunningham in *Happy Days*. After that series ended its six-year run in 1980, Howard devoted himself to life behind the camera, directing feelgood all-American classics such as *Splash!*, *Cocoon* and *Parenthood*. The toothy grin was still the same, but he had taken to hiding the loss of his famous ginger hair under a baseball cap.

Howard had first approached Tom Cruise about a film entitled *Irish Story* back in 1983. Other projects took precedence for both parties and the script would not reach the actor's office until 1989. Eighteen months later, the timing was right for Tom, who was searching for a strong romantic vehicle to counterbalance his usual 'tough guy' roles. And who better to play his love interest than his wife? Howard admits he was totally oblivious to Nicole Kidman's existence at that stage, but after some gentle persuasion he agreed to cast her opposite Tom; it would certainly help to play on the media interest in the relatively new couple.

The Cruises signed a reported £8 million deal for the Universal picture in March 1991. They arrived in Ireland that summer to absorb some of the local culture before filming commenced. During that time, the name of the film changed many times, from *Irish Story* to *Sure As The Moon* to *Distant Shores*, before its final title was decided upon: *Far And Away*.

With a budget estimated at around $60 million, *Far And Away* was a huge undertaking for the two stars and was by far Ron Howard's most expensive project to date. The six or so months of filming would take place in County Kerry, south-west Ireland, California and Montana.

In Ireland Tom and Nicole were initially ensconced in the honeymoon suite at the Westbury Hotel, then at the penthouse suite at Dublin's Berkeley Court Hotel. Finally, they took up residence in a small house close to the village of Ventry, where the first half of the film is set. A small gathering of thatched stone cottages had been reconstructed in the isolated spot, and the location itself was especially significant to Nicole, who later remarked, 'We shot *Far And Away* in the town where my great-great grandparents came from.'

During their stay in Ireland, the newly-weds buckled down to an intense schedule, starting filming promptly at 9 a.m. and sometimes not finishing until 11 p.m. Embracing Irish life as much as possible, Tom and Nicole were entranced with their picturesque surroundings and became regulars in the Paidi O'Se pub. For a while they considered buying a house in nearby Dingle; however, the ongoing threat of IRA terrorist attacks, which had prompted Tom to employ the services of three burly bodyguards, made them think twice about living in Ireland.

Predictably, the presence of the A-list couple attracted a steady stream of fans, who seized every opportunity to invade the set in search of autographs. Enormous screens shielded the set in Dublin, and an 8-foot wall was hastily constructed to conceal the filming at Kilruddery House in County Wicklow. Nevertheless, tabloid photographers did their best to take an 'exclusive' snap of the actors at work, one even attempting to break into their on-set trailer. The photographer was unsuccessful, but no doubt he would have been impressed with the temporary $750,000 lodging, with its marble flooring, fully furnished living area, kitchen and king-sized bedroom complete with satellite television.

One of the reasons the Cruises seemed fair game to the press was down to a rumour that Nicole was two months pregnant. The *Daily Mail* gleefully reported that she had supposedly told Tom the good news by asking him, 'What do you want for Father's Day, Big Daddy?' Tom, whose fertility continued to fall under scrutiny, had apparently commented: 'It's a miracle! She's pregnant and I did it! I'm going to be a dad. Hollywood can keep the Oscar [referring to his nomination for *Born On The Fourth Of July*]. The only award I really care about is having a kid of my own.' The news was left unconfirmed by their publicist and no bump emerged.

Back on the set, Tom and Nicole carefully considered how they could work happily together. Obviously they had the benefit of their experiences on *Days Of Thunder* to their advantage, but back then they were merely falling in love; now their relationship had changed. The prospect of overseeing a married couple, each a strong-willed individual, must have daunted their director.

Said Nicole: 'I had ideas that I thought were absolutely 100 per cent right, and Tom had ideas that he thought were absolutely 100 per cent right, and that's when Ron Howard would come in. It was great to have Ron because he's married; he's been married for a lot longer than we have, so he knows how to make it work.

'He said to us at the beginning, "I don't want you both going through each other and directing each other. I want you to always come to me so, if you've got an idea for Tom, give it to me and then I'll give it to Tom and vice versa." That set up a very good working relationship because we had to include the director and not go off and play married couples.'

Still, Nicole relished the fact that working with her husband made it possible for her to contribute to the film twenty-four hours a day. 'You can come up with an idea in the middle of the night and wake up your spouse and say, "Hey, I just got an idea for a scene." It really is helpful.' Although Tom could have been forgiven if he did not appreciate her midnight enthusiasm, he too enjoyed the experience of working with his wife.

'It's easy working with Nic,' he said. 'She's a professional – just a great actress who has the ability to turn a scene on its head and make it come alive. Enjoying the experience with my wife takes it to another level. I worked hard and covered a lot of ground each day, but somehow my life was fuller personally and that reflected professionally.'

It was clear to all on the set that the pair were still very much in love as they approached their first wedding anniversary. Tom was spotted supplying Nicole with constant cups of coffee and tenderly wrapping a towel around her shoulders in between takes to keep her warm.

Derek Wallace, a prop man working on the film, noticed that the Cruises were always canoodling, not caring who saw them. 'One of the drivers threatened to throw a bucket of cold water over them,' he says. 'I've never seen a couple so close or so ecstatically happy.'

Even Ron Howard noticed their frequent bids for privacy, observing, 'They'd disappear into the old trailer sometimes, so I think it was a honeymoon project . . .'

Watching the film in retrospect, it is plain to see that the Cruises really are having the time of their lives. Nicole looks stunning as Shannon, with her china-doll-like features romantically framed by orange corkscrew curls. She tackles the feisty role as the rebellious daughter of a landowner with vigour, proving in her first scene to be quite handy with a pitchfork. Tom, whose hapless character Joseph is neatly described as 'an especially odd boy', looks equally fresh-faced.

Both actors were obliged to adopt Irish accents for their roles, so Tom employed the services of a pair of locals and two dialect coaches, Sean O'Casey and Tim Monich, the latter an American.

'My first question when they asked me to do it was, "Why don't you hire an Irish person?"' says Monich. But Universal needed two of the biggest available names to guarantee the movie's success. Besides, a genuine Irish couple might have proved too hard to understand for the target mainstream audience, or, as Monich puts it, 'Universal did not want to be involved in having a film that wasn't intelligible to Americans.'

So Tom and Nicole bit the bullet and did their best to pull off a Celtic lilt, or 'Irish-lite', as it could be described. Despite both actors having Irish blood running through their veins (on Tom's side, the original Mapothers had emigrated to Louisville from south-east Ireland), this did not come easily, and their accents were uneven, to say the least. But they were willing to give it a go, and physically Nicole's colouring suggests a certain stereotypical Irishness, which did help.

Far And Away is set in 1892 during the rebellion of the Irish tenant farmers. Tom, as Joseph, is the rather bumbling son of a poor farmer in Ireland. When his father dies, leaving the family unable to afford the rent, their house is burned down by the landowner's minions. Joseph sets off on a quest to murder the landowner; the sight of the *Top Gun* star earnestly venturing forth on a small cantankerous donkey yields much amusement. Hiding out in the landowner's stable, Joseph is then discovered by Shannon, who thrusts her pitchfork in the general direction of his upper thigh . . .

This latest development brings about one of Ron Howard's favourite moments of filming. Joseph is taken into the landowner's house to receive treatment for his prong punctures and rests awhile in bed plotting his revenge, naked apart from what closely resembles a mixing bowl preserving his modesty.

'Tom was always great about that and he knew he'd be there naked with just this pot,' explains Howard. 'We *did* have a little black cloth over his groin section. When Nicole lifted the bowl in the scene where she thinks the character is asleep, we shot her reaction.' Two takes were filmed with the cloth in place, but Howard was unhappy with Nicole's expression. 'So I went over to Tom and told him to do one more take and slip the cloth away – just a joke between the boys – and we got a somewhat different reaction from Nicole . . .'

The third take did not disappoint and Nicole hid her true response admirably – her performance in that hilarious scene alone is perhaps worthy of an Oscar, considering – and, as she says, '*That's* the reaction you see onscreen. I suppose I *was* excited!'

Frivolities aside, the eternally feuding Shannon and Joseph escape their elders and head to America: they have heard that land is literally being given away in Oklahoma. They arrive in Boston, where they pretend to be brother and sister, and take on work to pay for the train fare to Oklahoma. Joseph earns his keep as a bare-knuckle boxer, engaging in some bloody fights.

'It was ferocious!' recalls the former wrestler. 'I didn't realize it would be so physical. I really took a pounding! I had knuckles going into my back and chest. I got hit in the ribs a lot too. For about a week and a half I was in constant pain.' Nicole watched squeamishly from the sidelines, at one point requesting Howard stop the action when it became too gory.

During their time in Boston, Shannon and Joseph overcome the class boundary and fall in love, although they hide their mutual attraction from each other until the very last moment. As Tom pointed out, 'We hoped that would work for people, to build up the tension so that one little kiss becomes a big thing.' But the kisses alone presented the director with a bit of a quandary.

'I think Ron was nervous about our kissing scenes,' said Nicole. 'He thought, "Gosh, how's a first kiss between these two going to work?" because all we do is kiss all the time.'

For a while Howard considered placing a ban on Tom and Nicole's off-screen smooching to ensure onscreen sparks, but in the end he realized that there was a certain freshness to their affection which came across naturally.

'I think that there was something in the newness of their love which they were able to really apply to this story – even though they were together and married,' he says. 'When Tom was looking at Nicole, it was very easy for him to remember the first time he really sensed her beauty or her magnetism, and I think the same was true for Nicole of Tom. So I learned how to give direction while they were kissing and I realized that they could actually take direction while kissing, and we didn't even have to make eye contact!'

Nicole remembers another aspect to those scenes, similar to Howard's missing-cloth innovation. 'We did a few takes and he had some crew standing by the monitor, giving us a rating on how hot it was on a score of one to ten, and on one case we got a ten – that's the one we used.'

Far And Away only really seems to settle into its stride about halfway through, when Shannon and Joseph begin to flirt and tease each other after having lived in Boston for a while. For Nicole, this was the beauty of the whole project. 'When you're acting with your husband there's a certain kind of easiness, because you know each other so well. That ease comes across onscreen, I know it does. When two people touch one another you can see it.

'If you don't know somebody, which is often the case with films, it can be very awkward to touch them. But when you know them, even the simplest thing, like stroking their hair, looks and feels more natural. Kissing on the screen is not as easy as it may seem, so it helps that you know somebody for a long time before you have to do those intimate things before the camera.'

Interestingly, alongside their obvious infatuation came a certain competitiveness. This revealed itself during the film's final scenes: the spectacularly realized Oklahoma land rush which involved some 800 extras, 400 horses and 200 wagons.

The shoot actually took place in Billings, Montana, and both Tom and Nicole were obliged to race their horses among the crowd. Screenwriter Bob Dolman recalls, 'Nicole would be riding, and Tom would ask the horse wranglers, "So how fast do you think Nicole is going?"

'"About 33 miles per hour."

'The next day he did the scene and came back to the guys and said, "How fast do you think I was going?"

'"You must have been going about 40 miles per hour."

'He looked over at Nicole and said, "*Yes!*". It was extraordinary.'

Nicole tells a different, slightly darker tale. 'At first on the horse, I was screaming. Everybody's laughing because they just hear this girl screaming,

"Whoa!" The horse would not stop and we got up to 37 miles per hour, which is very fast. Finally they pulled over and I was shaking.'

Although Nicole had already ridden in *Archer's Adventure* and counted horse-riding among her favourite activities, she found this high-speed chase quite alarming. Howard decided to tackle her panic by immediately ordering another take. 'The next time I took off I could control him and that's when I lost my fear of speed.

'Then Tom and I started a competition to see who could go faster. I'd be kicking and flying, and I'd stop and I'd ask the wranglers, "What did I clock in at?" and they'd say, "37 miles per hour – I mile per hour faster than Tom."'

Far And Away was intended as a vast, sweeping historical epic harking back to a more romantic era. On a technical level it was beautifully shot, the first movie since Disney's *Tron* in 1982 to be filmed in Panavision Super 70, producing a 65mm print with the extra 5mm taken up by John Williams's (*Star Wars, Empire Of The Sun*) splendid soundtrack. Visually, scenes like the climactic Oklahoma land rush rivalled the breathtaking buffalo-hunting sequences from Kevin Costner's recent *Dances With Wolves*, which had won several Academy Awards.

After the relative commercial disappointment of *Days Of Thunder*, Tom Cruise wasn't prepared to take any chances and personally oversaw post-production with a keen eye. Various sketches of his and Nicole's scenes had to go through Tom first for approval, and photographs for promotional posters had to be 'outstanding' to 'evoke a voluminous amount of interest and positive reaction', according to one strict memo.

Universal splashed out on a spectacular advertising campaign and Tom and Nicole embarked on a whirlwind PR tour. Incredibly, the thirty-page official publicity document omitted the very fact that the stars of the movie were married in real life. In addition, the actor and actress insisted on being interviewed separately, with their joint publicist explaining, 'They're separate people, with separate careers.'

Unusually for the time, the actor and actress also requested that journalists attending the press junkets should each sign a contract promising to use the ensuing material for promotion of the film only, even stipulating in which publications the text would appear. 'Cruise Control', as overseen by Pat Kingsley, Tom's notorious publicist, was a phrase often used in relation to Nicole's husband, and the tour gave a taste of things to come as writers who broke the rules were refused further access to either actor point-blank.

Finally, the film was ready to be released. Tom and Nicole made a spectacular appearance presenting awards at the last night of the Cannes Film Festival on 18 May 1992. Screaming crowds gave them a most enthusiastic reception as they drove up to the Palais des Festivals in an open limousine, accompanied by a police escort. Dressed in a long white gown with matching gloves, Nicole looked significantly bridal – perhaps in some way a symbolic advertisement for the film. *Far And Away* was released in America a few days later on 22 May, surrounded by much hype about its relatively newly-wed stars. It appeared in the UK on 31 July and subsequently received nominations at the 1993 MTV Movie Awards, for Best Action Sequence and Best Onscreen Duo.

Sadly, this is about as far as it got. The film's lack of commercial success had little to do with the two leads. Aside from their slightly skewed accents, Tom and Nicole's performances were entertaining and they certainly made a pleasing pair visually. Once their characters progressed to Boston, the real-life couple began to bounce off each other with an onscreen chemistry far stronger than in *Days Of Thunder*.

However, the film suffered greatly from less charismatic supporting acting, and the stereotypical representations of the Irish proved insulting at times. While light relief was occasionally provided with moments of humour (Nicole peering under the mixing bowl; Tom punching his disobedient horse to make him go), for the first hour or so it is unclear whether the story is supposed to be a comedy or perhaps even a farce. *Far And Away* could also have benefited considerably from harsher editing. And if 140 minutes seemed lengthy, viewers would later find versions shown on network television added thirty-five minutes of extra footage not included in the cinematic release.

Ultimately, *Far And Away* as a package failed to live up to the sum of its individual parts, resulting in an unforeseen lukewarm reception. At the American box office it took less than $47 million in the first four weeks, compared to that year's *Batman Returns*, which took $46 million in just three days. And the reviews were merciless.

'A doddering bloated bit of corn, and its characters and situations so hackneyed, that we can't give in to the story and allow ourselves to be washed away,' said the *Washington Post*, while *Sight And Sound* condemned it as 'unrepentant and vapid nonsense, celebrated with inappropriate splendour'. And the British press agreed. 'A bland, misguided, well-upholstered bore. The plot and characters sometimes seem to have been borrowed from a picture storybook for teenage girls,' said *The Times*.

Nicole Kidman stood by her work. She had gained valuable experience in being so closely involved in a major Hollywood movie. 'I've become more confident and I understand [the] film-making process more,' she said. 'But I could still sit here and pick everything I've done to shreds very easily, I don't think I'll ever be satisfied. However, I'm proud of *Far And Away* – I think that it's a great movie.'

As for working again with Tom, she said, 'What you see are real feelings and real love. There was nothing wrong in allowing that to show.'

13
The Ice Queen Cometh

In October 1991, as production on *Far And Away* was coming to a close, reports surfaced that Nicole had been rushed to St John's Hospital and Health Center in Santa Monica, Los Angeles. Apparently she booked in anonymously and was thought to have undergone 'minor abdominal surgery to remove scar tissue that was causing her pain'.

Later that winter, she flew to Australia for a private trip to catch up with her family. She went alone, as Tom had also been in the wars. Having survived gruelling fight scenes during *Far And Away*, he had now fractured a rib and broken a finger falling out of a tree in their Pacific Palisades garden. He stayed in Los Angeles, but telephoned Nicole every day.

Although she had no official engagements, Nicole's stay in hospital prompted her to spread some Christmas goodwill to the children in the Camperdown Children's Hospital in Sydney. After handing out a variety of gifts, she sat and chatted with some teenagers, promising to return the following February. The actress had specifically chosen that hospital because it was where Janelle had previously worked.

Clearly signifying their divergent careers, at the NATO/ShoWest Awards in May 1992 Tom Cruise won the International Box Office Star award, while Nicole Kidman was named Female Star Of Tomorrow. Nicole was still being referred to as 'Mrs Tom Cruise'.

The actress was to suffer greatly from criticism that by immediately signing on to do a romantic movie with her husband, she was simply cashing in on her position as Tom Cruise's wife. This was a serious blow which was to haunt her for some time.

'In retrospect, I probably shouldn't have done a movie with him so quickly,' she admitted later. 'I probably should have done more by myself to be seen independently. To work with Tom Cruise is a great thing, but I certainly don't want to be in every single film with my husband because it becomes a little myopic.'

For now, Nicole laughingly brushed aside rumours that she and Tom would be playing the Duke and Duchess of York (a fellow redhead) in a new onscreen pairing. It was clear that if she wanted to survive as an actress in her own right, she would have to take on a range of challenging roles that had nothing to do with her marital status. Whether or not Nicole realized at this stage that her career was in danger is open to speculation.

Despite the promise of *Dead Calm*, since arriving in Hollywood Nicole had only appeared in the lame *Days Of Thunder*, the poorly received *Billy Bathgate* and *Far And Away*, another relative box-office flop in which she starred opposite her husband. Directors seemed to be giving her a wide berth. Nicole failed several auditions to star in some potentially pivotal films, including *Ghost* and *Silence Of The Lambs*, which provided breakthrough roles for Demi Moore and Jodie Foster respectively; she also missed out on either of the strong female parts in the cult favourite *Thelma And Louise*, and the lead in *Sleepless In Seattle*, which set Meg Ryan up for life as the loveable, scatty, blonde romantic-comedy heroine.

'Rejection used to be very difficult to take,' says Nicole, 'but as an actor you learn to deal with that. I have missed out on stuff that I really, really wanted and have been so frustrated and upset, but in the end you just have to keep at it.

'My mum calls me tenacious. People can say things and it will hurt me, but I think my determination is there.' She would now be forced to rely on this tenacity.

'I went through a period when I didn't get any work for a year,' Nicole later admitted. 'It was a very tough time for me and I wanted to go back to Australia, but Tom's career was in America. I was willing to give up a lot of other things to keep my marriage.' Reminiscent of her honeymoon period, Nicole again found herself compromising for the sake of her husband.

Jane Campion advised the fourteen-year-old Nicole: 'Protect your talent'. It would be fifteen years before they would work together in 1996's *The Portrait Of A Lady*.

Right: For the role of Isabel Archer in *The Portrait Of A Lady*, Campion makes good use of Nicole's unconventional looks.

Below: Isabel is trapped in an unhappy marriage to Gilbert Osmond, played by John Malkovich.

Tom and Nicole adopted two children: Isabella in 1993 and Conor in 1995. 'I'd sit around and say, "I want to adopt a child", but never, "I want a baby in my tummy",' explains Nicole.

'I fell in love, madly in love,' says Nicole. 'I just kind of went, "Oh, forget my career, who cares?"' Was this the same woman who was demanding the right to have an independent career just a short year ago?

✯

Inadvertently, Nicole was coming across as The Ice Queen in the eyes of the press. Some of this was undoubtedly down to her otherworldly, inaccessible looks: her blanched skin, her imposing stature and the fact that she was rarely pictured smiling broadly. Additionally, it was leaked by 'those in the know' that Nicole was turning into a high-maintenance, demanding wife.

Despite the fact that Tom was celebrating his thirtieth birthday and Nicole was only just twenty-five, he was allegedly a hen-pecked husband. There were reports that she had insisted he give up his L.A. Dodgers season tickets in order to spend more time with her. She was also supposed to have doctored his wardrobe, giving some of his favourite clothes to charity shops and approving all his new outfits. But the other side of that particular story claims that the clothes earmarked for dumping were swiftly rescued by Tom and put firmly back in the closet, while the five Armani and two Versace suits chosen by Nicole remained in his wardrobe, unworn, in their plastic wrapping.

Tom's devotion to his wife often manifested itself in buying her numerous gifts, often expensive clothing, antique jewellery or cars. It was even suggested that he was trying to mould her to his tastes.

Nicole admitted she was still adapting to her new lifestyle as one half of an A-list couple. 'The first year was a little overwhelming, but you get used to it. I was lucky because I married a man who's incredibly sane and never allows the celebrity thing to go to his head.'

Of course, she also had to deal with the fact that Tom was an international sex symbol. 'I don't suppose I'll ever get used to seeing girls gazing at my husband lustfully, but at least they don't try to rip his clothes off.' Constantly questioned about her man, Nicole's replies soon became smug: 'I get to go to bed with Tom Cruise every night!' This 'cat that got the cream' attitude endeared her to no one.

Another contributing factor to the popular perception of Nicole being somewhat standoffish was that she was constantly having to defend and justify herself in interviews. The latest rumours were that she was again pregnant.

'Why do people keep saying this?' she snapped. 'At the Golden Globes I wore the tightest dress I could get my hands on but even then I have a little bit of a belly so I think it starts the rumours. It's funny, I'm not opposed to having children, just not right now.' Perhaps the exasperation in her voice was unsurprising given the constant interrogation she had endured on this subject.

Whatever image the public were being fed of the actress, they were going to have to wait a while before seeing the ice melt.

★

As it dawned on Nicole that she was in need of an image transformation, she readily accepted a part which had the potential to show her darker side (possibly not the best way to charm the public). 'It's a great female role and I'm really excited about it. It's a thriller with two men and a woman, similar to *Dead Calm* in that sense.'

Directed by Harold Becker (*Taps* with Tom Cruise, *The Onion Field*), *Malice* looked set to breathe life into Nicole's career and she relished the disturbing role. Starring opposite Hollywood heavyweights Alec Baldwin and Bill Pullman, Nicole was to play the role of a wife who takes an instant dislike to an intrusive male houseguest. The story did indeed sound familiar.

The elaborate, some might say over-complicated, plot twists and turns from the first to the final frame, and the gimmick was to see the film before someone spoilt the ending. The audience is required to pay keen attention to *Malice* as every detail without fail has a deeper significance.

Bill Pullman and Nicole Kidman make an attractively cosy couple (Andy and Tracy) who are renovating their house and hoping to start a family. We see them enjoying everyday life, including an intimate scene sharing a Chinese takeaway in bed. There are just a few problems threatening their happiness: college professor Andy is concerned about a serial killer at loose on campus; Tracy is suffering sporadic abdominal pains; and the couple lack the funds necessary for their domestic overhaul.

Cue the arrival of Jed (Alec Baldwin), an old high-school friend of Andy, who is now a first-rate surgeon and coincidentally looking for a place to stay – why doesn't he rent out the top floor of their house? The two men are drinking one night when Andy flippantly mutters he would give his right arm for $1 million. Jed questions whether he really would, and so introduces the premise of the film.

What follows is a series of far-fetched events: Tracy has an emergency bilateral salpingo-oophorectomy (removal of both ovaries and fallopian tubes to you and me); the surgery shows she was in fact pregnant; she leaves her husband and sues the surgeon – a certain houseguest named Jed.

The subplot of the college killer farcically proves Andy to be sterile, ergo not the father of Tracy's baby, and he plays detective, unravelling the very involved set-up which began years earlier. While he struggles to regain control of the situation, so too does the audience, piecing together the convoluted story and all its permutations.

Nicole does not feature for the middle third of the film, and when she reappears, Tracy is supposed to be a crazy woman, capable of anything since selling her fertility for $20 million. This is Nicole's opportunity to show that she can do more than act the happy wife, but, sadly, she fails to inject enough intensity to truly terrify. She has plenty of potential for hair-raising hysterics, but never quite manages to convey insanity. Equally, neither Pullman nor Baldwin fully establish their respective characters, which suggests that the intricate plot and direction are partly to blame. With all the divergent dynamics of the film, perhaps Becker bit off more than he could chew?

The critics certainly thought so when *Malice* was unleashed on the unsuspecting public in October 1993. 'A virtual scrapbook of elements borrowed from other suspense pics,' slated *Variety*. Indeed, *Malice* reeked of all the recent films that had jumped on the homicidal ex-lover/houseguest bandwagon after the success of *Fatal Attraction* in 1987: *Sleeping With The Enemy* (1990), *The Hand That Rocks The Cradle* (1991), *Single White Female* (1992) and, most obviously, *Indecent Proposal*, 1993's sordid tale of selling sex for money. London's *Evening Standard* put it a little more bluntly: 'One of the most shameless pieces of unadulterated trash.'

Nicole's adequate performance sank without trace along with the film and her heartless character failed to attract any attention – she continued to be overlooked as an actress.

While Nicole was struggling with her career at the end of 1992, Tom Cruise was busy rebuilding his reputation after the embarrassment of *Far And Away*. Following *A Few Good Men*, he was now filming the thriller *The Firm* in Memphis, Tennessee. But working did not detract him from his ultimate goal of becoming a father.

Whether or not the rumours of failed pregnancies and fertility problems were founded in truth, the fact remained that the couple had yet to conceive a child naturally. Impatient to move on to this stage of life, Tom and Nicole filed adoption papers in Palm Beach, Florida.

Although far removed from the couple's base in Los Angeles, Florida was one of the few American states to uphold a law preventing a mother from backtracking after surrendering her child for adoption. However, the receiving parents had to be resident in the area, a problem easily solved by the luxury condominium Tom had purchased there years earlier.

The Cruises' private file specified that a child would be placed with them from a 'broking' company, a children's home or through a private arrangement. Such papers were supposed to be protected by confidentiality agreements, but somehow, in their bid to become parents, the famous couple's secret was uncovered by the press. Fighting back, Tom and Nicole raged about an 'irreparable invasion of privacy' and told the media that they had now withdrawn their papers, due to the lack of sensitivity from journalists. This was in fact a red herring and the adoption process continued.

To their great joy, the New Year brought the anxious couple a new life. At the beginning of January, having just celebrated their second wedding anniversary, Tom and Nicole flew to a hospital in Miami. There they collected their daughter. 'There were tears of happiness in Nicole's eyes as she held the child close to her,' said the nurse who had cared for the unnamed baby.

The pretty 9-pound blue-eyed girl was born to a family who already had two children and couldn't afford a third. Tom and Nicole jumped at this opportunity and were delighted to hear that the baby's birth on 22 December 1992 had been without complication. Tom and Nicole called her Isabella Jane Kidman Cruise; Bella for short. The choice of the first name was not attributed to any family member, but the much-admired actress Isabella Rossellini, with whom Tom had worked recently on *Fallen Angels*. Tom was due back on set for *The Firm* and was sad to leave his instant family as they were just beginning to get to know each other.

The sensitive issue of adoption provided easy pickings for gossip-hungry journalists and the Cruises had to endure incessant idle speculation about their reasons for adopting.

'I'd always wanted to adopt a child,' Nicole explained time after time. 'I'd sit around and say, "I want to adopt a child", but never, "I want a baby in my tummy".' They were by no means the first Hollywood couple to do this – Kirstie Alley had adopted in 1988 – and in fact this was the start of a growing trend: Michelle Pfeiffer followed suit in March 1993.

'The adoption was a very spontaneous thing,' Nicole continued. 'We decided to adopt Isabella because the situation came up. The spiritual aspect of adoption is that it's so extraordinary that two adults and a baby find each other in such a huge world. That makes it very special.'

Nicole's response did not satisfy inquisitive minds and Tom's publicist was determined to quell the cruel and baseless rumours that her client was sterile. 'Tom and Nicole wanted a child *right now*,' said Pat Kingsley. 'The opportunity presented itself and they took it. They look forward to having other children of their own.'

Others wondered about the whole event coming so soon after Nicole's crystal-clear declarations in 1991 and 1992 that although she wanted a family, the timing wasn't right. It was also noted that this method had saved Nicole from interrupting her career with nine months of pregnancy and the customary race to regain her figure afterwards.

Later in January, the couple attended the Golden Globe Awards in Los Angeles, having safely ensconced Isabella with a babysitter. There they appeared very affectionate with each other and fell over themselves in their eagerness to talk about the new arrival.

'Becoming a father is the greatest thing that has ever happened to me,' beamed Tom. 'I have longed for a child. Now that I have little Isabella, I look at her and thank God every day for giving me such a precious gift. I adore her to death and I hope I will love and protect her to my dying day – I am ecstatically happy.' Nicole was reportedly heard to say that having tried to conceive 'for so long, we are making the most of Isabella now'.

The next question on the list was whether the family had any further plans for expansion, either naturally or with another adoption. Nicole patiently told the press that they were intending to both adopt more children *and* hopefully have some of their own. 'Whether that happens or not is not my obsession in life,' she said. 'I don't want to discuss it as it's very private and very personal. When it happens, it happens, and the truth is, I'd be so excited I wouldn't be able to keep my mouth shut.' That was a polite way of saying mind your own business.

Having fended off enough questions for one day, the protective mother was adamant that the subject of the child's natural parentage was strictly off limits and refused point-blank to discuss the matter. Instead, she elaborated on the ways in which Isabella had affected them. 'Obviously my life has changed,' she acknowledged. 'My career used to be the all-important thing. These days there is something else there too – something more important.'

Tom, who had been the most vocal about his desire to start a family, was not only a doting dad, but also fell in love with his wife all over again. 'Being a father is what I always dreamed of, only a hundred times better. She has changed my life.

'Seeing Nic with Isabella, I see a whole other side to her. Sometimes Nic forgets to turn the baby-speaker off, and I'll just sit there and listen to them. Those are the little moments in life when you stop and think, "I want to make sure I'll remember this forever. I'm a daddy."'

Once he had finished filming *The Firm*, Tom spent a considerable amount of time at home with Isabella. He was adamant that family was his priority, not work, and neither he nor Nicole would be absentee parents. 'Nic and I were never going to have a child and disappear off to work every day to leave her with a nanny. I mean, what kind of way is that to treat a child?' he asked.

For Nicole, however, the lure of improving her sinking career beckoned more urgently than motherhood. After all, she had not yet matched the impressive box-office run of her husband and did not share the luxury of his Hollywood clout.

By the spring of 1993 she had teamed up with Bruce Joel Rubin for the emotional roller coaster *My Life*. It was the screenwriter's directorial debut and, given his previous work, the subject matter was predictable: *Deadly Friend* revolves around death and revenge; *Ghost* continues this theme with some paranormal additions; and *Jacob's Ladder* further explores the supernatural. Accordingly, *My Life* exploits the notion of having one last time with a loved one – an idea memorably depicted by Demi Moore in *Ghost*, for which Nicole had ironically failed the audition three years earlier.

In *My Life*, Nicole plays Gail, the pregnant wife of Bob (Michael Keaton), who finds out that he has advanced cancer and only four months to live. Bob makes a videotape for his unborn child, during which the unresolved anger and web of lies that makes up his past unravels. Living on borrowed time, he is miraculously still alive for the birth of his son and survives long enough to be reconciled with his estranged parents.

Nicole was keen to work with Rubin and relished the prospect of such a stimulating role. 'I wanted to play the opposite end of the spectrum, a naturalistic character that I consider to be a very strong and nurturing woman,' she said. 'She's about to give birth to her child and lose her husband, so she has to be strong for her child and for her husband, and yet handle her grief.'

Striving to make the most of this opportunity, Nicole took her research very seriously. In real life, she had already suffered the emotional upheaval of preparing to lose a loved one to cancer. At the other extreme, she was eager to draw on her recently awakened maternal instincts. What she needed to do was learn about pregnancy and birth, not having experienced either firsthand. She contacted a local obstetrician during her quest, and late one night she received a surprise phone call. 'I was told that a woman was about to give birth without using drugs – did I want to come and see it?' recalls Nicole.

'So of course I drove over to the hospital. I stayed with this woman for eight hours, holding her hand in the delivery room. I was there through the whole thing until 8 o'clock in the morning, when she delivered a baby girl.' Nicole's scenes of labour are indeed some of her best, accurately portraying the pain, exhaustion and eventual overwhelming joy of the situation. She also managed successfully to 'glow' during her pretend pregnancy and began to waddle authentically as her bump grew. When Gail and an initially reluctant Bob see their child for the first time on the ultrasound, it is a particularly touching and poignant moment. Co-star Keaton tried to praise Nicole's performance but revealed, 'She doesn't really do well with compliments – she's good at changing the subject.'

Unfortunately, Nicole was not afforded many more moments to shine as her other potentially challenging scenes (breaking down to her mother, and Bob's final breath) are cut short, simply because this is primarily her husband's story. Gail is described by her mother as 'a saint' and Nicole uses the compassion appropriate to her character to excuse a very hushed performance. Judging by her speech in *Malice*, she did not need to disguise her Australian accent anymore and her persistent whisper only stresses her supporting role.

Although it tackles a delicate subject with sensitivity, there are too many implausible moments in *My Life* for the viewer to become fully engrossed in the film: the circus in the backyard, Gail not knowing the date of 'D-Day' (her husband's predicted death), Bob being so sprightly while on borrowed time. When *My Life* was released at the end of 1993, reviews suggested that Rubin was content to 'evoke easy tears' rather than address the issues in an overly sentimental chick flick. However, given the plot, his artistic direction, comprising dreams, flashes of pain, focus on conversation and scene overlap, resulted in a gentle documentary relieved with moments of surprising humour, rather than an all-out heart-wrenching weepy.

As Tom Cruise continued to consolidate his triumphs of the 1980s (his latest releases, *A Few Good Men* and *The Firm*, were both critically acclaimed and box-office smashes), Nicole became even more determined to prove that she wasn't only working off the back of his fame.

'I spent a long time acting before I met Tom, and as he once said to me, there are a lot of actors around with girlfriends who are actresses who aren't working. So I don't somehow think that studios are casting me in several-million-dollar films only to please Tom,' she retorted. In private, the thwarted actress must have been concerned about the direction of her career, but publicly she continued to play the doting wife.

In June 1993 Tom was honoured with his own star on Hollywood's Walk Of Fame.* Nicole set aside any feelings of inadequacy and put on a brave face. Unfortunately, the outfit she chose was far less successful. Wearing a shapeless, unflattering floral dress and a boater, with her hair in schoolgirl pigtails, Nicole resembled a *Brady Bunch* outcast – a dowdy housewife caught up in the wrong world rather than a glamorous actress in her own right.

After her surprising display of bad taste at the ceremony, Nicole showed good sense in hiring a personal assistant and wardrobe consultant. For one who had prided herself on not possessing a private entourage, Nicole now employed a veritable array of personal staff, not least since the arrival of Isabella.

As their increasing number of aides were witness to daily life with the Cruises, they were required to sign an employee confidentiality agreement. This was considered standard practice within the celebrity world, but even so this particular document was an involved seven pages with heavy penalties for contravening the terms of the agreement. In it, employees are made aware that their bosses are 'internationally well-known figures who will be seriously harmed, both professionally and personally, by the unauthorized disclosure of confidential information'.

Simply relaying any aspect of their job to a friend or spouse would cost the employee dear. The price for divulging material to be used publicly differed depending on the medium. Information appearing in a book had a $1 million minimum charge in America and a further $500,000 for each country in which it was published, whereas a U.S. network television broadcast would cost an extortionate $5 million per broadcast or $2 million per non-network broadcast. Recording a conversation carried an automatic $1 million fine. Gone were the carefree days when Nicole could pretend to be part of an ordinary couple.

* Ironically, just the previous Christmas Nicole had paid the International Star Registry in Illinois $45 to name a star in the Hercules constellation 'Forever Tom' for her husband.

14

You're My Isabel

It had been twelve long years since New Zealand director Jane Campion had first spotted the fourteen-year-old Nicole Kidman performing with great zeal in *Spring Awakening* at the Phillip Street Theatre in Sydney. While Nicole had gone on to become one of the brightest teen stars in Australia before leaving her home country to marry one of the biggest names in Hollywood, Campion had been working her way methodically up the directorial and screenwriting ladder.

Choosing her projects with great care, Campion typically spent years perfecting each film to which she attached her name. Like her previous television work, the three Australian-produced movies she had lovingly created focused on strong women – first came *Sweetie*, a deliberately off-balance exploration of the dynamic between two sisters. Next was *An Angel At My Table*, a compassionate biopic of an introverted writer incorrectly diagnosed as schizophrenic.

Finally, Campion's *pièce de résistance* came in the form of *The Piano*, a complex and powerful tale starring Holly Hunter as a mute Scottish widow who emerges from a repressed background into a fulfilled life, reconciling love with desire. *The Piano* had secured Campion's presence as a force to be reckoned with, winning many awards (including an Oscar for Campion in the form of Best Original Screenplay) and capturing the hearts of all who saw it. *Newsweek*, for example, described it as a 'riveting excursion into nineteenth-century sexual repression'. Many noted the feminist nature that was beginning to characterize the director's work.

Still only in her late thirties in 1993, Campion was flushed with success and riding high on the ecstatic reception of her latest venture. Unsurprisingly, she wanted more – and the world wanted more of her. As she pondered the direction her career should take next, she remembered *The Portrait Of A Lady*, the Henry James novel about Isabel Archer, a liberated American heiress who loses her independence to a cruel and obsessive husband in the 1870s.

The book had been a favourite of Campion's since her teenage years, and in fact she had considered adapting it for film well before commencing work on *The Piano*. Discussing its merits one day with a friend, she mentioned the tall, fiery youngster she had encountered in Sydney all those years ago, whom she'd advised to 'protect your talent'. Perhaps the timing was finally right to work with Nicole Kidman.

When word got round to the actress, she decided the role had to be hers. On an interesting parallel, her reasoning for this resolve also dated from her adolescence.

'I read the book when I was fourteen and I had such an affinity for the heroine,' said Nicole, although she admitted she'd needed to reread the book later in life to fully understand Isabel. 'In a career there are probably only three or four roles that make you go, "Wow!" And *Portrait* is one of them.'

In the book, the fiercely independent Isabel Archer marries Gilbert Osmond, who oppresses her spirit and forces her to recognize that her life lacks purpose. Nicole was resolute that, despite her current lifestyle, she could identify with the character. 'I have some understanding of that. When I was fourteen, living in Sydney, my aim was to grab life and run with it. I never want to get married and have children.' Her immediate response was to get straight on the phone to Campion and claim the part.

But Nicole was unprepared for Campion's reaction. Instead of being as enthusiastic and excited as the actress about the possibilities the book held for the screen, Campion appeared to have 'gone off' the idea. She had been disillusioned by the recent bombshell that period-drama moguls Merchant Ivory had decided on *Portrait* for their latest project.

As it happened, that company had been discussing the novel for over a decade, but according to Ruth Prawer Jhabvala, the screenwriter who has adapted three other Henry James tomes very successfully for Merchant

Ivory, they simply failed to get the project off the ground: 'We never had the money for it.' The setting of this particular James novel required filming locations of Italy and England, and at that point Merchant Ivory could only afford to shoot in America.

Jane Campion was unaware of these constraints, and she explained to Nicole that if they pursued the project, they might face tough competition.

'Well, that's OK,' Nicole replied, 'They can do theirs and we'll do ours.'

Already establishing an 'against all odds' theme that was to haunt the beginning of this project, Nicole's feistiness appealed to the older woman, who needed an Isabel Archer with indomitable strength of character. 'I must say I was quite shocked by her boldness and courage,' the director reflects. 'I don't think I would have done it at all if she hadn't made that call.'

The women ended their conversation on a high, determined to make it work. Kidman had the role. And then it all went awry.

'Jane saw some of my work that I did in America and decided that I didn't have the spirit,' said Nicole, after receiving quite a different phone call. 'It was almost as if she was saying that I had failed to protect my talent.'

'I became quite fiery, upset and emotional. I yelled at her and we had a terrible fight.'

Campion's doubts stemmed precisely from the various 'girlfriend' roles which Nicole had accepted in an attempt to break into Hollywood. The director's research into the actress's more recent CV – *Days Of Thunder, Billy Bathgate, Malice* and *My Life* – did little to assure her that Nicole had the gumption to portray a woman trapped in an abusive marriage, suffering extreme degradation and self-loathing. On the phone, admittedly embarrassed for being so open-minded about Nicole's ability in the first place, Campion told the enraged actress that she had made a mistake.

'I think it just came out,' says Campion. 'In the time that Nicole was in Hollywood, she'd made quite a few films which I didn't really think suited her. I started to feel unconfident about it and felt the only way really for it to work for me was if we did a couple of days' audition. Which is a *terrible* thing to tell someone when you've basically said, "Oh, you can have the part."'

Nicole reacted strongly, which, unbeknown to her at the time, went some way in her favour. 'She was quite clear in saying she was pissed off,' Campion recalls.

'It was very hurtful at first,' says Nicole. 'You go through your whole self-doubt as to whether you *do* have the talent.' Hanging up the phone, in her mind she revisited the decisions she had made over the last few years. It was hard to accept that the projects into which she had poured her heart and soul were condemned by a director she respected more than most; particularly one who had taken such a special interest in her at the beginning of her career. Surely the pairing was always meant to be?

Nicole began to ponder the true meaning of 'protect your talent'. 'I think I went through a stage when I didn't,' she was forced to admit. 'Now it means to me listening to your instincts, not being corrupted by what you're meant to do for success. You've got to make films based on the experience, not how they're going to be perceived. And it's hard to do when you get to a level where there's a lot to lose.'

Faced with failure, Nicole knew that there was no way she could give up now. 'Nearly losing the role was very upsetting,' she says. 'There were a lot of tears.' During one such tearful phone call, she reluctantly agreed to prove herself to Campion in any way she could.

The prospect of having to audition for a role like an unknown actress was devastating. Nicole had set her heart on the part for some time now, telling friends and family she would soon be making some definite changes to the direction of her career. Her husband, for one, was appalled at Campion's treatment of his wife, but was supportive in Nicole's decision to fight for her role.

'It *was* upsetting,' says Tom. 'Jane was wrong. You say, "OK, that's fate. I'm gonna do everything I can, but ultimately it's the director's picture." It was very unpleasant.' He encouraged his wife to meet Campion in Los Angeles and see what happened.

With two days of auditions ahead of her, Nicole was prepared for anything. The punishing regime the director dreamed up did not disappoint. Under Campion's exacting supervision Nicole performed countless scenes from the book, underwent many hours of improvisation and was even required to join Campion for a night out go-go dancing to see if the two tenacious personalities could indeed work together on an intensely personal basis. As they bid their farewells, it was still unclear whether or not she had got the part.

Yet another tearful phone call was on the cards, but this time Nicole wasn't taking no for an answer. She'd jumped through enough hoops.

To her credit, Campion was pleased.

'Well,' she said. 'The way you're talking now is really good. I think that Isabel would be like this. You're my Isabel.'

'I started crying,' says Nicole. 'It was kind of like breaking my spirit and then putting it back together, which is what happens to Isabel too. Jane really likes her actresses to desperately, passionately want to be in her films, and she likes to put you through hard work to see if you have the stamina. I know Holly [Hunter, star of *The Piano*] has a similar story.'

'It was very confronting, but it created an incredibly real basis for the relationship,' muses Campion. 'It brought a level of honesty to our relationship. We decided to go ahead and became close.'

Unfortunately for both women, *The Portrait Of A Lady* was then put on hold indefinitely.

'I was cast a year in advance and I'm not allowed to work for a year because I'm preparing for that role,' Nicole would say in early 1994. 'It will be shot in Italy, in Lucca, and in London. I know Jane quite well. I'm a huge fan of hers and I think she's one of the most brilliant directors of her generation.' She had clearly overcome any residual feelings of animosity towards her director.

But Campion, soon to fall pregnant, had yet to finish the script and her entire schedule was rocked when her baby boy died soon after his birth. As Campion recovered from her tragic loss, eventually becoming pregnant with her second child (a healthy daughter, Alice, would be born in 1995), Nicole was left to forge ahead on her own.

After all the heartache of landing the role of Isabel and now with a goal in sight, Nicole decided to put her enforced time off to good use. August 1993 afforded the Cruises a brief family holiday, yachting around the coast of Italy, but then she set to work. With the revelation that she had not 'protected her talent' fresh in her mind, Nicole enrolled in New York's famous Actors Studio to join the ranks of leading actors who practise the Method.

At the turn of the twentieth century, Russian actor and director Konstantin Stanislavsky pioneered a new technique to help actors prepare themselves for specific roles by drawing on personal experiences that correlate with their characters. Lee Strasberg, the influential acting teacher, subsequently developed this technique further and made it widely available through his classes in America during the 1930s. But it was the foundation of the Actors Studio in New York in 1947 by Elia Kazan, Robert Lewis and Cheryl Crawford that widely popularized the Method (so called because Strasberg did not like the term 'system').

Strasberg continued his teachings in the new venue. In his own words, the Method is 'an open-ended and fortuitous voyage'. It incorporates relaxation and intense training of the emotional memory bank to enable the actor to have instant access to their senses. The Method was employed by revolutionary actors of the 1950s such as Marlon Brando, Shelley Winters, Paul Newman and James Dean. It then experienced a revival among modern-day greats including Robert De Niro, Harvey Keitel, Al Pacino, Dustin Hoffman and Faye Dunaway. With over two hundred Academy Award winners and nominees having passed through the doors of the Actors Studio, Nicole had undoubtedly taken a step in the right direction and she credits this experience as having changed her whole life. 'Being an actor means maintaining your integrity, maintaining your relationship with your emotions and experiences so that you have the capability to put them onscreen,' she explained.

Nicole went through much soul-searching during this time and found it a great comfort to be in a relationship with a fellow actor, someone who could understand her frustrations and fears. 'We help each other,' she said of Tom. 'We really give each other a lot of support in each other's careers. To be involved with an actor, and I've been involved with actors mostly, it really helps.'

The actress was also aware that her new bond with her daughter, the responsibilities of motherhood and the fresh emotions she was experiencing were all good acting fodder. 'It makes you more sensitive,' she said of becoming a parent. 'It gives you a depth and selflessness that, particularly as an actor, you just don't have. It does open a lot of feelings that maybe you're not dealing with or maybe haven't realized were inside you.'

After their summer holiday, while Nicole was ensconced in New York, Tom bent his rules about being an absentee father. He started filming *Interview With The Vampire: The Vampire Chronicles*, which looked set to be a huge hit with its all-star cast and a script adapted from Anne Rice's much-loved cult novel.

In September 1993 Nicole and Tom joined forces with Greenpeace to support Sydney's bid to stage the 2000 Olympic Games. The celebrity couple spent £150,000 producing a five-minute promotional video of an environmentally sound Olympic village, complete with solar-powered lighting and water heating. The film was to be shown to the international Olympic selection committee against competing proposals from Manchester, Beijing, Berlin and Istanbul.

Nicole was campaigning for both Australia and green issues. 'With the Olympics we have the opportunity to start the next century with a renewed commitment to our fragile earth,' she said. 'I grew up in Sydney and it would be wonderful if my home town could provide an environmental role model for the world.'

The Cruises then flew to France so that Tom could appear at the annual film festival in Deauville, where he was guest of honour. They made the most of their time abroad, stealing a short second honeymoon in Paris, occupying two suites at the Ritz. The devoted parents savoured spending time with nine-month-old Isabella and only let their hair down one night, dancing until the early hours at trendy club Neil's. The paparazzi were keen to secure rare photos of the Hollywood stars and find out more about their secret family life.

'I get edgy with Isabella,' confided Nicole about the latest press attention. 'She doesn't have to be public, too. We want to make her life as normal as possible. We're involved parents, we don't believe in armies of nannies. Isabella travels with me everywhere I go, and that's a lot because I love travelling.' She insisted that they were like any regular parents besotted with their child. 'We have the video camera out all the time, taking film of her. One of the great things for this new generation is that they will have the opportunity to see themselves growing up.'

However, Tom and Nicole were unlike most parents in that their baby was adopted. 'You're not seeing yourself duplicated,' marvelled Nicole. 'You watch and say, "Oh my, she's athletic or musically inclined or whatever." Destiny comes into play. It's quite magical.'

Despite earlier comments about wanting to wait before having a family, Nicole found she fell naturally into the role. 'I like being a young mum,' she declared. 'Suddenly that maternal thing kicks in and that's it. Isabella smiles, or you see her sleeping, and you melt. I'd like to have more kids.' The experience made her grateful for her own secure childhood and she telephoned Antony and Janelle simply to thank them, hoping that she could be as successful a parent.

With a plan of action for her faltering career now in place, Nicole couldn't be happier. Seeking a different challenge before work with Jane Campion commenced, she undertook a hostess slot on the American comedy show *Saturday Night Live* on 20 November. Although terrified by the prospect of working in this new medium, she pulled it off with her usual aplomb, starring in skits alongside Mike Myers and Christina Ricci.

Determined to stand on her own two feet, Nicole even turned down the prestigious opportunity of appearing on the front of *Vogue*, because the magazine requested a photo shoot of Tom and Nicole as a couple. 'The *Vogue* cover was not of interest to me because it looks like I'm riding on his coat tails,' she said resolutely. 'I'm over-defensive about it.'

However, Nicole agreed to appear inside the magazine, in a piece celebrating old movie stars. She revelled in dressing up as Carole Lombard, Marilyn Monroe, Marlene Dietrich and Lucille Ball. 'I met Nicole ten years ago when I was guest editor of *Vogue*,' says Baz Luhrmann, now a respected director. 'She struck me as this incredible firecracker – funny, a bit out of control. It wasn't how most people saw her. I recognized the moment I met her that who we think she is has nothing to do with who she actually is.'

The Cruises spent New Year's Eve with Neil Jordan, the director of *Interview With The Vampire*. Jordan invited the little family to Ireland to attend a party at his home in Dalkey, just outside Dublin. Delighted to return to the Emerald Isle, of which they had such fond memories, Tom and Nicole joined in some traditional Irish folk dancing and Guinness-drinking. Despite their earlier reluctance to move into IRA territory, they apparently browsed around local properties with a view to buying. They returned to America in their private jet, named 'Sweet Nic' for good luck – but Tom's latest film was to bring him mostly misfortune.

Old rumours once again came back to haunt Tom Cruise with the 1994 release of *Interview With The Vampire*. Brad Pitt takes the moody lead of Louis in this adaptation of Anne Rice's novel about a two-hundred-year-old vampire reminiscing about his life. His story begins when he is converted to vampirism by the wickedly decadent and bisexual Lestat (Cruise). Louis does not adopt Lestat's debauched ways but is forced to indulge in his blood-sucking habit to achieve immortality.

It is less the gruesome vampire lifestyle that caused such a stir, more the perverted, kinky aspects of the movie. Paedophilia is hinted at as the cast consisted primarily of four handsome leading actors with an eleven-year-old girl (Kirsten Dunst) the only female in their midst. Moreover, the sexually ambiguous nature of Lestat (modified from the original character in the novel, who transcends gender) created the biggest fuss. England's *Independent On Sunday* declared it 'the most candidly gay movie to come out of mainstream Hollywood'.

Lestat's cavalier attitude and dubious blonde wig, combined with the homoerotic subtext and gothic wantonness, quickly fuelled the ongoing 'Tom Is Gay' campaign. Worse still, this speculation came at the time Mimi Rogers decided to set the record straight about her own sexuality with the aforementioned *Playboy* interview, naturally dragging her ex-husband into the equation. For the second time in their three-year marriage, Tom and Nicole were forced to publicly confirm their sexual preferences.

'We're both heterosexual,' said Nicole clearly. 'We have a lot of homosexual friends and neither of us would shy away from having a homosexual film role. I think it is something that is very important in society.

'Tom's not gay, to my knowledge. I can assure you my husband is no monk. He's the best lover I've ever had and he's a very sexual guy.' As a mother, Nicole was embarrassed about being so explicit, but felt it was required as the slurs were putting a strain on their relationship. Tom used his junkets for the film to squash the latest gossip. 'I feel very angry about it,' he said, protecting his family. 'I just try to remind Nicole – it's like a mantra: "You have me, you have the kids. It doesn't matter what anyone else thinks." I know it's all part of it, but sometimes it's hard.'

To add insult to injury, the critics launched another attack on Cruise's religion. Suggesting that Tom's throaty voice in the film was achieved using Clearsound, a box of tricks conjured up by technicians at the Church of Scientology, it was once again alleged that the Cruises were ruled by the religious sect. Nicole simply retorted: 'No one is going to tell me what to do.'

This did not quell rumours that Tom had recently turned down the lead in *Indecent Proposal* because his religion is firmly against gambling, which formed the crux of the movie. Other parts he had declined were analysed, including *Edward Scissorhands*, a fairytale fantasy, and *Backdraft*, with its A-list cast. In fact, Tom had covered all these topics earlier in his career (in *The Color Of Money*, *Legend* and *Top Gun*), albeit before he converted to Scientology.

The further suggestion that Tom refused *Bright Lights, Big City*, *Rush* and *Pulp Fiction* on the basis that Scientology is strongly against drugs also seems unlikely; staunch Scientologist John Travolta willingly stepped into Tom's shoes in the latter film, famously reviving his career.

The rest of 1994 afforded the family some time to recover. Following Jane Campion's devastating loss earlier that year, Nicole devoted precious time to motherhood. Their everyday life was neatly summarized by Tom: 'We do a lot of things, we're very active. We go to museums, we read, we have a lot of common interests. We spend time with family and friends. We go to movies and plays. I mean, I don't go to special screenings, I go to the movie theatres just like anyone else.'

If the Cruises wanted to get away from being a normal couple 'just like anyone else', they could now escape to their new secluded country home. The couple had recently bought a four-bedroom house with a tennis court in several acres of land for a reported $2.5 million in the exquisite resort of Telluride, Colorado, where they got married.

Tom, in particular, was nostalgic about the place and became involved in the local community, attending various charity benefits. He organized a family holiday there for his and Nicole's fourth wedding anniversary, flying Antony and Janelle over from Australia and arranging for private skiing lessons.

The celebrity-rich but sleepy town afforded the couple genuine anonymity, and other than long hikes and skiing, being able to spend quality time alone with each other was its main attraction. 'We are the type of couple that likes to be together all hours of the day,' said Tom. 'I really like that feeling of being at one with Nic, and I think she appreciates that closeness and harmony.'

If their lives were ever in the slightest danger of becoming tedious, Tom could be relied upon to do the unexpected. 'If someone's a pure gentleman that's a little boring,' explained Nicole. 'He has a side that's exciting – you never know what's going to happen next. I don't think I would have married someone where I could have predicted what he was going to be like in forty years' time. I have no idea what he's going to be like – I can't wait to see.'

15

A Barbie Doll
Gone Wrong

Towards the end of 1994, both actors found themselves simultaneously busy. 'Working hard doesn't matter if we both love our work,' said Tom. 'We share it together. Nic reads my scripts and I trust her ideas and her taste. Not that we agree on everything, but I respect her viewpoint, so she challenges me.'

Tom was about to star in *Mission: Impossible,* and Nicole would play Batman's love interest in the third film based on the cult comic strip, *Batman Forever.* It was a return to type for both. While Tom's movie was set to reassert his position as action hero, Nicole's character may appear surprisingly reminiscent of the impossibly young and beautiful neurosurgeon in *Days Of Thunder.*

Defeating versatile actress Sandra Bullock (who had already portrayed the cartoon character Bionic Woman) to win the part of Dr Chase Meridian, Nicole took on what was essentially another 'intelligent girlfriend' role. 'I know, I know, she doesn't look anything like a criminal psychiatrist,' concedes director Joel Schumacher. 'But it's my Gotham City and I can do what I want! I've had my eye on her since *Dead Calm.* You meet a lot of beautiful people in this business, but there's something almost luminous about her. I wish I had a clause in my contract that said Nicole Kidman had to be in every one of my movies.' Schumacher was apparently determined to work with Nicole because of her arresting features rather than her finely honed acting abilities.

The part had landed in Nicole's lap, and, although it went against her new-found, Campion-inspired work ethic and Method technique, she jumped at the chance to be involved with the caped crusader. She postponed a trip to Australia in favour of the job — after all, she had not worked for almost two years.

For the first time onscreen, Nicole Kidman appears as a grown-up sex symbol. With straight, sleek blonde hair and cocky self-assurance, she smoulders as Chase romances both Bruce Wayne and his alter ego, Batman. 'She's constantly trying to seduce him,' says the actress. 'She wears black slinky dresses, has perfect hair, perfect red lips, and talks in a deep, husky voice. It's definitely a heightened reality. Really over the top.'

Overtly playing for the camera as a glamourpuss, Chase lures Batman with a fake call-out and engages him in flirtatious banter, telling him she always falls for the wrong kind of man. Then she encounters Bruce Wayne. He mistakes her athletic grunts during boxing practice for cries for help and breaks down her door. Getting off on the wrong foot, they discover a mutual attraction and she is intrigued by his complex character. Torn between the two men, Chase doesn't realize they are one and the same until she is captured by Batman's archenemies, The Riddler and Two Faces. She is, of course, rescued by our hero and finally comprehends his dark secret.

Throwing herself wholeheartedly into the rather limited role, Nicole trained for her brief boxing and fight scenes, and also studied some of the original cartoon strips. 'Jim Carrey gave me some stuff. It's amazing, with the weird angles and strange writing — some incredibly strong images,' said Nicole, obviously new to DC Comics. 'There's something cool about Batman.'

Although *My Life* co-star Michael Keaton had previously donned the superhero's cape, he bowed out this time (rumour has it because the supporting characters had too many scenes), to be replaced by Val Kilmer (*The Doors*). Aided by his sidekick Robin (Chris O'Donnell), Batman fights archrivals The Riddler (Jim Carrey) and Two Faces (Tommy Lee Jones); some say the star-studded cast carried the show.

Another difference from the two previous *Batman* films was the change of director. Schumacher took a lighter stance compared to Tim Burton's very dark approach to Gotham City.

'I liked the idea of doing something comedic,' says Nicole. 'Batman was one of those situations where you get to laugh a lot. I'd say to Val Kilmer, "Make sure you move your head otherwise I'm going to get make-up on your black mask." You have no idea how hard it is to kiss a man in a black rubber suit!'

Batman Forever did little for Nicole in terms of her bid to be taken seriously as an actress, but she did at least escape the rut of boring supporting roles. Not only did she shine in her new capacity as 'temptress', but she also succeeded in linking her name to a cult series and branching out into stylish comedy. Working with Val Kilmer, another Method advocate, was good fun. 'Val has a quirky sense of humour, and we laughed a lot,' Nicole recalls. This may not have been a popular friendship as far as her husband was concerned – Tom and Kilmer had played bitter rivals in Top Gun and it is said the ill feeling was mirrored offscreen.

Although she received no Oscar or BAFTA nominations, Nicole did pick up a Blockbuster Entertainment Award as Favourite Actress – Action Or Adventure and was nominated for the MTV Movie Awards' Most Desirable Female. Apparently she also wore an impossible thirty-five pairs of shoes as Chase, all of which she was allowed to keep. The film itself broke all box-office records in America on its release in June 1995, and the theme song, 'Kiss From A Rose' by Seal, also became a huge summer hit. Nicole's face was back on billboards where it belonged.

The good news about Jane Campion's second pregnancy further delayed filming of The Portrait Of A Lady, and so Nicole found herself at a loose end.

After four years in her husband's shadow, she was reasserting her individuality in earnest. While the frivolous Batman Forever marked her first real blockbuster appearance, she still craved a powerful lead role. Then she heard about Gus Van Sant's next project, To Die For.

Van Sant's career had undulated from the distinguished Drugstore Cowboy in 1989 to the massive flop Even Cowgirls Get The Blues in 1993, but the quirky and controversial director was determined to succeed this time with his trademark visual flourishes and skilful way with actors.

Joyce Maynard's novel To Die For was a black comedy based on the life of New Hampshire newly-wed Pamela Smart. Transformed into a satirical screenplay by Buck Henry (The Graduate), the adaptation portrays an insatiable small-town television weathergirl, Suzanne Stone, as she embarks upon her unscrupulous pursuit of fame, ultimately persuading her teenage lover (Joaquin Phoenix) to murder her husband (Matt Dillon). Interestingly, the producers had originally slated Meg Ryan for the role of Suzanne, but when she pulled out, the part became available.

Judging by her recent work, Nicole was not the obvious substitute, but her sheer enthusiasm for the character prompted her to pick up the phone.

'Look, I've read the script,' she said to the producers, begging them to consider her.

'No, there's no way you can do this,' they replied emphatically. 'You're not funny enough, you're not American.' It was the same old story – she'd heard it all before.

'Now the fun begins,' muttered the stubborn actress as she replaced the handset. Nicole plagued the production company with calls until she was finally given Van Sant's home telephone number in Portland, Oregon.

'I thought, "Well, he's probably not going to cast me, but I may as well give him a call. The least I can do is just talk to him,"' she says. 'We talked for an hour, and I told him it would be a chance that no one's given me in America.

'I talked about the script, I talked about my feelings in relation to it and what I thought it meant to me, and how I thought it was very funny and very black.

'He called me back two hours later and gave me the role. He's renowned for bucking the system, and I appreciate that.' Van Sant had bent over backwards to convince the producers that Nicole could fill the part – now all she had to do was prove him right.

Describing Suzanne as 'a Barbie doll gone wrong', Nicole had the unenviable task of depicting a thoroughly disagreeable character, her only similar role to date being that of Tracy in *Malice*. 'I certainly don't fear playing somebody the audience dislike – I relish that,' she says. 'I think they're among the most interesting characters to play. De Niro or Pacino, or any of the great male actors, play unlikeable men the majority of the time.'

As she studied Suzanne Stone, a woman obsessed with life in the lime-light, Nicole did not miss the intentional dig at her own status. 'I found it very funny, and of course ironic, in the sense of who I am. I saw the burn-out in playing a character who's obsessed with celebrity,' she recalls.

'You're nobody in America unless you're on TV,' says Suzanne, 'because what's the point of doing something worthwhile if nobody's watching?' This, rather than a vehement hatred of the prying paparazzi, was the mental attitude that the actress had to adopt for this challenging part. And she knew just how to do it.

'I spent three days in a Santa Barbara motel watching television continuously,' she explains. 'It is incredible what television does to your mind, it has a hypnotic effect. Those shows are so addictive – you *know* you shouldn't be watching them, you *know* you should be reading a great novel, but you *can't* stop!

'In the States you can watch talk shows twenty-four-hours-a-day and you see people on them saying the most bizarre things, revealing their deepest, darkest secrets in front of millions of people. It's that "fifteen minutes of fame" thing. That's now becoming the norm. Suzanne may only be a character in a movie but you need only tune into *Oprah* or *Ricki Lake* to realize just what a biting satire it is.'

Admitting, 'I didn't go out, just ordered room service, and found myself shouting at the screen,' Nicole clearly had a lot of fun researching this particular role, but says it's not something in which she could indulge too often.

Van Sant tells the murderous tale of *To Die For* through individual documentary-style disclosures, compelling the audience to piece the parts together. Nicole is dazzling as Suzanne from her first mesmerizing monologue, amply displaying that she understands the full range of her character's numerous facets: she is sexy, funny, dense, determined, naïve, blunt and in-your-face. She thinks, talks and breathes television. She is ruthlessly ambitious to the core.

Looking remarkably different with a straight blonde bob, Nicole discarded her now-immaculate sense of style. 'I really changed the way I look in real life so I could create her,' says the actress. 'It was a lot of fun. We would just say, "Well, this doesn't match this, so let's put it together" – yellow shoes with pink suits!'

With brazen cockiness, Suzanne tells her story in a very open, yet confidential manner. Desperate to further her career, she orchestrates her honeymoon so that she can attend a celebrity seminar. Here she learns a valuable lesson – she can wield tremendous power with her femininity. On her return she channels her energies into getting an assistant's position at the local cable television station. But this is not enough.

Suzanne aspires to become a television reporter and produces documentary footage for the station. 'For *To Die For* I learned to edit film and I shot the little film in the film,' Nicole explains. Gus Van Sant was curious about a notebook in which the actress scribbled endlessly, in acute preparation for each scene. 'It's like doing your homework before you take your exam,' she continues. 'It may not come up in the exam but you want the confidence to go in and feel you know it all.'

While waiting to be discovered, Suzanne talks her way in front of the camera; oozing sex appeal, she delivers the late-night forecast. But she is not a sunny weathergirl; she possesses a very dark side. It is not long before she starts to see her humdrum husband as a dead weight holding her back. She opts for anonymous murder rather than the scandal of divorce and enlists the help of an odd assortment of teenage groupies. After the event, Suzanne turns on her accomplices with a jolly brutality but, without spoiling the ending, she upholds Nicole's moniker as the Ice Queen.

Suzanne's thoroughly disreputable nature appealed to Nicole. 'Even though people perceive her as a very evil character, I really adored her,' she says. 'But she isn't a caricature. We all know people with Suzanne's qualities, though maybe they haven't gone as far.

'And there's something quite endearing about the way Suzanne takes a situation and makes the most of it.' Perhaps Nicole had become too involved in her Machiavellian personality – unlike on the set of *Billy Bathgate*, she refused to come out of character once filming had finished.

'I don't like the feeling that when the camera starts rolling, you're suddenly performing,' she says. 'So I spoke in my American accent from the minute we started rehearsal to the minute we finished the movie. You didn't have to call me by my character's name or anything – it's just that I walked and talked differently. I perceived things more intensely.'

It was maintaining this intensity that prompted Nicole to ban her husband from the set. She had previously always allowed him to visit but, as this starring role demanded significantly more time and attention, she did not want to be distracted. The same would be true for her upcoming work on *The Portrait Of A Lady*.

'When you're creating a complex character like that, you don't want the person who knows you inside out standing there watching you. A lot of it is about losing yourself, so when somebody's there who knows you so well, it's restricting. You need to be focused, you can't be talking in between takes.

'It sounds like I'm strict, but he understands. When I'm working I like to concentrate and get on with it. I don't like to fart about. Also, he's a very forceful presence on a set, and it's distracting to people.'

So was Tom's absence due to her diligent work ethic, his overwhelming charisma – or perhaps Nicole's erotic love scenes? The steamy scenes with Joaquin Phoenix again reveal the actress's relaxed attitude to nudity, which clashed with Tom's own convictions, and it was rumoured that he asked that a double be used. Maybe the racier sections were cut, as less of her anatomy is seen than in previous films.

Simultaneously, some said Nicole was unhappy about a passionate clinch Tom shared with Emmanuelle Béart in *Mission: Impossible*. As an action hero Tom had few love scenes, but surely the same rule had to apply to both husband and wife? When asked about the green-eyed monster, Nicole said: 'I feel secure enough; I trust him – if I didn't, I probably *would* feel jealous, but I do trust him. You just have to be committed.'

Trust didn't come into it for Tom: he was just plain uncomfortable with the whole idea. 'Love scenes make me nervous,' he said. 'It's very strange to get in bed with someone you don't really know. They're embarrassed and I'm kinda going, "Are you OK?" It's no fun at all. That's the way it is.'

Frequently present on each other's film sets, Tom and Nicole were thought to be exceptionally possessive over each other. Whatever the press thought now, it would not be long before the Cruises' sexual jealousies would be pushed to the limit.

Gus Van Sant was vindicated. Not only had his conviction about Nicole's abilities paid off, but she proved a delight to work with. 'She had a very authoritative view on the story,' he reveals. 'She was really a great ally on the set. We never had any disagreements. We mostly just had fun. It surprised me how much I was laughing.'

There was more enjoyment to come, as critics showed a renewed and re-evaluated interest in Nicole when *To Die For* premiered at the Cannes Film Festival in May 1995.

Variety heralded the movie, 'Witty, energetic and splendidly acted, this handcrafted curio will find support among the specialized, adventurous-minded audiences who have patronized the director's work in the past.' But instead, it was mainstream audiences who took it to their hearts, finding the film far more accessible than anticipated when it appeared that autumn, and this stopped it from being released straight to video, its rumoured fate.

While Van Sant regained recognition as a director, his leading lady was acknowledged with a nomination for Best Actress at the 1996 BAFTA Awards. This was only the beginning: Nicole won the Golden Globe Award for Best Actress – Comedy Or Musical, the Seattle International Film Festival Golden Space Needle Award for Best Actress, the National Film Critics Association Award, the London Critics Circle Awards' Actress Of The Year, and Best Actress at the Empire Awards.

She was also receiving welcome attention from Hollywood directors and was inundated with offers, including the female lead in the thriller *Kiss The Girls* opposite Morgan Freeman. Her performance no doubt allayed any concerns Campion might have harboured about casting her as Isabel Archer.

Nicole was relieved finally to be interviewed about her work rather than her husband. 'It was very tough for me just to be seen as Mrs Tom Cruise. Don't get me wrong, I don't think being married to somebody that you're in love with is a burden, but being judged in a particular way, that is something I don't like. I hope *To Die For* gives people a better image of what I'm about as an actress.

'It's difficult, you don't get offered a lot of things, you have to take opportunities and create other opportunities with it. But in the last year and a half it's started to change.' Nicole's success was well timed, as Tom's career was reaching ever more dizzying heights; she easily could have been lost to celebrity wifedom forever.

But the altered attitude towards the actress was not confined to public opinion. Looking back, she candidly admits that there was a tangible shift in the Cruise–Kidman balance of power as she began to assert herself as a person: 'I said halfway through the marriage, "I don't want this now, I want your influence but I kind of want to find out who I am."'

Nicole's next little project seemed a complete contradiction to her focus on reviving her career; a younger sibling for Isabella. Again opting for adoption, Tom and Nicole broached another tricky issue when they became the proud parents of an African-American boy.

Named Conor, perhaps as a nod to the couple's Irish ancestry, he had been born on 17 January 1995 and officially became a Cruise on 6 February. The bi-racial baby was destined to cause even more furore than his older sister. 'I don't think there is a racial problem,' stated Nicole. 'It just comes through education – being aware of it, and once there's awareness and the ability to educate, then people can formulate their own opinions and their own ideas. I think the most important thing is treating your children as individuals and giving them the best education possible.' Perhaps Nicole's beliefs were a little idealistic; a few months later she would be horrified to find herself and Conor the target of racist taunts in London.

Again, Nicole was obliged to provide reasons for adopting her child and answered succinctly: 'It is fate completely. I just believe, for whatever reason, that these two children were meant to be in our family.' As with Isabella, she refused to be drawn on any details about the natural parents, but said that they would always be very open about the fact that the children were adopted and would help them find their biological families if they so desired: 'We're not afraid to talk about it,' she said.

Her comments about having her own children were a little more candid this time around. 'Obviously I would love to give birth to a child as well, absolutely. I would like to experience that. But if I don't, it's not going to destroy me.

'Two kids are a lot; I hear that when there are three, you're outnumbered! At least when there are two, you're OK – you grab one and I'll grab one.'

But, as with Isabella, Conor wasn't going to halt her career. 'My mother worked through my whole childhood and she gave me a strong role model,' said Nicole. 'Any woman who works and has a child knows that it takes planning and juggling.'

16

A Very Uncomfortable Emotional State

Work commitments pandered to the couple's wanderlust when Tom and Nicole relocated their family of four to England in the spring of 1995. He was finishing filming *Mission: Impossible*, while she prepared for *The Portrait Of A Lady*.

Organizing her maternal duties around her career, Nicole was determined to stay true to her earlier statement – 'We don't have armies of nannies'. Baby Conor was still at home, but Isabella was now old enough to attend a local nursery school during the day, and initially her famous parents took it in turns to drop her off and pick her up. It would not be long, however, before Nicole would hire a second personal assistant and a nanny to help her out, but to her best abilities she oversaw their upbringing herself.

'I believe in lavishing children with love, but being strict and having rules and boundaries,' she said. 'As my father, who is a psychologist, always said: "With love, but firm". I think that's the key to it.'

The couple started by renting an eleven-bedroom mansion, complete with gym and indoor swimming pool, in central London's exclusive Holland Park. As the move became more permanent, they looked to buy a property in the leafy county of Hertfordshire. Something about England made Tom and Nicole feel more comfortable – perhaps the natives were less starstruck than Americans, or maybe the stereotypical British reserve afforded the celebrity family freedom from adoring fans invading their privacy. They marvelled about how they could stroll through the main shopping streets and parks with their children without being mobbed.

Nicole had been fortunate to experience similar ambivalence in her home country. 'Australians are not as impressed with success and the trappings of fame as other nations, say, Americans,' explains director Bob Weis. 'In fact it can work the other way round: people who are too successful, too in the public eye get a negative reaction to them.'

London offered genuine anonymity, and there was a particular dark-panelled pub off King's Road in Chelsea that Nicole frequented with her husband. 'In London it's quite weird,' she said. 'We'll walk in the street and go to a pub and the normal people, they don't give a shit.' Tom even became one of the faceless joggers in Hyde Park before he got hooked on the rollerblading craze, in which he tried to encourage the rest of the family to participate.

Down-to-earth Nicole thought it was self-indulgent for famous people to brush off their fans. 'You've got to be willing to sign autographs and chat with people or you'll be miserable. People who fight it end up flipping out,' she said, but remained adamant that there is a line which should not be crossed: 'You've got to have some level of privacy. You become ferocious in your [family's] protection, like a mother tigress.'

Like Janelle some twenty-five years earlier, Nicole found herself facing the feminist dilemma of which toys to allow her children. She felt strongly that guns should not be allowed, while Tom, who was still blowing up film sets, didn't see a problem with them. 'Like any couple with kids, we sometimes get into heated discussions about how to raise them,' said Nicole.

Tom was otherwise proving a superb dad, putting to rest all his fears and feelings about his own father and parenthood. 'I loved my father very much,' said Tom. 'I sometimes think what it would have been like for him to see me with my children. When I look at them, I realize there is no possible way that a parent can't love his children.'

Nicole was grateful for the physical help he provided. 'Tom was really hands-on in nappy-changing,' she said. 'He would make sure I had the nappies and bottles when I was taking the kids out. I'm a little more vague with that stuff. I walk around a little blurry – I should be wearing glasses and I don't.' Furthermore, she reported, 'He sits with the mothers in the playgroup, he goes to the playground – he'll be the only guy there!'

Maintaining their 'normal' lifestyle, the couple were seen out and about in London during the summer when Nicole turned twenty-eight. Accompanied to the tennis by Antonia, the Cruises enjoyed the Wimbledon Men's Final between Boris Becker and Pete Sampras, watching from the players' box.

Tom and Nicole still preferred more dangerous sports themselves, and their passion only increased as they sought greater thrills. Tom piloted his own aircraft, while Nicole was known to perform aerobatics: 'I've been out doing arabesques on the wing. It's silly, but fun,' she laughed.

Moving from the heights of the sky to the depths of the ocean, Nicole found a more peaceful pastime. 'I like getting away, being removed from the world. That's why I like scuba diving – it's a whole different world under the water. It's a place where there are no words, just signals. It is very beautiful, very serene, very quiet.'

But she swore it was not a permanent state of mind, 'It's funny, I can go from being incredibly frenetic to the opposite, where I just sit around, sleep a lot and daydream.'

The arrival of Isabella and Conor forced Cruise and Kidman to rethink their priorities in life. Nicole in particular felt motherhood had changed her considerably. 'I am somebody who is attracted to dangerous things,' she acknowledged. 'It is something I have to fight in myself, especially now that I've got kids.' In an attempt to tone down her activities, she swapped skydiving for rock-climbing, but Tom let slip the latest adventure they hoped to try: 'In Australia you can dive with the Great Whites, and Nic and I want to do that. Sharks eat people – it's the thrill of extreme sport, you'd be like a deer in headlights!'

After *Mission: Impossible* secured Tom another box-office smash (taking over $400 million worldwide), his next role in *Jerry Maguire* earned him a second Oscar nomination. It seemed he could do no wrong. Nicole, in the meantime, was finally realizing her dreams of working with Jane Campion, although the timing with Tom's career was not ideal.

'We try to plan it so we work at different times,' said Nicole. 'But if there's a role which will change my life forever then we work it out. I've wanted to do *The Portrait Of A Lady* for years. Family life is about commitment, about saying, "We're going to make this work, no matter what."'

At the end of 1995, Campion was at last ready to commence filming. Gaps in the cast had been filled with some of the most eminent names in the business; Richard E. Grant, Barbara Hershey, Sir John Gielgud and

Shelley Winters among them. John Malkovich would play Nicole/Isabel's domineering husband, Gilbert Osmond. It had been a long time coming and all involved hoped it would be worth the wait.

At Jane Campion's request, Nicole had taken considerable time off to prepare herself for the harrowing task ahead. Although she had received her director's blessing for *To Die For*, it wouldn't have been right, at least in Campion's eyes, for the actress to immerse herself in another persona immediately before becoming Isabel.

When it came down to it, Campion didn't even want Nicole to be herself.

'When I filmed *The Portrait Of A Lady*, Jane Campion said: "I don't want you going out to dinner at night and having a lot of fun and then coming in thinking you're going to be able to do the part. It's not that kind of part, and I don't want that sort of performance,"' Nicole recalls. 'So I did the role in a very uncomfortable emotional state, and I did not feel like going out at all. I would spend days on set where I would be slapped with a glove by John Malkovich.'

Filming started in London, before moving to Lucca in Tuscany for the Italian scenes. Nicole prepared by reading the novel three more times and studying the immense depths of her character with her director. In her attempts to identify with Isabel, a spirited young woman who spurns two good proposals for the sake of remaining an individual, only to succumb to the evil Osmond and end up in a loveless, oppressive marriage, Nicole listened constantly to Nina Simone records, the diva who was herself a figurehead for basic human rights.

'I used every resource of my being to play Isabel Archer,' says Nicole. 'I actually ran through scenes with Tom, so he played the Malkovich role in our bedroom.' Unable and unwilling to leave her character behind at the end of each day's shooting, the actress also insisted on wearing a corset to physically feel Isabel's 19-inch waist, thus conforming to the nineteenth-century opinion of how a woman should appear.

It is important to note that Jane Campion's *The Portrait Of A Lady* is more an adaptation than a faithful rendition of Henry James's novel. Campion chooses to assert that the conflicting notions of womanhood haven't really changed over the last century, for example opening the film with a montage of modern-day Australian female characters discussing love.

The story is compelling, if exasperating at times. Isabel Archer, a beautiful young American woman, is orphaned. It would make sense for her to marry, therefore acquiring both security and, in the opinion of the time, a purpose in life. Rejecting the advances of her first suitor in

America (Caspar Goodwood, played by Viggo Mortensen), she visits wealthy English relatives and is approached by Lord Warburton (Grant). To Isabel, Warburton signifies all that is safe and sheltered in life: she wants to strike out on her own. Astounding her family (especially her sick cousin, Ralph, who is equally smitten with her), Isabel refuses this second proposal.

On inheriting a small fortune from Ralph's father, she embarks on a tour of Europe, commencing in Rome. There she re-encounters the duplicitous Madame Merle (Hershey), a matchmaker with an agenda. Merle introduces her to the malevolently reptilian Osmond, an idle fraud posing as an artist. Blinded by love, Isabel rejects all her former ideals and accepts his marriage invitation, taking on his daughter, Pansy, into the bargain. The story then advances three years and Isabel is visited by Ralph, who is horrified to find his beloved trapped in a relationship of great cruelty and just about to discover the true nature of her situation.

Clearly a tough taskmistress, Jane Campion at first harboured some lingering reservations about her leading lady. 'I always thought that, somewhere inside me, *I* was always best for the part,' the director said, tellingly admitting aspirations to being in front of the camera. 'Until about halfway through, when Nicole started doing stuff which I couldn't even imagine. She was surprising me and surprising herself. And that's what I wanted for Isabel – to be surprised.'

As the cast and crew progressed to Lucca, the job of recreating an accurate Isabel Archer didn't get any easier, despite the warmer climate. 'Making *The Portrait Of A Lady* in Italy wasn't about glamour,' Nicole recalls. 'It was about getting up and there's no hot water in the little villa so you've got to have a cold shower at 5 a.m. so that you can be in the make-up chair by 5.30, and you're freezing your tits off in the shower going, "Oh noooo . . ."'

By now, Nicole's fervent dedication to her craft had won the respect of everyone involved. 'She never stopped working and getting inside her character's head,' recalls Viggo Mortensen. 'You look at some of these people and wonder why they have done so well. With Nicole, it was clear. She has all the talent, but never lets it get in the way of hard work. She's also down-to-earth and could tell jokes very easily. The film crew fell in love with her.'

And it seems Nicole wasn't afraid to share her jokes with her formidable director. 'With a woman director, you tend to feel that you can express some of your feelings more openly – or at least I do,' she revealed. 'You sometimes get ideas that maybe a man wouldn't discover. A good example of that is the scene on the bed in *The Portrait Of A Lady* where I fantasize about the three men kissing me, loving me. Every woman who sees that goes, "Oh, *I've* had that fantasy." I don't know if a male director would have done that . . .'

The two women grew closer as the shoot went on. Nicole's focused diligence rivalled anything Campion could have hoped for. Over Isabel's corsets she had to wear large, cumbersome dresses and Nicole was even worried that the movement of her skirts would detract from her performance.

'She can be murderously challenging in her perfectionism,' Campion sighs. 'Take twenty: "Are you sure that's good enough?" We're going [wearily], "Yeah" . . . And then afterward, she'd say, "You hate me because I was so awful."

'That's what's so enchanting about her: just when you're thinking, "Oh my God, I can't take another minute of this," she knows exactly what you're thinking and says it: "You hate me, don't you?" And of course you *don't* hate her, you're just thinking, "Oh, enough, enough!"' Ironically, Nicole's voluminous skirts served another unfortunate purpose. When Tom, who was taking his turn at parenthood, was finally allowed to visit the set and bring Isabella, the little girl was so confused by the costume that she didn't even recognize her mother!

'It's the most personal film that I've made,' says Nicole of *The Portrait Of A Lady*. 'There are films that you make and they're not you. This film has a part of me.

'We're dealing with the dark side of attraction. Why do you choose the person that is wrong for you, when you should ultimately be searching for the person that's right? Jane and I both have had relationships like that. I find that fascinating, the incredible power that one person can have over another, because someone else can be the most perfect person for you, and for whatever reason, there's no sexual attraction, *something* is missing . . .

'The abusive emotional relationship with Osmond relates very much to today. Anyone can be in one of those relationships – and you can't get out.' The five weeks that she spent shooting the scenes of Osmond's merciless abuse marked a time when the actress transcended her role and *became* her character.

It was terrifying for Nicole. She simply couldn't understand how she had allowed the part to get to her to such an extent, although the rigours of working for Jane Campion and her own tireless perfectionism probably played a big part.

'I was playing an abused wife,' said the actress, who, reminiscent of her time in *To Die For*, found it hard to 'snap out' of character. 'You feel a lot of shame when you go home at night because of the things that are being done to you when you're on the set. I started to live Isabel. As much as you say, "No, no", it enters into your psyche, and you're not aware of how much until after you finish. There was an inbuilt humiliation I felt every single day.

'If you can enter the dark side of life and come through it, you emerge with more strength and compassion. It went beyond a film experience, this was a life experience for me. It taught me to approach life seeking honesty and to not fear emotion. A lot of the time you walk around thinking, "I've got to be together, I've got to be sane." Isabel says, "If I feel upset I'm going to cry."'

Indeed, when Nicole was finally set free from the horrors of becoming Isabel each day, she collapsed into bed, where she remained for a fortnight, diagnosed with 'emotional stress'.

Nicole's mother offers some insight into the perils of Nicole's working too hard. 'She takes on too much,' says Janelle. 'Sometimes I think she's a bit frail. You know, there are people who know when to stop and look after themselves a bit more.'

The Portrait Of A Lady was all set to be the thinking theatregoer's picture of choice when it was released on 24 December 1996. But it split critics and its audience straight down the middle.

One reaction was that Nicole's insightful performance was worthy of an Oscar, or at least a nomination. Having proved herself in *To Die For*, she was now fast ascending the ranks of Hollywood power. However, Henry James enthusiasts and theatre purists condemned what they perceived to be a gross 'miscasting' of the central roles and damned Campion's 'absurdly mannered' follow-up to *The Piano*. Consequently, the $20 million production turned out to be a horrific financial disappointment, grossing less than $10 million in theatres and through video sales worldwide.

Perhaps it was all part and parcel of Hollywood's habit of raising a director to the greatest heights and then hurling him or her to the darkest depths. Or maybe the Kidman name alone was not yet capable of drawing the masses.

To be fair, *The Portrait Of A Lady* isn't an easy film to watch. Campion flings the viewer in at the deep end, during Isabel's second proposal, and if you haven't read the book then working out the storyline so far is quite a challenge.

Nicole's looks are also a shock. After the modern montage, the opening shot is an unforgiving close-up of Isabel, and the beautiful actress appears positively ugly. Without the benefit of make-up, she has winged eyebrows, an odd groove on the underside of her nose, frizzy brown hair and bloodshot eyes. With her strange, triangular-shaped hairstyle and corsets giving her a waist only just thicker than her neck, she seems awkward, angular. Her astonishing appearance begs the question: is Isabel sufficiently attractive in character and countenance to cause so many men to fall for her?

Yet as an actress, Nicole excels in portraying confusion and pain as a free spirit imprisoned in a loveless union. Considering her situation and public image, she is surprisingly and pleasingly sensual in the more private moments – smelling her hand, stroking her neck. Clearly, electricity exists between her and the odious Malkovich – it's just a shame that Campion only includes a couple of scenes showing them together before they marry, so the viewer is left questioning the intrinsic power of this largely unexplained attraction for the remainder of the movie.

The overall impression of the over-long, two-and-a-half-hour film is one of coldness, which is presumably intended to reflect the painstakingly constructed Jane Austen-style goings-on, but it begs another question – does the audience identify with and even like Isabel enough to feel compassion for her? Even the ending is unsatisfactory: in the book Isabel returns to Italy, but the film closes on her confusion in England and those unfamiliar with the story will be left wondering what happens next.

'It was hard when people criticized it,' said the actress, who had sweated blood for the project. 'The film meant a lot. But as a person, it's good to go through, too, I suppose. You hope it's going to be wonderful and everyone will love it, and when that doesn't happen, that's OK. I still love the film, and am very proud of it.'

But the after-effects of the negative response to *Portrait* and the extreme emotions of the last three years in general eventually overcame Nicole. Exhausted, she would take another six months off from any acting work.

'I think that character will always be with me,' she says today. 'This was the first psychological, really deep role that I've ever had to dive into at a level where it taught me something about myself. Or Henry James and Jane Campion taught me something about myself . . . that it's all right to be emotional and vulnerable and all those things that lead you to a deeper understanding of yourself.'

17

Four Near Funerals And A Wedding

W hile Nicole recuperated from the emotionally draining experience of *The Portrait Of A Lady* at the beginning of 1996, she manifestly turned down all work offers bar one. Her close friend, director John Duigan, had once again called in a favour. He required her services for a miniscule cameo in his latest project, *The Leading Man*, a romantic comedy featuring one of Duigan's other favourite actresses, Thandie Newton, as well as rock star Jon Bon Jovi in his first principal role.

The Leading Man follows the adventures of hot new Hollywood actor Robin Grange (Bon Jovi), treading the boards as a novice in the West End and indulging in all the adulterous backstage shenanigans that accompany him to London. Nicole's fleeting appearance comes at the end of the movie as a presenter on a television broadcast of the Oscars. Her blink-and-you-miss-it scene could only have taken a couple of hours to shoot, so by and large Nicole managed to keep her no-work promise.

Instead, Nicole and Tom decided to spend quality time with their family, relaxing far away from the demands of directors, critics and the like. The first opportunity to do this was at the wedding of Nicole's sister,

Antonia, now twenty-five, to her twenty-seven-year-old boyfriend, sports marketing entrepreneur Angus Hawley.

In January 1996 the Cruises flew into Sydney for the pre-wedding celebrations, in which they were heavily involved. Nicole, who had been given the responsible role of matron of honour by Antonia, organized the hen party, while her husband generously splashed out on an elaborate stag weekend for his brother-in-law-to-be at the Sanctuary Cove in Queensland. Using Tom's private jet as a taxi service, the bucks partied in high style, and reports trickled back to the Kidmans that the actor had 'invested' over $45,000 in one casino alone.

After the hangovers had subsided and the men were safely returned to Sydney, the wedding took place in early February, in the chapel of Antonia's former school, Monte St Angelo, in North Sydney. Originally she had wanted the ceremony to be held in St Mark's Church, a grand setting in Darling Point which had previously hosted the doomed marriage of rock star Elton John to Renate Blauel, but the church had been unable to guarantee the high level of privacy required by a family including two huge celebrity names.

The big day was a grand affair, attended by 160 people. Nicole, clad in a long pale-blue silk dress, was accompanied by Isabella, now three years old, looking sweet as a flower girl. Graciously, Nicole did her utmost not to steal the show and papers made a point of commenting that she refrained from making a speech so that all eyes would remain on her sister. The crowd went on to a lavish reception at Sydney's Museum of Contemporary Arts and partied until the early hours of the morning, but Nicole and Tom bid their farewells early in order to check on baby Conor, who was too young to join in the festivities.

Journalists commented on the physical similarity between the bride and her famous sister. Nicole frequently describes them as being 'like twins' and, although Antonia's healthy good looks and long dark hair are a contrast to her sister's famous alabaster complexion and strawberry-blonde locks, their statuesque figures and facial features are indeed alike. Says Antonia of the three Kidman women: 'When we're together we're all stooping and trying to be the smallest.'

'When I was younger, I was absolutely scared of being compared to Nic,' she reveals. 'I felt that I didn't have an identity. I didn't feel confident.' Nevertheless, like Nicole, Antonia could not resist the call of the screen and at the time of her wedding was working as a researcher on the Australian television programme *This Is Your Life*. Over the next few years she was to ascend into the ranks of presenting, and eventually became a well-known face on cable television introducing *The Cover*, a modern women's lifestyle show, and *Premiere*, a programme about films and their stars. For the latter, she would interview Tom Cruise in 1999, but, interestingly, she has yet to appear with her sister.

✸

The night after Antonia and Angus's wedding, Nicole attended the Australian premiere of *To Die For* (already a box-office hit in America and England) at the Verona Cinema in Sydney. Her hair dramatically straightened and held back with a large Alice band, she made no secret of the fact she would be taking the next six months off to be with her family. This was to be her last public appearance for some time. The next day she was spotted with Tom and the children frolicking on the beach, incognito in matching sunglasses and baseball caps, which produced the first snaps of Conor with his famous parents.

Tom and Nicole then spent the spring and summer of 1996 travelling. Of course, a holiday for the Cruises was far removed from the average worn-out parents' requirements of lying on a beach in the sun, sipping cocktails. They set off with some close friends on a yachting tour around the Italian coast, hoping to pack in as many perilous sporting activities as possible. Amazingly, the beginning of their holiday was relatively peaceful.

One might be forgiven for wondering why Nicole would want to return to Italy so soon after her gruelling experiences while filming there for *The Portrait Of A Lady*. But since her first visit during her extended tour of Europe as a seventeen-year-old, Italy remains one of her favourite spots in the world and a country to which she is drawn year after year.

'That's the place I want to retire – there's something so wonderful about the country,' she said. 'And I speak Italian. I had to put those six years of Latin at high school to use, so I had three lessons a week and even did homework! I've learned to speak enough to get by. Tom stands beside me in a restaurant and says, "What's happening? What are they saying? What's that pasta called? Order me some!" Italian food is great.'

Sailing down from Lucca, the Tuscan town which had been the Italian setting for *Portrait* and was the place where Tom and Nicole would annually rent a villa for their holidays, the party progressed to Rome. Unfortunately, the celebrity couple found themselves unable to go out in public in this more cosmopolitan city without being mobbed.

'We couldn't walk down the street in the daytime because of people coming up,' said Nicole. 'So the way we saw Rome was to sleep during the day and go out at night, when it's much quieter and darker. We'd break out of the hotel room and run around at 3 o'clock in the morning, and just do it that way! We would always see places at night, it's a way of dealing with being really well known but still being able to see cities like Rome. I'd lived in Rome so I knew it quite well but Tom had never been there and I wanted him to see it, and we saw it by moonlight – aah!

'Anyway, we broke into the Colosseum! Tom climbed into the Colosseum illegally, climbed over those huge bars with spikes. I was screaming, "What are you doing?". . .' The daredevil pair managed to escape detection and continued their Italian experience by sailing south to the tiny volcanic island of Stromboli, just off Sicily.

One day, while Tom was out at sea scuba diving, Nicole decided she wanted to take a closer look at the semi-active volcano that gives the island its name. Hiring a guide whose attitude suggested he was fairly laid-back, the actress dressed casually in chinos and sneakers without socks, rather than hiking boots, and set off. New to mountain-climbing (and obviously ill-advised by her guide), she left without taking so much as a drop of water with her.

The hike took longer than anticipated, hindered by Nicole's poor choice of footwear, which gave her blisters. By the time they reached the top the sun was setting, and as most of the ground around them was covered in black sulphuric ash, it soon became impossible to see their surroundings. Panicking, the guide suggested they should attempt to slowly make their way down the other side of the mountain – a much shorter route, but far more dangerous in the dark.

'There were moments there where, if you put one foot wrong, you fall and you're dead,' shuddered Nicole. 'I like to do things that are dangerous. But this was stupid, I admit it.'

When, inevitably, the amateur climber fell and sprained her ankle, she insisted that they stay put. It was safer and less painful to camp out and hope for discovery. Cold, hungry, thirsty, in tears and far from any signs of civilization, Nicole was forced to face the possibility that she might never see her family again. 'I just remember thinking, "So this is how I'm gonna go. Wow, I would never have predicted it to be this way."' By then, she had been missing for eight-and-a-half hours.

Meanwhile, Tom had reluctantly returned from his diving trip when the fading light was no longer able to penetrate beneath the waves. Horrified that his wife had failed to return from her hike, he assumed she must be stranded. Tom's immediate concern was to find Nicole. As if in a scene from *Mission: Impossible*, he raced up the mountain to rescue her. 'He *ran* to the top in an hour and a half, which is usually a three-hour hike,' marvelled Nicole. 'I *know*, very corny . . .'

But Tom could not find his wife. It seemed all was lost when, in the early hours of the morning, Nicole's cries were heard by two Italians, who were in the area after doing a spot of skydiving. They led the exhausted actress and her shivering guide back down the mountain to safety.

On a yacht moored nearby, they helped Nicole radio her frantic husband, who was by now halfway down the other side of the mountain, still desperately searching for his wife in the dark. 'It was like one of those scenes out of a bad movie,' said Nicole. 'I was sobbing, "Thomas, Thomas!"'

When the stricken adventurer was finally reunited with his bedraggled wife on board the boat, he was shocked by her unexpected reaction to seeing him. All he wanted to do was rush her back to their yacht and wrap her up in cotton wool, but seemingly the prospect of starving to death up a mountain had brought out Nicole's best table manners.

'I kept saying to him, "Thomas, these are *very nice people*. If they offer you coffee, you *must* accept!"' Bewildered, Tom stared at Nicole, searching her face for signs of sanity. Had she perhaps started a fever?

There was nothing for it but to pacify his rambling wife (and the hospitable Italian boat owners). The action hero downed the steaming coffee in one swig, no doubt burning the roof of his mouth in the process. 'OK!' he declared, clapping his hands in typically no-nonsense fashion. 'We're outta here!'

Many people might have considered that these reckless and dangerous pastimes were, well, simply too *dangerous* to continue, especially after nearly losing one's life as a consequence. Not Nicole.

'Now that I've survived it, I'm kind of proud of it,' she laughed. 'The people we were with said, "We're inviting you back! This is fun, this game: 'Celebrity Search And Rescue', we're gonna call it!"'

Nineteen ninety-six proved to be Nicole's year of near-death experiences. She went straight from sailing to skiing in Colorado.

'I dislocated my shoulder skiing – but it wasn't my fault,' she insisted. 'I was on a black run, which is rated difficult, behind double black which is the hardest, but I classify myself as an intermediate. This 6 foot 4 guy, screaming, "Get out of the way!" came down the mountain and pummelled me . . .'

No stranger to danger, Nicole 'nearly died' again some years later when her helicopter had to make an emergency landing in Sussex, England, and narrowly missed some live power cables. She also admitted, 'I've driven on the wrong side of the road, barely nicking the car in front of me.' It seemed that the thrills of Hollywood were insignificant in comparison to Nicole's real-life escapades.

✸

Although Nicole had purposefully and publicly taken six months off after *The Portrait Of A Lady*, the offers of work did not stop rolling in. Almost immediately after she had hung up Isabel's corsets, a proposal had come in from producer Steven Spielberg. He offered her the lead in the debut feature of DreamWorks SKG, the new studio founded by the powerful triumvirate of Spielberg, Jeffrey Katzenberg and David Geffen.

The Peacemaker, a topical thriller set against the background of Bosnian unrest and the Russian underground crime scene, was primarily an action vehicle for the actor George Clooney, then best known as Dr Doug Ross on the medical television drama series *ER*. '*The Peacemaker* will be the first real test to see if I actually have any mettle for this,' he said of his upcoming role.

The movie was to be directed by Mimi Leder, whose work, also on *ER*, had won her an Emmy; this was her first full-length cinematic feature. Filmed in Slovakia, Macedonia and New York between May and September 1996, *The Peacemaker* was based on investigative reports by Andrew Cockburn and his wife Leslie, who were co-producers for the project. The plot involved Serb, Croat and Muslim terrorists, stolen nuclear warheads and a deadly cat-and-mouse chase against the clock all the way from Slovakia to Manhattan.

Spielberg wanted Nicole for the part of Dr Julia Kelly, the acting head of the White House Nuclear Smuggling Group and a nuclear physicist to boot – a character loosely based on Jessica Stern, who served as a consultant for the movie. Opposite her, Clooney would play Lieutenant Colonel Thomas Devoe, an intelligence officer with the U.S. Army's Special Forces. Nicole would be the reluctant, uptight bureaucrat, Clooney the handsome rogue. United, they would save America from nuclear holocaust. 'It's not a love story,' says Clooney. 'They are adversaries at first but they must learn to work together.'

For Nicole, it was yet another return to the world of brainy babes (*Days Of Thunder*'s neurosurgeon and *Batman Forever*'s criminal psychiatrist spring to mind) but it would certainly provide light entertainment. Acknowledging that *The Portrait Of A Lady* had been the hardest film she had made to date, in an emotional sense at least, Nicole decided that *The Peacemaker* would be the perfect way of easing herself back into acting after her long break.

'This was my way of having some fun. I wanted not to have to work every day, and to be able to go out at night and dance,' she says.

It was also possible that she had acquired her husband's penchant for thrilling physical roles, and her fans were about to witness another slice of the high-spirited marital competition first glimpsed during the horse races of *Far And Away* – who could go faster? So she accepted the part and spent just eight weeks filming over the summer, revelling in the stunts and high-speed car chases required to save the world.

Becoming good friends with notorious practical joker Clooney was a pleasing sideline. He was an interesting choice of sparring partner, especially as an odd twist of fate had recently crowned him the third Batman, after Nicole's erstwhile co-stars Michael Keaton and Val Kilmer had retired from Gotham City. It was a phone call from Clooney that had eventually persuaded her to take on this new role in the first place.

To her great relief, the trickster exempted her from his usual on-set pranks, and an easy, playful friendship ensued. Clooney was famously commitment-phobic, but Nicole bet him $10,000 that he would be a father by the time he was forty. With the patter of tiny feet markedly absent at his birthday celebrations in May 2001, Nicole dutifully honoured their wager. 'I got to collect on it,' laughs Clooney, 'and she did send me a cheque for the amount. I sent it back to her with a note saying: "Double or nothing – check back with me when I'm fifty!"'

Over the last three years, the world had been keenly observing the much-hyped creation of the DreamWorks studio, which would oversee the funding and production of films, cartoons, television shows, music and computer games. Certainly, as its first cinematic offering, *The Peacemaker* had a lot to live up to, and critics marvelled at the studio's choice of director and stars. Leder, Kidman and Clooney were all well-respected professionals within their fields, but none had the Hollywood bankability of, say, a Quentin Tarantino, a Julia Roberts or (dare one mention) a Tom Cruise.

With its 110 special effects, Hans Zimmer score and Calvin Klein wardrobe, ultimately *The Peacemaker* was a success on its release in September 1997, despite critical put-downs along the lines of *Time's* 'standard action-film stuff'. Clooney basically revises his *ER* role as loveable, twinkly eyed maverick Lieutenant Devoe, stealing scene after scene from Nicole as Dr Kelly – the boring voice of reason. Not that the strong-willed brunette doesn't give her all; it's just that up until the surprise ending (containing more holes than a slice of Emmenthal but just as cheesy), her part is quite weak in comparison.

Nevertheless, as the film grossed more than $100 million worldwide, it seemed that Spielberg, Katzenberg and Geffen had got it right. It was now expected that their stars' pay packets would rise into the higher brackets of the Hollywood elite. Leder undoubtedly built on her success by directing the big-budget sci-fi movie *Deep Impact*, and Clooney was soon attracting acclaim in *Out Of Sight* and *The Thin Red Line*.

In time, Nicole would live to regret reverting to type as a scientist with sex appeal, dismissing *The Peacemaker* as professionally unsatisfying, but for now she was a hit, and was nominated by the Blockbuster Entertainment Awards as Favourite Actress – Action Or Adventure.

★

While Nicole was off waging war on terrorists, her husband was fighting an unpleasant battle of his own. *Bunte*, a German magazine with an estimated weekly circulation of 650,000, published what they claimed was an interview with Tom Cruise in July 1996. Within the 'exclusive' question-and-answer report, Tom was directly quoted as saying that he had a 'zero sperm count' and that infertility had ruined his life.

Tom was understandably furious and lost no time in issuing an official response. To the public, Pat Kingsley stated, 'Not only is it not true, but he didn't say it.' To *Bunte*, Tom raged that they had acted 'out of greed and with total disregard for the personal and professional harm it causes', and promptly filed a seven-page lawsuit at the Los Angeles Superior Court claiming $60 million in damages.

'Cruise is *not* sterile,' said the lawsuit. 'He has a normal sperm count and can produce children.' Such suggestions could have 'a devastating effect' and were 'calculated to hold him up to ridicule among a significant part of the public'.

Unfortunately for *Bunte*, the timing of Tom's legal threats was perfect. During the past year, the magazine had embarrassingly lost a lawsuit to Princess Caroline of Monaco for an equally fictitious interview supplied by a inventive freelance journalist. In that instance they had been ordered to pay the princess 180,000 DM. The fact that the powerful actor's claim for damages was over 500 times the amount of the previous settlement was enough to make *Bunte* back down whimpering.

Incredibly, at the time the magazine complained noisily, using the fact that they were by no means the first to print this speculation as good reason for fabricating Cruise's words. After the event, *Bunte* released a statement revealing they had no proof of their allegations, let alone anything as concrete as a cassette recording of the 'interview'. The deputy editor of *Bunte* was fired, they printed a front-cover retraction, and Cruise dropped the suit.

One can only begin to imagine how Tom's wife might have been affected. The Cruises were decent people, and parents at that. Exactly *why* did the media continue to hound them on such issues?

'Whether I give birth to a child or not, is not even an element that exists now,' was Nicole's jaded response. 'If more are added to the family, more will be, but that's a very personal thing. It isn't anybody else's business.'

Tom had the final say about all the aspersions, past and present, cast on both his fertility and sexuality, in an interview published in *Premiere* that summer. He made no bones about his feelings on the matter:

'Let me make this very clear. Basically, it's attacking my relationship. I think it's absolutely disgusting that someone would say it. It's ridiculous, it fucking pisses me off. This is my relationship and I am being called a liar about it. I've called lawyers. I say, "You want to say that? Fine, go ahead, you fucking prove it."'

The couple, who were due to celebrate their sixth wedding anniversary in December, defiantly maintained a united front in public, posing together lovingly for photographers at the premiere for *The Portrait Of A Lady* in October 1996. In between nuzzling his wife, Tom told reporters, 'Every day I am with her, I still have this magnetic attraction to her – I can't keep my hands off her.' The only thing that marred this event was that their taxi launch was stopped for speeding by Venice's water police.

Although Nicole was well established in her career as an actress, she never forgot her childhood ambition of becoming a writer. During the filming of *The Portrait Of A Lady*, she kept a journal detailing her experiences and might often be found scribbling down her thoughts. In 1996, when she met up with John Duigan for *The Leading Man*, she put forward a proposal: 'I told him we should sit down and write something together, because I'm having a lot of ideas. But I don't know if I have the discipline to put it all together.'

Bitten by the creative bug, Nicole was perhaps inspired by Tom's links behind the scenes. Back in the summer of 1992, he had teamed up with his CAA agent, Paula Wagner, to form his own production company. Wagner, a former New York actress and playwright, had represented the actor for over a decade and, with her husband, Rick Nicita (Sam Cohn's successor as Nicole's agent), became a close friend. The company was called Odin, after the king of the Viking gods, and Wagner shouldered most of the business responsibilities, allowing Tom to be the 'talent'.

Now, Nicole began to wonder what it would be like to become involved with a film from its conception. After discussing this with one of her other favourite directors, she bit the bullet and, together with Jane Campion and her husband Colin, bought the screen rights for the 1995 novel *In The Cut* by Susanna Moore.

Described by the *New York Times Book Review* as a 'ferociously uninhibited erotic thriller', *In The Cut* is about a female New York University professor, who unwisely becomes involved with a detective working on a brutal murder case which has taken place in her apartment building. Drawn ever more deeply into the investigation, things become dangerous for the heroine and she is soon fighting for her life as a consequence. Although the basic plot might sound fairly run of the mill, *In The Cut* was notable for dividing reviewers' and readers' opinions with its sexually explicit language, pornographic scenes of sadism and violence, and undeniably gory ending.

At first it was implied that Nicole would star in the movie version, and much was made of Tom's supposed prudish outrage that she should jeopardize her career for such a vulgar role. In time, however, Nicole would reveal that her intentions were instead to co-produce the movie with Campion, who was also writing the screenplay. She stood by the erotic themes of the story, indicating that she wholeheartedly believed the film would portray women taking control of their sex lives rather than simply succumbing to the perverted demands of men. Although it seemed that she would not be working on this script herself, she continued to dabble in writing, and as late as 2001 would reveal that she was adapting another book into a screenplay.

18

Desire, Obsession, Sex And Infidelity

Stanley Kubrick, the enigmatic and brilliant writer and director of films like *2001: A Space Odyssey* and *A Clockwork Orange*, hadn't worked on a movie for over eight years. The film world had almost given up waiting for the next glimpse into his strange artistic mind. After 1987's bleak *Full Metal Jacket*, a disturbing take on the Vietnam War which itself had come after an eight-year gap, Kubrick sought a new project that would bring him back into the very living rooms of his viewers. Something with which they would be able to identify, if only through their uneasiness.

While shooting *Dr Strangelove* in the early 1960s, the director had watched some pornographic movies with his colleague, writer Terry Southern, and remarked, 'Wouldn't it be interesting if an artist were to do this with beautiful first-rate actors and good equipment?'

Half a dozen years later, Kubrick bought the film rights to Arthur Schnitzler's 1926 novella *Traumnovelle* (translated into English as *Dream Story* or *Dream Novel*). Fascinated with Schnitzler's perceptive observations on the human psyche, Kubrick said at the time, 'It's difficult to find any writer who understood the human soul more truly and who had a more profound insight into the way people think, act and really are, and who also had an all-seeing point of view — sympathetic, if somewhat cynical.'

In *Traumnovelle*, Schnitzler, an Austrian author who counted Sigmund Freud among his closest friends, had created a sinister and occasionally explicit tale of carnal competition, jealousy and paranoia between Fridolin and Albertine, a married couple who are both psychiatrists. The brief text, set in Vienna at the turn of the last century, revealed opinions that were considered shocking at the time, and explored the couple's dark *doppelexistenz* by using their struggle to distinguish between sexual fantasy and reality.

Kubrick would spend over thirty years deliberating over whether or not the novella would translate successfully on to celluloid. He was by no means the first; among others, Billy Wilder had tried, and failed, to adapt the story. But the brooding subject material seemed to echo Kubrick's own signature style perfectly: deeply symbolic, icily formal, often sexually disturbed and so detached as to be almost clinical.

Over the years, Kubrick had shown *Traumnovelle* to all the writers with whom he worked, to no avail. Having finally reached a mutual understanding of his goals with screenwriter Frederic Raphael, the pair adapted the book together, retitling it *Eyes Wide Shut*. Fridolin and Albertine became Bill and Alice Harford, and the setting was fast-forwarded a hundred years to millennial New York. The twists and turns of the couple's individual sexual odysseys remained essentially the same.

Aware of the need for voyeurism both within the film and from its audience, Kubrick realized that to use a real-life married couple would fulfil both briefs spectacularly, stretching the actors beyond the usual call of duty. The practised chemistry between the two leads was imperative in itself, as Nicole Kidman had once said: 'When two people who know each other touch one another, even the simplest things, like stroking their hair, look and feel more natural.'

For a while, Kubrick considered Alec Baldwin and Kim Basinger for the roles of the Harfords. Basinger would have been an interesting, if more mature, choice as Alice, since her CV included the steamy *9½ Weeks* from a decade before. But the title role really belonged to Bill Harford, as the story is viewed mainly from his perspective. Unfortunately for Nicole's one-time co-star, Baldwin was by no means a match for the ratings guaranteed by, and the intrigue surrounding, one Tom Cruise.

So Kubrick sent off two faxes simultaneously to Mr and Mrs Cruise, mentioning the name and basic details of the script and asking politely if they would be interested. At the time both actors were busy with other projects (Nicole was deep in the throes of *The Portrait Of A Lady*), but they both expressed their enthusiasm for the roles and keenness to work with such an acclaimed film-maker. A few months later the finished manuscript arrived, marked for Tom's attention.

'He flipped over it, and then I read it five days later,' recalled Nicole. 'And then we had to give the script back. When it comes to films, our tastes tend to be quite different. But in terms of the Kubrick movie, it took us about two seconds to say "Yes". And that was it.'

During the first break in their respective schedules for many months, in winter 1995 Tom and Nicole flew by helicopter to Kubrick's rambling home in St Albans, Hertfordshire. It was an unusual setting for a meeting with Hollywood's top couple, but as Nicole explained, 'since Stanley doesn't travel and he lives in England, we had to go to him'. In other words, Muhammad came to the mountain.

Together they discussed Kubrick's vision of the movie and a proposed schedule. It seems that, in the light of their shared fascination for the director, the Cruises didn't think once, let alone twice, about the implications of *Eyes Wide Shut* being their third movie together in the space of just over five years.

Nicole was especially pleased. For some time now she had realized that the success of her movies depended to a certain extent on the director pulling her strings, and she was finally in a position to be more discerning about her roles. The actress relished the prospect of being associated with Kubrick, whose genius was largely uncontested and whose reputation for provoking controversy was legendary.

With its specifically marital premise, *Eyes Wide Shut* would also challenge her acting skills enormously – a taste recently acquired during her harrowing time with Jane Campion.

'This is dangerous subject matter,' she admitted. 'Even Stanley had been frightened by it. He'd wanted to make this movie when he was a young man, but his wife said, "Let's not go there, not at this stage of our marriage."'

'But Tom and I decided to take the plunge. It meant talking to each other about jealousy and attraction for other people – things you usually skirt around or pretend aren't there. It would be difficult and, at times, very confronting. It was something that was going to either draw us closer together or pull us apart.'

Nicole later confessed that the themes alone made her distinctly nervous. 'I was reading an interview with Susan Sarandon talking about working with her partner Tim Robbins, and there was such an intensity about the project, they decided to live apart while making it,' she mused during the film's early stages. 'I don't know whether it will come to that between me and Tom, but we'll have to see.'

No doubt the job posed the threat of creating problems for the close-knit couple, but they were resolute. Nicole also benefited at this stage from strong support from her parents.

'When they heard I was doing the film, they enrolled in a two-day university course on Kubrick,' she said. 'They packed a little lunch each day, and saw all his films, which they loved. I thought that was quite special.'

During Kubrick's first meeting with Nicole and Tom, he had outlined a preliminary shooting schedule of roughly six to eight months. This was a reasonably lengthy estimate, given that Nicole had rattled off her performance in *The Peacemaker* in a third of the time, but not strikingly unusual. However, setbacks arose almost immediately, and Kubrick would not be ready to direct for a full year. Filming officially started on 4 November 1996 in and around London, on a budget speculated at $65 million.

Tom and Nicole's patience would prove a great asset over and beyond the course of *Eyes Wide Shut*. Waiting for a year at the start may have caused minor problems with other engagements in their personal and professional lives, but this was just the tip of the iceberg. Shooting would continue on a daily basis right up until 31 January 1998, and even then they would be called back eight weeks later for miscellaneous retakes. After their performances were finally in the can, they would stay in regular contact with Kubrick as he embarked on the extensive editing process. No one could have predicted at the beginning that *Eyes Wide Shut* would not premiere until mid-July 1999, meaning the project took a total of four years out of the Cruises' lives. For Kubrick, of course, overseeing this labour of love from the outset had taken nearly ten times as long.

The obvious reason for all the delays was the director himself. The term 'perfectionist' didn't really do him justice.

'He gives new meaning to the word meticulous,' Jack Nicholson had famously disclosed after working with Kubrick on *The Shining* in 1979. His co-star, Shelley Duvall, had been less forgiving, claiming that her experiences with the director had played havoc with her sanity.

Nothing could have prepared Tom and Nicole for Kubrick's painstaking technique. For one short scene he would oversee an unrelenting series of takes, usually amounting to around fifty but often coming in at double that number. For actors as experienced as Tom and Nicole, this was abnormally excessive.

According to the producer, Jan Harlan, Kubrick was in fact using a highly expensive method of filming the rehearsals, just in case the call of 'Action!' should fail to elicit a great movie moment. But, either way, there would be no breaks, no let-up. Nicole and her husband may have believed they couldn't draw any more emotion out of an already torturous scene, or that they had already hit their marks several times. It didn't matter. Kubrick was a man obsessed.

'It's true, he is a perfectionist and that's scary,' said Nicole. 'He expects you to dedicate yourself to the film 200 per cent, and nothing less will do.

'I've got to say, though, the thing about working with him is that you know you're working with someone who cares. He lives and breathes movies. And he makes so few that he enjoys the process that much more; he wants to exhaust all the possibilities. And the kind of actor that I am, I love that. I find it much harder to work with a director who says, "Hey, great, let's move on."'

By now, the on- and offscreen couple were anxious that their third movie together should be a success. They were committed to avoiding their previous critical derision at all costs. The potential demise of their respective careers rested fully in the hands of their director.

'People say Tom and I don't hit it off onscreen and in *Days Of Thunder* I can see why,' Nicole revealed in a moment of surprising candour. 'But with Kubrick we've had the chance to explore new things as actors. If he feels he's not getting it, then he does a lot of takes.'

Warner Brothers' fast-disappearing funds were preserved to some degree by working with just the tiniest of crews, making what was already a deeply personal movie even more intimate for those involved. 'It's almost like making a student film,' Nicole commented.

Says the film's stills photographer, Manuel Harlan: 'I think it was probably hard for most people not to be slightly in awe of the charisma, and above all the enormous energy of this man. But there was no normal hierarchy within the film crew; it was just Stanley – "the guv'nor" – and then everybody else. He got to know everyone personally [some of the crew had in fact worked with him as far back as *Barry Lyndon* in 1975] and he has dealt with everyone, from the production designer to the chippie, on a one-to-one basis.

'As he said, "Don't talk to the suits – talk to the guys doing the job." I think that it was because of this level of professional intimacy that everyone was willing to bend over backwards.'

Still, no matter what Nicole said about the profound experience of working with Stanley Kubrick, even her tolerance must have been sorely

stretched at times. Like Ron Howard before him, Kubrick always intentionally dealt with the Cruises separately and his control over his leading
lady extended far further than the perimeter of the set.

'When you work with Stanley, you live the way he wants you to live,'
said Nicole, feeling a certain sense of *déjà vu* about her experience with
Campion. 'He wouldn't want me to leave the house. He would get anxious
if I was going out.' Although, as Nicole herself admitted, her role was
only a third of the size of her husband's, she was ordered to be on constant standby, just in case Kubrick decided he needed her. 'He wanted me
to be so dedicated – I mean as every director does, they don't want to
think that any other films exist in the world, other than the film you are
working on.'

Nicole went on to say that she enjoyed the company of this most
extraordinary man so much that, during the many empty hours when her
presence was not required, she would go and sit in Kubrick's office just to
absorb his personality. Then, when he was around, she found they could
chat for hours about anything and everything: '. . . politics, war, airplanes,
computers, Peter Sellers – you name it, he knows about it!'

Manuel Harlan feels that the popular conception of Kubrick as a mysterious, withdrawn character is unfair. 'I think it stems from his dislike of
personal publicity. He shunned it mostly because he felt he wasn't any
good at it,' he says. Like Nicole, the photographer has a dramatically different personal opinion of the director. 'He was a great raconteur and had
a hilarious sense of irony and black humour, as well as a developed sar-
castic streak that he could use to devastating effect, usually accompanied
by a very boyish, mischievous twinkle in his eyes.'

Still, for all Nicole's enthusiasm and admiration, she never really gave
the impression that her feelings for Kubrick were especially warm – as
they had been for, say, Jane Campion.

'Jane was very tactile – she'd hug you and give you a lot of emotional
support,' Nicole revealed. 'Kubrick is different – for a start, he doesn't
come and hug me.' Whatever Kubrick's method of supporting his actors,
it obviously worked for Tom. 'Although he was demanding, he also wanted
everyone to have a good time,' he recalled. 'When Nic and I were having
a rough time, he'd always be on hand to reassure us.'

While Stanley Kubrick gradually developed a certain relationship with the
actors in *Eyes Wide Shut*'s lead roles, problems evolved with the supporting
cast. The comings and goings of various big names provided almost as

much excited tabloid tittle-tattle as the erotic subject material and ever-increasing length of shooting. As filming went on, key members would be dropped and replaced.

In the film, Bill Harford finds himself disturbed yet aroused by his wife's sexual fantasies involving other people. In Kubrick's initial version of the script, this leads to each psychiatrist having an affair with a patient, played by Harvey Keitel and Jennifer Jason Leigh. Both actors were known for their relaxed attitude to onscreen nudity, in *The Piano* and *Last Exit To Brooklyn* respectively.

Keitel quit *Eyes Wide Shut* early on, amid a flurry of rumours suggesting he had become tired of having to do so many takes of one particular sex scene with Nicole. When asked to explain what went wrong by reporters, he issued a terse 'No comment'. Nicole's version of events was that Keitel left amicably due to scheduling problems. He was immediately replaced with Sydney Pollack, an actor with whom the director had maintained a long-term telephone relationship. Typically in the bizarre world of Stanley Kubrick, the film veterans had never met until this moment.

Pollack, who played the completely revised role of Dr Victor Ziegler, was a most welcome addition to the fold. The Academy Award-winning actor and director had worked with Tom before, directing him in *The Firm* and co-producing Cruise's own directorial debut, an episode of *Fallen Angels*.

'Talking about working with Tom Cruise is boring,' Pollack once ventured amusingly. 'It'd be much more interesting to say that Tom Cruise is really unpredictable, but to say that he comes to work every morning with a smile on his face and can't wait to get started, that he takes direction, that he will work until he drops – that's boring, but that's the truth.'

The second casualty of war was Jennifer Jason Leigh. Long after she had completed filming her part as a patient's daughter in *Eyes Wide Shut*, the actress was recalled by Kubrick to reshoot several scenes in London. She informed him that this was impossible as she had moved on to David Cronenberg's *eXistenZ*. Her replacement, the Swedish actress Marie Richardson, was called in to shoot the entire role from scratch.

And so the original six-month timetable sprawled into a staggering two-and-a-half years, the longest shoot in major studio history.

'This is the first time since we've had the kids that we are working together,' said Nicole during the making of *Eyes Wide Shut*. 'It's almost like discovering a different aspect of our relationship, and different things about each other as actors.'

There was no question in either actor's mind that their roles in *Eyes Wide Shut* were light years away from their previous work on *Days Of Thunder* and *Far And Away* in terms of emotional involvement and testing their relationship.

In *Eyes Wide Shut* Alice Harford (her role revised from that of a psychiatrist to an ex-art entrepreneur) torments her husband by telling him she is invariably unfaithful to him in her fantasies. Disgusted by her frankness (brought on by a large helping of marijuana), during the course of that night Bill surprises himself as one sexual opportunity after another presents itself. He resists them all but cannot stop himself from attending a mysterious and masked upper-class orgy, shot in Highclere Castle. There he learns much about his sexuality as a voyeur, but gets into mortal danger when his identity as an uninvited guest is revealed to the revellers.

'Filming *Eyes Wide Shut* could have destroyed our marriage, but instead it brought us together,' said Tom after the event. 'Nic and I have good communication, but with issues such as the ones this film confronts, you really have to discuss everything.

'There are a lot of things we brought to the picture and I think Stanley appreciated it. He knew what it cost us to go through with the scenes. It was very demanding emotionally and physically for both of us, and there were times when Nic and I were uneasy with each other. I don't like to bring work home, but sometimes, because of the characters and the nature of the scenes, it was very difficult not to think about it and become slightly obsessed with it.'

The incident which caused the most friction was the sequence where Alice shares her fantasy of making love to a naval officer, arguably the most explicit scene in the film. Although it only lasts for ninety seconds onscreen and is split into a handful of fifteen-second clips, under Kubrick's direction it took three whole days to shoot to his satisfaction. These were the only three days of the entire two-and-a-half-years when Tom elected to stay away from the set.

'That was definitely hard,' recalled Nicole. 'It came at the beginning of the movie and Stanley wanted it to be harsh and gritty looking, almost pornographic. He didn't exploit me, I did it because I thought it was important to the film. The film deals with sex and sexual obsession and the scenes could not have been of me in a bra and panties pretending to have sex with somebody. It had to have a graphic quality to it.

'We filmed a lot of stuff; some of the footage was used and some of it wasn't. I certainly wouldn't have done it for any other director and, yes, it was a little difficult to go home to my husband afterwards.'

Desire, Obsession, Sex And Infidelity   169

As *Eyes Wide Shut* centred more on Bill Harford's sexual explorations than anything else, Kubrick's use of Nicole was primarily to capitalize on her physical appearance. The very first scene is a gratuitous glimpse of Nicole naked bar a pair of high heels, seen from behind. Within the opening sequence viewers are also treated to shots of her using the toilet just inches away from her husband. Here Kubrick was able to accurately portray the intimacy and ease of a couple who had been together for several years.

'Sometimes it would wear on me,' admitted Tom of the director's openly physical use of his wife, who was also to be shown topless and in a see-through vest. 'We really had to take time to try and be kind to each other . . . The fact that we're married made the film easier for Nic and me to do. I was glad we'd been married for several years by the time we did it; it would have been much more difficult to look at that stuff when we were young newly-weds.'

They were refreshingly candid in relating their characters to their real-life partnership and the media lapped it up.

'This is a woman who's not unhappy in her marriage but she's bored and wants more,' said Nicole of Alice. 'I don't think there are many women who can't relate to that at some stage of their lives with their men. She also sees her husband flirting with other women and gets jealous. Do Tom and I get jealous? Of course we do! It's only normal if you care about the person you're with.

'What counts is how you handle jealousy. Tom and I do OK, and I know that I married a good man.' This was notably more upfront than her previous protestations that trust always overcame envy within the boundaries of their marriage.

While some papers reported the couple's words faithfully, less reputable sources, intrigued by this marital confrontation, launched a virtual plague of rumours. Kubrick had made it clear to his tiny cast and crew that absolute secrecy was crucial, and in their desperation to know what had been going on all this time, tabloids seized on the merest unconfirmed whisper. *Eyes Wide Shut* was blatant pornography. Harvey Keitel had become a little too close to Nicole. She and Tom had researched their filthy roles by visiting live sex shows, taking addictive drugs and poring over sado-masochistic photographs. Their marriage had become a 'passionless shell' and they were sleeping in separate beds. The stream of lurid stories was relentless.

By the time shooting of *Eyes Wide Shut* wrapped on 31 January 1998, the constant speculation coupled with Kubrick's ongoing demands had taken its toll on the Cruises' health. As well as nursing a broken foot, Tom had developed a stomach ulcer which he was at pains to hide from both his director and the press for fear of provoking predictable 'Kubrick Made Me Ill!' headlines. He was not alone in his physical suffering: Nicole was developing rather worrying twinges in her abdomen.

Only eight weeks passed before the couple received a telephone call from Kubrick, who was characteristically unsatisfied with some of the scenes he was editing, specifically their location. Both actors were recalled and the whole process started up again.

To their credit, Tom and Nicole were so committed to *Eyes Wide Shut* they literally dropped everything to return to Kubrick in London (something which Jennifer Jason Leigh failed to do, costing her her role), although it should be noted that they were obligated to do this under the terms of their contracts. For Nicole this meant temporarily interrupting a more lightweight project she had accepted during her long year on standby – the film *Practical Magic*. Her quote – 'Working with Stanley is an honour. I would do it again in a second' – was being tested to the letter.

A few months later, Kubrick called it a day on set. Tom and Nicole were free to regain control of their lives and explore other career paths. As with her time as Isabel Archer in *The Portrait Of A Lady*, it would be a long while before Nicole was able to fully digest the episode and put the more traumatic events behind her.

'The whole thing is so personal that it is hard to talk about it without getting upset,' she said as late as the following year. 'It was a bleak, intense experience. Emotionally I am still very connected to it. I couldn't imagine doing this film with anyone but Tom – I'm so glad it was him.'

But the world would have to wait for over a year before the fruits of Kubrick, Cruise and Kidman's labour was revealed. The director immersed himself in the technicalities of editing the thousands of hours' worth of footage, hitting a stumbling block along the way when he tried to pass the orgy sequence off as less than X-rated. 'Truth of it is that Stanley couldn't really understand the ratings system,' his friend Julian Senior from Warner Brothers later revealed. 'He had signed a contract with Warner to deliver an R-rated movie and he looked at that sequence again and again.'

The remarkable scene, which involves an expansive uninterrupted panning shot lasting over a minute, clearly showed an array of human body parts that would present a problem for discerning American audiences. While the U.K. and Europe would pass the film for cinematic release in Kubrick's original format, it was proving impossible to keep the U.S. censors happy. As he struggled over the editing, time marched ever onward.

19

A Strange,
Cocooned World

Tom and Nicole's lengthy sojourn with Stanley Kubrick forced them to relocate to Hertfordshire in 1995. They needed to be near the director's house in St Albans and close to the studios – they also wanted to enjoy the English countryside during their extended stay. Being Hollywood film stars, the couple had some specific requirements, as local estate agent Jim Falconer recalls: 'Mr Cruise wanted somewhere secluded, accessible for London, with efficient security.'

Aided by Kubrick, the Cruises finally found a property to rent that matched most of their requests, and in November 1996 the family of four moved into a twenty-room Georgian mansion set in 50 acres near Shenley. The English town is well used to celebrity spotting, due to its proximity to Elstree Studios, the filming location for *Star Wars* and *Indiana Jones*, among other big movies.

Already almost perfect, the house needed just a few alterations for the safety-conscious parents; the upstairs windows were childproofed. Reports that they spent tens of thousands of pounds getting the house ready mentioned some more enjoyable additions, such as a personal gym for the adults and a slide for the children.

'I hate living in big houses – somehow they just seem too big. It was sort of like the house out of *The Shining*,' said Nicole of their new home. But she didn't have to worry about being alone and scared: she was now accompanied by an entourage which included bodyguards, personal assistants, personal trainers, a French chef, and not one but *two* nannies. One of the helpers was Peter Crone, who often accompanied Nicole when she was out and about in London, providing both protection and companionship.

Free from the pressures of Hollywood, the couple were determined to lead a normal life outside filming, and first on the list was Isabella's and Conor's education. 'Tom and I don't intend to spoil our children,' said Nicole. 'They won't be treated with kid gloves. They'll go to normal schools and we'll allow them to be their own people.'

One neighbour whose child shared classes with the new Cruise recruits remarked, 'It says a great deal about Tom and Nicole that they chose to send their children to a normal, local fee-paying school – certainly nothing flashy.' Even more surprising to the residents was that the parents took turns with the school run when possible, rather than letting the staff take over.

'We developed a different perspective on life, rather than being in L.A. and talking about movies all the time,' said Nicole of their time in Hertfordshire. As with the children's rota, they endeavoured to blend in with their new surroundings. 'We try not to live in a goldfish bowl,' said Nicole. 'We go to the park with the children, or to the pub, and nobody notices us.' Well, not quite: they were spotted in nearby restaurants and even shopping at a local supermarket. However, as the pair had previously experienced, the great British reserve meant that they were not hassled by strangers and the locals became used to seeing the famous faces in their midst. 'They're such a delightful couple,' their neighbour continued. 'They've tried to integrate themselves into the local community without any fuss.'

Nicole felt it was important to establish a routine. If that meant getting up after only four hours' sleep to take her daughter to school, then so be it. 'They won't be children forever and I don't want to miss this part.'

With both Tom and Nicole working on the same film, and such an emotionally charged one at that, there had to be some ground rules. So what was it like to have two actors filming and living together?

'It certainly allows us an understanding of each other's work processes,' said Nicole. 'We don't discuss choices in our work, because that's a very instinctual thing. Generally we try to keep it separate because otherwise it becomes too strange. We try to make our household as normal as possible for the children.'

Fortunately for the husband-and-wife team, who celebrated their sixth and seventh wedding anniversaries during the filming of *Eyes Wide Shut*, when they weren't stressed by work, their feelings for each other still ran deep. 'He fascinates me still,' said Nicole. 'I can sit with him and know what he's thinking from a glance of an eye. Another time I can look at him and think, "My God, I would never have thought that he would say that, or react that way".'

During the filming of *Eyes Wide Shut*, Tom and Nicole made a concerted effort to look after their personal relationship. Tom occasionally prepared romantic nights for his wife, tucking the children into bed, drawing a scented bath and lighting candles. Nicole was grateful that he displayed his affections so openly; she admitted, 'He's very romantic, more romantic than I am. He buys flowers, he writes letters . . .'

Women envious of not only her handsome husband, but also her slim figure would be livid to know that the actress never dieted – 'I'm renowned for eating cake'. During hectic filming schedules, Nicole had trouble keeping her weight up. Tom knew that at these times the way to his woman's heart was through her stomach, and he would bake her his secret-recipe chocolate-chip cookies.

When he was feeling particularly generous, Tom would indulge Nicole's passion for vintage accessories. 'He knows I love antique jewellery,' she explained after he produced an exquisite Victorian diamond ring.

Perhaps Tom was trying to make up for the fact that he spent a lot of 1997 busy filming. 'When you're working you get a little spoiled and then it switches,' said Nicole. 'I think you must have equality in a relationship for it to work.'

Try as they might to preserve a healthy balance, as Nicole was required on set far less than Tom, she naturally assumed the main household role. This imbalance undoubtedly led to tension between them, as Tom was constantly tired from a long, hard day with Kubrick, whereas Nicole had often had a pleasant, leisurely day.

'On the film *Eyes Wide Shut* I got to live a lot because I had a lot of time off,' said Nicole. She used the spare hours while the children were out of the house to brush up on her Italian, but it was the quality time she was able to spend with her son and daughter that she most enjoyed. Juggling her two careers, actress and mother, was not always easy, but during this period Nicole amply succeeded. The trio spent a lot of time out in the garden enjoying the sunshine, and Nicole revelled in seeing Conor grow into a toddler, improving his mobility and vocabulary daily.

Nicole took the opportunity to introduce Isabella to her love of horses. They paid their £100 annual membership at South Medburn

Equestrian Centre and the pair attended mother-and-daughter riding lessons. 'They're a delightful family,' said Harold Rose, whose wife Margaret ran the centre, 'and we're very pleased they chose to ride here.'

Like Janelle, Nicole acquainted her daughter with music at an early age. 'Isabella and I are big fans of Vivaldi,' said Nicole. 'I once took her to a church in Vienna for a concert of his music. She whispered to me, "Mummy, is it all right if I dance?" How could I say no? So in this great, imposing church, there was this cute little tot pirouetting in the aisle.'

Indulging her travelling bug, Nicole visited several European cities during 1997, as well as much of the British Isles. One weekend Tom whisked her away for a romantic break in the windswept Scottish Highlands, in his private plane stationed nearby at Elstree Aerodrome. Venturing to the wilds of West Yorkshire, Nicole revisited the land of her favourite authors. 'I'm fascinated by the Brontë sisters,' she says. 'My mum and I walked up on the moors where they lived. Jane Campion and I did it as well. It was beautiful. There's something about the place that you know inspired great writers.'

Continuing her literary exploits, Nicole enrolled in a poetry course in the Lake District. 'I love Wordsworth's poetry. When I had a week off from the film without Tom, I went to Wordsworth's cottage. To be able to do those walks and see those vistas that inspired some of the greatest poems of all time was breathtaking.' Clearly having fallen in love with the area, Nicole later returned with the rest of the family. 'We love hiking in the Lake District. It's beautiful and so lush. We stay in a quiet little guest-house with the kids.'

Always one with itchy feet, she talked of her plans for future adventures. 'I think that eventually, when we're older, Tom and I would basically like to retire. Go hiking in the Himalayas, go to China. We have a whole dream to explore the world. Yes, we're exploring the world now but it's not like I can walk down the street and see stuff.' Their more immediate plans included hiking, perhaps in Nepal, when filming finally finished. But when she read *Into Thin Air*, Jon Krakauer's riveting firsthand account of the catastrophic expedition up Mount Everest in March 1996 which left eight people from the experienced climbing party dead, Nicole had second thoughts.

Nicole attended just a few obligatory industry functions during her time in Hertfordshire, including flying in for the sixty-ninth Academy Awards, sadly to present, not receive, an Oscar. At the lavish ceremony on 24 March 1997, Nicole took to the podium to announce the award for Best Achievement In Editing. Discreetly, she reached for her glasses. 'I had to put them on to read the monitor,' she remembers. 'I copped a lot of shit for that . . .

'"Why was she wearing glasses when she was wearing a beautiful evening dress?" *Please!* I had to read. I couldn't believe it – there was judgement made on wearing glasses.' Nicole doesn't just dislike contact lenses; she actually likes her specs.

Although filming *Eyes Wide Shut* was nowhere near completed at this time, Nicole was quizzed about her involvement and her next steps. 'Just to have this opportunity, as an actor, to be in this film, is just *wow!*' she exclaimed. 'I think that's when you say, "OK, after this I'm taking a break," because I went from Jane Campion to Stanley Kubrick, and it was incredible. It can only go down from here.'

There was speculation that Nicole would appear as the leather-clad Emma Peel in the cinema version of the British sixties cult television show *The Avengers*, possibly due to her recent affinity with the country. But as nothing came of this, perhaps Nicole did not deem working with the relatively new and unaccomplished director Jeremiah S. Chechik a suitable next step.

Nicole celebrated her thirtieth birthday in the summer, for which Tom splashed out on a £17,500 emerald-studded necklace. As Kubrick's crew moved from the Home Counties to Pinewood Studios in Buckinghamshire, the couple chose to commute in a Warner Brothers helicopter each morning rather than relocate. Commenting on the insular world within the movie, Nicole said, 'That was exactly how we lived – we didn't see many people. I look back on it and I think, how did we exist for about a year and a half?

'Tom and I had a trailer that we shared, we also had a smaller room and I would go into that room a lot and read. We were existing in a strange, cocooned world.'

Nicole's blinkered existence was rudely shattered on 31 August 1997. She watched in horror, along with the rest of the world, footage of the car wreckage that claimed the life of Princess Diana. A shy, beautiful and statuesque mother of two, only six years older than Nicole, the princess died being chased by the paparazzi. The circumstances seemed too close for comfort. Having met Diana five years earlier at a movie premiere, Tom and Nicole attended the funeral on 6 September. Shaken, Nicole was anxious to return to the loving bosom of her family.

'After Princess Diana died I came out to Australia,' she recalled, 'but I was just hounded by paparazzi. So I actually went on a radio program and said, "Listen, please leave my kids alone so that they can go to school here, so that they can have a normal life." And they did, they left the kids alone.

'At this point I would have to say that Australia is the easiest country for us to be in.'

With houses in Los Angeles, Colorado and London, Nicole felt the need to establish roots in Sydney and the Cruises bought a luxurious harbourside property at Darling Point. She undoubtedly felt more relaxed living close to her parents and sister and was even heard denigrating their Pacific Palisades place, describing it as an 'ugly fortress'. Determined not to feel the same about her new Australian base, Nicole spent some time adding the feminine touches that turn a house into a home.

'I'd like to work in Australia again,' she said. 'There are some fantastic young directors there now. But it's very hard for actors there, because there's not enough films being made.' It wouldn't be too long before this dream was realized.

Although they had been living under the same roof for the bulk of 1997, Tom and Nicole hadn't been able to spend much time together due to Kubrick's excessive filming demands. When *Eyes Wide Shut* wrapped at the end of January 1998, Tom, feeling exhausted and ill, had hoped to take a break, recuperate and relax with his wife.

But while he had been working hard, Nicole felt she had slipped into a lull and readily accepted a part in a new film. She flew to America at the beginning of January, before Tom had even finished work, to be on standby for shooting *Practical Magic*. Tom instead planned a skiing trip with his brother-in-law Angus, and bought his wife some beautiful Indian jewellery to congratulate her on completing one film and starting another. The family managed to celebrate Conor's third birthday together in modest style with a cake, a movie and dinner.

Before Nicole could immerse herself in her new character, she had health concerns of her own. She had worried about hereditary cancer since her mother's battle with the disease in 1985: 'The memory is still there,' she said, 'and the fear – for her and for me.'

Now, as she suffered increasingly excruciating abdominal pain in February 1998, it seemed her greatest fear could be a real threat. She sought professional advice at the UCLA Medical Center in Los Angeles with Dr Jonathan Berek. After consultation she was booked in for surgery to remove an abnormal growth on her ovary. Although this was considered a minor medical procedure, Nicole was nervous – more about what they might find than the ordeal itself.

The two-hour operation was straightforward and Tom remained by her side throughout, but the worry was not over. The couple stayed in the hospital overnight, anxiously awaiting the pathology results.

After a sleepless night they were reassured by Dr Berek that the cyst was benign; there was no sign of cancer. Nicole was taken out to the car in a wheelchair, where she was snapped by the paparazzi looking weary but relieved. More concerned with the last twenty-four hours than the press, she turned and gave the surgeon a grateful embrace before being taken home by her husband.

Having photographers hassling her at such a testing time was the last thing the actress needed, and Pat Kingsley condemned the behaviour of the press as 'an invasion of privacy'. Besieged by reporters for comments, she later confirmed, 'The operation was entirely successful and Nicole is in the best of health.'

Her wellbeing was naturally at the forefront of Nicole's mind at this time, and it has been suggested that this particular scare prompted her to favour holistic medicine and natural remedies. What is certain is that the couple had quite a shock and despite the strain the last year had put on their marriage, they clearly still needed each other. Tom splashed out on a new private plane, a Gulfstream IV jet complete with a Jacuzzi and cinema, to ensure that they could easily be together wherever they were in the world.

Thankfully now restored to full health, Nicole was ready to commence work on her next film. As she watched her husband notch up hit after hit at the box office, Nicole had become concerned that his career would always eclipse hers.

'He was doing these extraordinary roles and I felt like such a loser,' she said candidly a few years later, reflecting on this period. When asked directly at the time if she felt that her career came second to Tom's in their marriage, she bluntly responded, 'Sometimes, yes. Definitely. But I do it willingly. That's my choice.'

Now her choice was to make a change. Over the last few years she had picked her roles with a keen eye to the overall benefit to her career, and this latest project was no exception. As well as providing some much-needed light relief, after so many supporting roles she was thrilled to be playing one of two strong female leads in the kooky feature *Practical Magic*.

Griffin Dunne had been acting in and producing films since 1975 and was a notable figure in contemporary independent film-making. Although this was only his second turn as director, after *Addicted To Love* the previous year, Nicole was happy to be working with him. It was in fact her co-star, Sandra Bullock, who suggested that Nicole play her wayward sister.

'It's so rare to have two women on film that support each other and love each other,' says Bullock. 'When I read this I said this is a great opportunity to show two women who are completely opposite. When we were deciding who should play the part, I just kept coming up with Nicole.'

Both women are tall and slender, with pale skin and an elongated face framed by long hair: perfectly believable as sisters. 'She's a real head-turner,' says co-star Aidan Quinn of Nicole. 'She walks into a room with a sense of humour and a bounce in her step – and a nice smirk on her lips.'

But, unlike *Batman Forever*, this casting was based on more than looks alone. Given Nicole's tortured performance in *The Portrait Of A Lady*, it might have been hard to envisage her in a light comedic role. 'I knew people would be surprised by seeing Nicole in this,' says Dunne, clearly sold on the idea.

'When I first met her she was wildly funny. I thought, "Nobody has seen Nicole like this!" She's *Aussie*.

'She's just one of these great women and she's always been thought of as very classical and period, and a highly serious, trained actress. She is all that, but she's also hilariously funny so I loved playing with that surprise.' Indeed, Dunne succeeded in projecting Nicole's true personality onscreen. She is funny, sassy, enchanting, compassionate and comfortable with children.

Filming got underway in the early spring of 1998, not in New England but on the opposite coast on the San Juan Islands in Washington State, only narrowly missing the rages of El Niño.

Set in New England in the 1960s, *Practical Magic* is based on Alice Hoffman's novel and follows the doomed love lives of Gillian and Sally Owen. The twist is that the women are witches, haunted by their ancestor's curse that kills any man with whom they fall in love.

The sisters remain close when Sally (Bullock) settles down, happily married with two daughters, while Gillian (Nicole) pursues the wild life – drinking, dancing and smoking. Then she meets Jimmy Angelov. Originally a Texan redneck, Jimmy's character was rewritten as a mysterious Transylvanian when Dunne recruited Croatian Goran Visnjic (*Welcome To Sarajevo*) for the role. As Gillian's relationship intensifies, Sally's world is rocked when her husband falls foul of the Owen curse.

The sisters' psychic link is put to the test when Sally tries to rescue Gillian from Jimmy, who has turned nasty. They pull together in an *Exorcist*-style scene where Gillian is possessed. Nicole handles this departure well, assuming Jimmy's deranged stare.

Practical Magic is a fun fantasy with a dark edge; ultimately it is down to the two actresses to draw the audience into their bewitching world. The deadly mishaps are offset by cute comedy and mischievous magic. A standout scene is saucy Gillian confronting Sally's stuck-up parents group, swivelling her hips and purring, 'I'm back – hang on to your husbands!'

Nicole and Sandra certainly seem affectionate as siblings, drawing from their own strong bonds with Antonia Kidman and Gesine Bullock respectively. 'They had such an innate understanding of what being a sister is,' says Dunne, 'that their chemistry from day one of rehearsals was always there. They just love to play and they'd mix it up and try different things. They had a great rapport. They are very different in background, but somehow they acted like sisters who'd known each other all their lives.'

Curious about the world of witchcraft, the actresses researched the subject and developed a more open-minded view of the ancient art. But their on-set dabbling led to some spooky events. 'We were filming a scene where we have brought a coven together and we had just reached an integral part where the women begin chanting together,' recalls Bullock. 'All of a sudden, the door started slamming. Everyone saw and heard it, but we had no idea how it could be happening.'

The sinister scenes were enhanced by some expensive technical wizardry; much of the $60 million budget was invested in stunning special effects, notably during the exorcism. The mechanics also enabled the six primary female characters to fly off the roof during the bustling Hallowe'en scene – the finances were spared here as they employed more than a hundred locals in home-made costumes.

Relatively new to directing, Griffin Dunne was happy to receive some input from Nicole, who was still recovering from Stanley Kubrick's draining despotism. 'Nicole is constantly pushing a little further and further,' said Dunne. 'She'd just come off *Eyes Wide Shut* so she was used to about seventy or eighty takes. She could still be getting warmed up, whereas Sandy nailed it the first two or three times. It would always be different for each of them.

'One thing they have in common is they react to what they're given and what the moment is – so if Nicole did something different, Sandy would bounce it right back in a completely different way. The further Nicole went, the further it pushed Sandy.'

Shooting was completed in just a few months and the film was released in the autumn of 1998 – in time for Hallowe'en and long before *Eyes Wide Shut* would see the light of day. The film did not fare as well as Warner Brothers had hoped and was only a modest success. This could well be due to the fact that *Practical Magic* was just the latest in a recent line of *Witches Of Eastwick*-style entertainments aimed at teens – *Buffy The Vampire Slayer* (1992), *The Craft* (1996) and the television series *Charmed*, which premiered in October 1998. Although essentially a chick flick, this romantic comedy had a contemporary soundtrack and appealed to adults rather than teenagers. Overall, critics and Nicole's fans were pleased to see her as a feisty main character once more.

During the customary series of interviews to promote *Practical Magic*, reporters used the film's mystical theme as an excuse to quiz Nicole on her religious beliefs. She admitted that she had been exploring Buddhism during her spare time over the last year, but she would always retain her Catholic roots.

'There's a little Buddhism, a little Scientology, I was raised Catholic and a big part of me is still a Catholic girl,' she said. 'There are still things that will stay with me for the rest of my life in relation to my Catholicism,' namely 'the tradition and the ritual'. This was obviously in direct contradiction to Tom's devout beliefs.

Scientology, which had been banned in the 1960s in Nicole Kidman's home country of Australia, was now being attacked in Germany to the extent of attempting to ban performances by followers, including Tom Cruise and John Travolta. Although her husband unwittingly became involved in the scandal, Nicole kept her distance and claimed only limited knowledge of the affair. 'I think it's very odd,' she said. 'One of those things where you just say, "Why?" I think it's upsetting and it's certainly discrimination.'

20

Pure Theatrical Viagra

Since work had begun on *Eyes Wide Shut*, Tom and Nicole had experienced some ups and downs in their marriage. They worked hard. They worked apart. They were stressed. They both suffered illnesses. Consequently, they argued about everyday things, just like any normal couple.

But unlike any normal couple, Cruise and Kidman were household names and their every move was considered newsworthy. Therefore, when a reporter happened to get wind of one such spat it was splashed across the front pages of tabloids all over the world.

Photographer Eric Ford used a modified Radio Shack scanner to illegally eavesdrop on a mobile-telephone conversation between Tom and Nicole. It was taped during a very low point early in 1998, when Nicole was on the set of *Practical Magic*. The argument, if the transcript is to be believed, revolved around Tom always being tired, the gestures they made for each other and spending too much time apart.

'You know exactly what I'm talking about,' she accused.

'No I don't, Nic. Tell me what I haven't done. I didn't go out to the set tonight to see you.'

'Not tonight, Tom. Have you done anything? Have you come out to the set once? OK? Have you sent me a rose? Have you –'

'Have you sent me a rose?' he snapped back. 'I came home with two roses –'

'Did you give me anything? Did you give me a note, did you give me a bunch of flowers?'

'Nic, did I get any flowers when I came back from *Eyes Wide Shut*? I was waiting here, I had the candles lit, I had a bath ready for you.'

'I don't really want this, OK? I don't want to spend my whole dinner break on the phone yelling.'

The conversation incorporated plans for Conor's birthday and Tom's skiing trip with Angus, but finally they resolved matters, making a few jokes and signing off with an 'I love you' each. All very mundane stuff.

Mundane that is, unless your private life is headline news. Ford had managed to sell the scandal to the *Globe* for $2500, and the article printed in June that year claimed Nicole had told Tom their marriage was 'hanging by a thread'.

Pat Kingsley quickly issued a statement, making it clear that the conversation was inaccurate, taken out of context and spliced to sound like an argument.

Nicole was a little more upfront: 'We were fighting about how many people to invite to our son's birthday party and about which one of us was more tired and who was working harder. Quite boring, actually.' Even if the transcript was based on truth, it was a shocking invasion of privacy.

'We've turned the other cheek and held our heads high, but now it's offensive and we're going to sue over it,' said an irate Nicole. But it was not the paper they were suing for publishing the article, but Ford for taping the phone call in the first place.

Ford pleaded guilty to one charge of federal wire-tapping (intercepting and recording a phone conversation) in March 1999. He was sentenced to six months in a correction centre, three years' probation and a $3000 fine. He was the first recipient of such a verdict.

Although the conversation showed their more human side, this was not the type of coverage the Cruises wanted. But if their marriage could survive this sort of attack, surely it could survive anything?

After the latest bad press, Nicole was anxious to improve her image and used the opportunity of refreshed media interest as a sounding board. A new tone of gratitude was added in her bid to appeal to the public.

'My marriage is one thing that brings me total satisfaction,' she said, in complete contrast to the recent tabloid article. 'Now I'm absolutely comfortable being Tom Cruise's wife.

'We've had a wonderful life, an extraordinary life, and we're incredibly privileged to be able to earn money and have these careers. It's all beyond my wildest dreams.'

As always, it was Isabella and Conor who made their parents the happiest. 'We spend as much time with our children as we can,' she said. 'They have totally altered my perspectives. As parents we are offered unconditional love and we take care never to jeopardize that.'

The proud father was also besotted with his young charges. 'Our kids are wonderful,' said Tom, revealing that television was now off limits. 'It's much more fun to read to them. Having two actors as parents has its advantages; Nic and I are able to play all the characters in their books.'

The acting bug did not appear to have bitten the youngsters. 'I don't know if Bella will be an actress,' he continued, 'right now she says she wants to be a bear when she grows up. Conor wants to be a pilot and I've been taking him up with me in my plane since his second birthday.'

One subject the parents had to tackle with their children was their adoption. Drawing on the honesty which had been a constant feature of her own childhood, Nicole told them, 'No, you didn't come from my tummy, but you came from my heart.'

In 1998, her obvious love for children was extended when she became an auntie. When Antonia gave birth to Lucia, incredibly both Nicole and Tom were on the phone throughout the entire labour, offering words of encouragement. Nicole, of course, had only ever witnessed a birth for the sake of her art and had no personal experience, but as the bond between the sisters was so close it was natural that she would want to help.

Tom and Nicole were conscious that their celebrity naturally had repercussions for the kids. 'With famous parents, I think it's going to be a hideous burden for them,' acknowledged Nicole, 'but it's something we're aware of and are helping them to deal with.

'I hated that unconventional stuff because as a kid you want to conform. Now it's happening to me – our kids are already embarrassed by me being an actor. My daughter says to me, "Please don't come in, Mummy" when I drop her off at school.'

Even a simple task such as going to the local shops caused a fuss. 'Tom and I always get recognized in public,' said Nicole, 'although we try not to let it spoil our lives. I go out in sweat pants and a baseball cap, but I always get noticed because I'm 6 feet tall – which tends to give me away. Tom gets it no matter what he does. I say, "Why don't you wear a wig?" And he says, "Then it'll be 'Cruise Caught In A Wig'". So you just pull that base-ball cap down, avert your eyes and hope for the best.'

Nicole was always determined to succeed as a working mother, but sometimes her nomadic lifestyle made it difficult. While she had benefited from a stable upbringing, Tom conversely strived for the security he lacked as a child. It is curious, then, that the couple insisted on moving their children wherever their work dictated, enrolling them in local schools and disrupting their lives. While they undoubtedly provided Isabella and Conor with as much love as was humanly possible, the constant uprooting must have been unsettling.

'I'm always trying to recreate my childhood for Isabella and failing because we're moving all the time,' Nicole confessed. 'I had friends that I'd known since I was four years old, and I have to realize that Isabella isn't going to have that. I can try and make it similar, but it's never going to be the same. And that's sad.'

As hard as it was for the children, Nicole did not find her combined role easy either. 'It's tough being a woman, having kids and working,' she declared, voicing the opinion of women the world over. 'I think it's important to let people know how hard it is for me, because women read these things and think, "My God, *she's* managing to do it all . . ."

'I'm kind of managing, but God, it's exhausting. If one of the kids has a cold and you've got to be up with them in the middle of the night, then get up for work at 6 a.m. the next morning, then that's what you do. You just hope they can put on enough make-up to cover your lines.'

Who would have thought that the glamorous film star ever worried about looking rough? Having established herself as an actress, Nicole now tried to alter the public perception of her as a perfect, unattainable woman. Ultimately, she wanted to assure her audience that if push came to shove, her children came first.

'If it came to a choice between having a career or being a mother, I would give up my career – I wouldn't even think twice about it,' she said. 'I get so much joy out of just lying in bed and reading to my children, seeing their faces light up. That stuff is priceless.

'You can be in the worst mood, having had the worst day. You come home and there's a smiling face painted with cat's whiskers going, "Mummy, look what I made today." It just puts why you're working into perspective.'

So why was Nicole continuing to work? She didn't need the money. She'd made it clear that it put a strain on her marriage and family life. And she had successfully proven herself to be a respectable actress in *To Die For*, *The Portrait Of A Lady* and *Practical Magic*.

'Acting is my passion. It fascinates me. I adore it,' was her concise rebuttal.

More specifically, Nicole was now looking to tread the boards once more. The perfect opportunity came in the form of Sam Mendes' production of *The Blue Room* at the Donmar Warehouse, the cutting-edge London theatre.

'My last play was *Steel Magnolias* in Sydney and I was quite keen to get back onstage. Why would I choose to do a mediocre film role when I could do something like this?' she enthused.

'I think of it as a wonderful experiment,' she continued, excited at the prospect of working in something so different. 'The Donmar is a theatre that says, "We're going to experiment, try something new, take risks." That's what theatre should be about: to push and challenge yourself.'

There was no doubt that this would be a challenge. The play signified a return for Nicole to the world of Arthur Schnitzler, as it was leading British playwright David Hare's adaptation of that author's *La Ronde*. Like Stanley Kubrick, Hare wanted to update the original drama, which had stunned 1920s Vienna, and therefore incorporated Elvis Presley records and modern scenarios. But his greatest modernization was to portray all ten characters with just two actors.

This alone would require dedicated hard work. Not only did Nicole's roles range from teenage prostitute to French au pair, politician's wife, cocaine-sniffing model and domineering stage diva, but she also had to master several accents. Her co-star, Iain Glen, similarly changes from macho cabdriver to naïve student, philandering politician, aristocrat and narcissistic playwright.

To compound matters, Nicole and Glen were forced to become very intimate very quickly, as they rehearsed the saga depicting a daisy chain of sexual couplings bridging class divides.

Both were rarely out of bed, let alone off stage. Discarding their various outfits ten times, their unions were performed in stage blackouts, accompanied by an electric buzzer and a sign displaying each carnal duration – varying from zero minutes for the trigger-happy student excited by the politician's wife to a drug-fuelled two hours and twenty-eight minutes between the politician and model.

Talented director Sam Mendes went to great lengths to ensure that his two actors were comfortable with their radical roles. 'Nic and I had to simulate just about everything,' recalls Glen. 'You have to approach those scenes with real delicacy, and make sure no one is made to do things they don't want to do. You have a rehearsal period to try to get to know each other.

'Sam Mendes got me to massage Nicole's shoulders, and she'd do the same to me. Then, when it came to massaging her shoulders in the play, it didn't seem strange. Nic and I got on very well and we were just really lucky.

'The truth is that you're just trying to do what's required in a scene. And if you need to be very much in love, or in lust with each other, or take your clothes off, that's what you do.'

As challenging as it was for Nicole, she believed the audience would be equally tested. 'I think they will find it very confronting, considering the content of the play. It's very sexual, emotional and right there. We're dealing with desire, obsession, sex and infidelity. It's perhaps what concerns us emotionally for the next century. It's a circle where we move on and see the ghosts people bring from other relationships to their relationships now.'

★

Sam Mendes and Iain Glen were veterans of the stage, but as Nicole had already admitted, she was a little rusty, having only worked on camera with limitless takes for the last decade.

Despite her great enthusiasm, Nicole struggled under the stress of such an exposing play. 'It was a ten-week rehearsal and at around the end of week three, I remember Nic and I looking at each other and admitting that we really didn't know what we were doing,' says Glen. 'We got really down about things – there was this collective moment of doubt, and we decided we had to work extra hard to get things right. Nicole may be a major star but she's just like everyone else, with her own insecurities.'

David Hare witnessed Nicole's gradual transformation. 'At the dress rehearsal of the first preview you could see her technical limitations,' he says. 'Two weeks later, by the time the play opened, they were gone.

'In two weeks she'd learned how to be a stage actress. She absorbs everything and learns very, very fast. You don't see that richness of physical texture in British acting, that incredible amount of brush strokes. There was a famous saying about John Gielgud, that he acted from the neck up. Nicole acts all the way down.' Which was just as well considering how much was on display.

Suffering from a more serious case of stage fright than Glen, Nicole had an alarming last-minute panic attack. 'Before the play opened in London, I freaked out,' she says. 'I phoned my dad in Sydney and said,

"I'm terrified. I have to pull out of the play. I can't play five different characters. There's no way I can learn all the accents. What was I thinking?" He just talked me through it for forty-five minutes.

'I came off the phone, took deep breaths and said, "I can do it."' Revealing that the opening night was a daunting prospect, Nicole kept reminding herself why she accepted the job: 'You never get the chance to play so many varied characters on film.'

Interestingly, money certainly hadn't been a factor in this particular venture. Nicole and Glen were both on Equity minimum – a mere £250 for a demanding eight performances per week.

Overcoming her nerves, Nicole made her West End debut at a preview on Thursday 10 September 1998. It was a relentless one-and-a-half hours. Furthermore, the Donmar is a particularly small theatre, positively tiny. The onstage nudity was rather foisted upon the audience, not least when Glen cartwheeled naked across the stage! Nicole, never one to shy away from showing all on film, hid only her most private parts under a blanket. Theatregoers were rigidly frisked for forbidden cameras – with numerous confiscations.

Nicole became an overnight sensation. The normally reserved British critics fawned over the Australian actress, penning endless lines dripping with praise for her full-on flirtation with nudity. She was described as 'achingly beautiful' and her acting as ripe with 'bravura, skill, real feeling'. Charles Spencer's casual remark in the *Daily Telegraph* that her performance was 'pure theatrical Viagra' has since become legendary.

Whatever the critics' choice of words, it was clear that Nicole had finally, once and for all, proved herself to be more than just a pretty face – she was a genuinely first-rate actress who could deliver the goods. Her accomplishment in *The Blue Room* won her the 1998 *Evening Standard* Theatre Awards' Special Award, and she was nominated for Best Actress at both that event and the 1999 Laurence Olivier Awards. Bringing some much-needed vitality to London's stage, her lead was shortly followed by Kathleen Turner, Jerry Hall, Amanda Donahoe and Linda Grey in *The Graduate* at the Gielgud Theatre. The combination of a respected director, an award-winning thespian, a Hollywood film star and the racy subject matter ensured *The Blue Room* was a sell-out during its run from 23 September to 31 October.

Based once again for a long stretch in England, Tom and Nicole bought a new property, this time a £2 million nine-bedroom Georgian place in Dulwich, South London. It was literally around the corner from Iain Glen, his wife Susannah and their son Finlay, and the two families quickly became close, a friendship which continued after the show finished.

'I met Tom for the first time when he turned up to watch us performing the play at a preview,' recalls Glen. 'He was such an extraordinary bundle of brilliant, positive energy. You couldn't have a more enthusiastic and generous person as a friend.'

And his wife? 'From the moment I met Nic, she struck me as a natural, fun-loving Aussie girl who just happens to be famous. She's one of the funniest people I've ever met, as well as one of the most glamorous. Nic and Tom are wonderful people, very generous and warm.'

Indeed, the alliance led to the couple offering to help raise funds for a full-time cast for Dundee Repertory, the small British theatre whose artistic director is Iain's brother, Hamish Glen.

'If I believed all the cruel gossip about them, then she'd be a cold, porcelain bitch and he'd be a homosexual Scientologist,' observed Iain Glen about his new friends Nicole and Tom. 'This couldn't be further from the truth.

'People think there's something too perfect about them and they're almost too good to be true.' Glen pinpointed the chief reason why the couple were a constant target for attack: jealousy. Sadly, during Nicole's reigning month in the West End, they were the subject of another spurious aspersion about the nature of their marriage.

This time it was London's *Sunday Express Magazine*. Regurgitating and remixing old theories, the article cruelly alleged that Isabella and Conor had been adopted as a 'fashion statement'. Celebrities might be considered by some to be fair game, but their children are surely innocent bystanders. Tom and Nicole were, needless to say, furious.

'This is not OK,' Tom fought back. 'My kids go to school, and they have friends, and things go out on the internet. Stop it. It is not OK.'

Nicole was also concerned about her children hearing such scandal in the playground. 'Rumour becomes truth within twenty-four hours and you start to go, "Hold on, this is a complete and utter lie." We turned the other cheek for so many years,' she said. They were now determined to seek legal proceedings each and every time: 'I tell you, it changes them — they think twice before they go and print some scurrilous gossip.'

Libel damages were awarded against the magazine and its former editor Richard Addis, thought to be in the region of £100,000 each for Tom and Nicole and £150,000 in costs. Present at the High Court hearing, Tom said afterwards that the money would be donated to charity: 'I don't take a lot of pleasure in being here, but it's the last recourse against those that printed vicious lies about me and my family and I have to protect them.' More meaningful to the actor was the public apology agreed to by the paper, admitting that the story was 'entirely false'.

Just one month later, the marriage was again under the microscope. The phenomenal success of *The Blue Room* had secured a transfer to the Cort Theater on Broadway, again for a sell-out run. Because Nicole and Glen flew out to New York alone prior to the opening on 13 December, the tabloids assumed that they were conducting an illicit affair. This common co-stars' curse had notably never befallen Nicole before.

Glen found himself fielding questions about his onstage intimacy with Mrs Cruise. 'Tom and I didn't really have any conversation about the scenes. He didn't say, "Hey, you're kissing my wife",' he told the press, re-iterating that they were all good friends and neither his wife nor Nicole's husband was jealous, or had any reason to be.

With all the extra hype, tickets reportedly changed hands for ten times their face value and Hare's play quickly became the fastest-selling non-musical show on Broadway. During the three-month run in New York, Nicole stayed at Tom's Manhattan apartment, although she complained about the noise: 'I need earplugs to get to sleep.' This lack of relaxation offstage did not help her fend off the flu-like infection she picked up towards the end of February. It was supposedly serious enough that although she continued valiantly onstage, she was being hooked up to an IV drip offstage. Whether or not her illness was that debilitating, she was forced to bow out for the final week of the run, unable to speak.

With *The Blue Room*, Nicole had achieved a personal goal set when she first moved to Hollywood in 1990, albeit a little late: 'Five years from now, when I'm twenty-eight, I hope to have done many more films and also some theatre on Broadway.'

21

Russian Roulette

The Blue Room caused quite a stir and consequently attracted notable figures in its audience on both sides of the Atlantic. 'In London, every single night there would be someone important in the audience,' says Iain Glen. 'And on Broadway it even went up a notch on that. All sorts of directors and actors came to see it.'

'When *The Blue Room* took off it was fantastic. Suddenly all the directors and producers were more interested in working with me,' says Nicole. 'The stuff that seems kind of strange and unusual tends to be the stuff that I do better now.'

Baz Luhrmann was one director bowled over by Nicole's performance when he saw the play in New York. The revolutionary film-maker behind *Strictly Ballroom* and *William Shakespeare's Romeo + Juliet* had the beginnings of a new project in mind. He looked for a leading lady who possessed an old-fashioned, effervescent screen star quality to carry his highly camp comic style, backed by serious dramatic ability to enact the grand tragedy. He contemplated several actresses, including Catherine Zeta Jones, but on seeing his fellow Aussie onstage, he knew she was 'the one'. He decided to approach her.*

'I couldn't get in the stage door for the thronging crowds – there were maybe two hundred people at that stage door,' he recalls. The following day the determined director sent the actress a dozen long-stemmed roses.

Accepting the beautiful flowers, Nicole assumed they were from her husband; it would be another of his typically romantic gestures. Instead, the card from Luhrmann read simply: 'She sings, she dances, she dies. Please meet me.'

'When a man sends you twelve red roses, what are you to do?' asks Nicole. 'I met him. He showed me this incredible book of all the photos and sketches and ideas he had. But there was no script. They were still writing it. Baz didn't need to sell it that much.'

Having followed Luhrmann's career, Nicole was enticed rather than repelled by his experimental style.

'I respond primarily to the director, because cinema is a director's medium,' she explains. 'People like Baz, Jane and Stanley are considered dominant personalities, unyielding in the way they direct. But they're not. I've found that they want actors to contribute. They feed off that. They don't want puppets. And I love being around those minds.' Luhrmann's project would take a while to get off the ground as he still needed to find his hero, but that suited Nicole, who was in dire need of a rest.

On 2 March 1999, Tom and Nicole arrived in Manhattan to view the long-awaited *Eyes Wide Shut*. More than three years after their first contact with the inimitable Stanley Kubrick, they were finally allowed to see the result of their collective labour of love.

At just before midnight, the couple watched the film in a private screening room, accompanied only by two studio bosses. Famously, even the projectionist was required to turn his back.

As the film finished running, Nicole sat staring at the screen in silence, stunned by what she had just seen. 'We had put so much of our life into it,' she explained, 'and to finally watch it, it was just surreal. We watched it again immediately.'

* Interestingly, in 1999 Nicole and Baz Luhrmann were both being chased to star in and direct respectively the film of the musical *Chicago*. Catherine Zeta Jones has since won the role of Velma Kelly, and the film will be directed by Rob Marshall.

Kubrick rose early on 3 March in England, anxious to hear what his protégés thought of the finished product. Having watched the film twice, the Cruises finally left the New York cinema in the early hours of the morning. At about 8.30 a.m. British time, Kubrick was put out of his misery as Tom called from the plane to say they both loved it. Sadly, Nicole had developed laryngitis from her infection during the Broadway run of *The Blue Room* and could not join in the conversation. Hoping to rest for a couple of days, she planned to call Kubrick later that week.

As soon as her voice returned, Nicole called the Kubrick residence, on 7 March. She was devastated to discover that the seventy-year-old director had died during the night. 'I never got to talk to him,' she says.

Still reeling from the shock, the Cruises attended Kubrick's funeral in London on 12 March.

'Making this film remains a great memory for us,' said Nicole at the film's premiere. 'Unfortunately our director is not with us, so that takes a lot of joy out of it. He was like a father to me.'

The buzz of anticipation surrounding the release of *Eyes Wide Shut* increased tenfold after Kubrick's death, as everyone wanted to see the cult director's swansong. But the American censors were still struggling to accept the minute-long panorama of the orgy scene. It was mooted in the press that another director might tinker with the film, executing some minor edits. But the Cruises were not going to allow a soul to tamper with Kubrick's legacy.

'Stanley showed us a final cut five days before he passed away. He wouldn't have shown it to us if he wasn't happy with it,' said an indignant Nicole. Tom backed up his wife, threatening anyone who tried to change things: 'They're going to have to get through me – no one is going to touch it.'

However, in true Kubrick fashion, the late director had foreseen the difficulty. He had realized that if the censors were unrelenting, Warner Brothers would be in an unenviable position. How could they justify releasing such an expensive film with the restrictive NC-17 rating, which many cinemas would not show, many papers would refuse to advertise and many video shops would not stock? As a last resort, Kubrick had devised a way of curtailing the offending scene rather than cutting it altogether, which would have disrupted the flow of Bill Harford's perusal of the mansion. Warner Brothers' Julian Senior remembers Kubrick saying, 'The only way to do it is to cover up the offending images electronically. If Spielberg can do a herd of dinosaurs, we can certainly do that.'

So Kubrick digitally inserted strategic figures to detract from the actors' naked shenanigans. This camera trickery pacified the censors and while the U.K. and the rest of Europe saw Kubrick's original vision, America viewed this technologically sanitized version.

Finally, some four months later, the world premiere of *Eyes Wide Shut* took place on 13 July 1999 in Los Angeles. Tom and Nicole were both present to promote their project.

Nicole looked stunning, if a little nervous, in a two-piece backless vintage trouser suit from Steinberg and Tolkien. Clinging to each other for support, Tom was spotted whispering to his wife more than usual. Nicole later explained, 'I panic in front of the cameras. My hands start shaking and I have trouble breathing. Tom would always whisper to me that everything was all right.'

Try as she might, the actress was unable to hold back, and she shed a few tears for the late director. 'The film, Stanley and the whole thing is so personal to us,' she explained falteringly. 'It's very hard to talk about. I'm usually quite articulate but I find it hard, more than any other film, to talk about in any depth without getting upset.'

Tom was more affected by his parents' reaction. 'When I showed the movie to my mother, she and my stepfather were both shaking,' he said. 'She just hugged me and said how incredible it was, what a moving piece of work it was.'

Proud family members are bound to praise their relatives' work – the real tests were the critics and audience, both equally important.

Speculation surrounding *Eyes Wide Shut* was somewhat misleading – the atmosphere of secrecy surrounding the shoot had led to inaccurate plot leaks, and the outrageous trailer insinuated that it was little short of a private porn flick for Tom and Nicole. The temptation to see Kubrick's final masterpiece while simultaneously peeking into the sex life of such a gorgeous couple proved irresistible, and American audiences swarmed to the cinemas. Unfortunately, when word spread that the film did not live up to these expectations, box-office figures quickly dropped.

Warner Brothers hoped that viewers on the other side of the Atlantic would be more appreciative. On 3 September Tom and Nicole attended the British premiere in London's Leicester Square. Playing to the 5000-strong crowd, the celebrity couple caused their bodyguards to panic as they emerged from the limousine 200 yards from the cinema entrance to walk among their fans, signing autographs, chatting and shaking hands.

Visibly more confident than at the American premiere, Nicole beamed, 'The response has been incredible throughout Europe and we are totally amazed with the response we've got here in London. We believe the film is going to do really well – we can't see why not. It's a great movie.'

Eyes Wide Shut is certainly characteristic of Kubrick's idiosyncratic style: dark, brooding and disturbing. Similarly to *2001: A Space Odyssey*, *Eyes Wide Shut* will never date – the story of Bill Harford's marital dilemma and sexual exploration, eerie music and even the couple's costumes are all timeless. However, the dialogue soon becomes irksome, with its incessant repetition and stilted, lethargic quality. It's all integral to Kubrick's portrayal of Harford's dreamlike state, both real and imagined, but as the film is so long the audience are required by default to be patient.

Regrettably for all involved, the critics were largely unimpressed. 'It's a slow-moving drama that's irritating and exhilarating in turn,' said Jonathan Ross, one of the fairest reviewers. 'There is much to dislike about *Eyes Wide Shut*. The dialogue is stagey. The plot is confused and fails to hook you. The characters are uninteresting and the situations they are placed in are absurd . . .

'It's not a great film, but it's filled with ideas, symbolism and characters, the like of which you see too rarely in the more straightforward movies we've got used to.' Nicole escaped relatively lightly and garnered some of the film's best notices for her portrayal of a bored, sexually adventurous wife.

★

General circulation of *Eyes Wide Shut* brought with it other, fairly inevitable problems for the Cruises. As the rumours had spread during filming, they predictably reappeared with a vengeance on its release.

Further to the suggestion during shooting that the Cruises' marriage had become a 'passionless shell', the American magazine *The Star* now claimed that the loveless couple required coaching from two sex therapists to convincingly perform their steamy scenes. According to the ludicrous article printed on 30 March 1999, Kubrick had insisted on using the services of Wendy and Tony Duffield, at £1250 per day, to instruct the stars, who 'failed to produce any sparks' for the camera.

Although Nicole once said, 'I was willing to do things for Stanley that I won't ever do again', this was not one of those things. Once again, Tom and Nicole were outraged. 'We have two kids who are going to school and coming back with stories,' repeated the exasperated mother. 'For their sake, we have to stand up and say, "This story is a lie." It's as simple as that. Our marriage is fine.'

When *The Star* refused to retract the story, the couple issued a twelve-page lawsuit stating that neither party had ever met or heard of the Duffields, and that the allegation exposed the actors to 'ridicule and derision given that they are married to each other'.

By setting yet another legal action in motion, the Cruises opened themselves up to the possibility of a public court case, scrutinizing every intimate detail of their personal lives. However, as with previous lawsuits, the magazine eventually settled, issuing a full retraction and donating an unspecified sum to charity.

Frustrated and appalled by the relentless bad press, Janelle Kidman stood up for her daughter and son-in-law. 'It's a shame that people say so many bad things about their marriage,' she told the press. 'They're a great couple and wonderful parents. If you get Nicole and Tom telling a story together, you'll laugh until the tears roll down your face.'

As both Tom and Nicole received considerable criticism for their roles in *Eyes Wide Shut*, they looked to other projects to maintain earning power.

Since 1995, Tom's career had gone from strength to strength, and in 1999 he notched up another Oscar nomination, this time for Paul Thomas Anderson's epic *Magnolia*. Furthermore, he was already engrossed in the sequel to *Mission: Impossible*. Tom preferred to play safe and rarely pushed back any boundaries in his career. He tended to stick to the roles he knew best; soldier, lawyer, sportsman, secret agent. As a result, he consistently retained his position as one of the most bankable Hollywood stars, but rarely challenged himself as his wife had done.

Equally, as hard as she might try, the more adventurous Nicole had yet to match the guaranteed financial success of her husband's career.

Filming for the ingeniously titled *Mission: Impossible II* took place in Australia, and Nicole was pleased to relocate her family. 'We have a place in L.A., but home is Sydney, our furniture is in Sydney. I'm very close to my family and we want our kids to have an Australian identity.' Tom too was pleased with the move. 'It's a beautiful place,' he said. 'A lot of people on the set knew Nic from when she was a kid. The only problem was the weather – it rained for twenty-eight days straight.'

Nicole was determined that she would not be separated from her husband, nor he from their children, following the last few demanding years which had placed an enormous strain on their family life. When she was then offered a role in the dark romantic comedy *Birthday Girl*, based in the late Stanley Kubrick's home town of St Albans, England, her resolve was sorely tested.

Careful to look after both her career and her marriage, the actress was willing to accept the part only on the condition that the Roman town was recreated in Australia for the interior shots. British director Jez Butterworth was remarkably amenable, saying, 'You might as well be on the moon when you're shooting on sets,' and was happy to move heaven and earth to accommodate the actress.

'I couldn't believe that they did that,' says an amazed Nicole. 'But it actually worked out for the film because it saved a lot of money, because it is much cheaper to shoot in Australia.'

The story's setting was purely coincidental, but Nicole readily acknowledges the attraction. 'We'd spent six months living in this house just near St Albans and that's partly why I really loved the script when I read it.'

Birthday Girl was a Butterworth family affair: Jez's brothers Steve and Tom were co-producer and screenwriter respectively. Of the five Butterworth siblings only one was a girl, and so the boys shared a room and were rather forced to be close. 'Working with my brothers is everybody's worst nightmare,' says the director, 'but it works because we share a sensibility.' Growing up in St Albans, they were keen to redress the lack of films based in the area. 'England is a little bit ashamed of its Home Counties,' explains Butterworth, 'as if it is embarrassed about everything being a bit middle class. But we love it.'

Fond memories of the town aside, Nicole was also intrigued by the unconventional plot line. Geeky bank clerk John Buckingham is unlucky in love and, resorting to desperate measures, orders a Russian bride from an internet site titled 'From Russia With Love'. John gets more than he bargained for with his beautiful fiancée Nadia. She drinks to the point of vomiting, chain smokes and despite the website's promises, doesn't speak a word of English. John wants to return her, but cannot contact the company. Nadia's two 'cousins', Yuri and Alexei, then descend upon the unsuspecting John and the three wreak havoc as the truth behind their relationship is unveiled. The mild-mannered Brit finds himself caught up in the Russians' dangerous and mysterious world, ultimately torn by love.

Nicole found the prospect of playing Nadia fun – perhaps the part seemed not too dissimilar from the wonderfully wicked Suzanne Stone in *To Die For*. But she was well aware that she was not being offered leads in the obvious blockbusters.

This was only Jez Butterworth's second turn at directing, and he teamed Nicole with an unlikely cast. John was played by Ben Chaplin (*The*

Thin Red Line; yet to appear in *Lost Souls*), still a relatively unknown English sitcom actor. With an Australian in the lead Russian role, it was somewhat unusual then to choose two Frenchmen as her cousins. 'They're best friends, so I was just buying that,' says Butterworth of Vincent Cassel and Mathieu Kassovitz. 'When they show up in the film, I think you do get a sense that they are enjoying performing for one another.' To round off the confusion over continents, the Russian-sounding music is in fact Croatian hip-hop.

Always one to savour a challenge, Nicole was actually a little nervous, as the plot called for her to speak very little English. That did not mean she had few lines, but that many were in Russian. So she took a crash course in the language.

'I had such fun with that role,' she remembers. 'I was in Sydney when I was preparing for the part, so off I went to Bondi, where the Russian community is based. I met this woman in a café there and asked her to teach me Russian. I ended up spending every day with her.

'She was really strict, really tough on me. She would say, "You don't sound like you are from Moscow. You sound like you are from the country." So, she taught me how to speak the language and taught me a lot about Russian culture.

'I thought I was going to be really bad speaking Russian, but I actually fell in love with the language. I was able to improvise in Russian by the end which I was very proud of. I don't mean to sound pretentious but I would love to learn it properly, to be able to perform Chekhov in Russian. Can you imagine actually being able to read Pushkin in Russian?' Most people can't, but Nicole has cited this aspiration since the age of twenty-one.

To give her character a darker and more realistic image, and perhaps distance herself from her natural-looking role in *Eyes Wide Shut*, Nicole dyed her hair dark brown. Her altered appearance enabled her to walk more freely in local shopping malls, particularly during the brief period she spent in Hemel Hempstead, England, shooting the exterior scenes.

Filming soon overran and *Birthday Girl* went over its allotted time scale – not quite to the extent of *Eyes Wide Shut*, although the lasting effect was the same. Nicole was too busy to continue because she was booked to promote her last film and then due on set for her next. When she became available, Vincent Cassel was then tied up, and so on. 'The trouble with actors,' bemoans Butterworth, 'is they go off and do other people's films and you have to wait for them to come back.' Almost a year passed before Butterworth was finally able to finish shooting some troublesome scenes, and then there were a few editing problems. The film was destined not to see the light of day until 2002, some three years later.

As a comparative newcomer to the world of celluloid, Butterworth was thrilled to have landed the Hollywood A-lister in his quirky feature. 'I got Nicole to do it because we sent her the script and she liked it,' he says simply. '*Birthday Girl* was quite hard because you take two characters and push them as far apart as you humanly can halfway through the film, and then attempt to bring them back together in some sort of meaningful way. At the same time it's a trifle, just playfulness really, and it doesn't really want to be massively profound.'

Similarly to *Eyes Wide Shut*, *Birthday Girl* suffered from misrepresentative publicity upon its eventual release. Ben Chaplin described the general scenario thus: 'John's got this really tall, good-looking Russian in his house, and she doesn't speak any English – so they can only communicate physically.' Even though Nadia does discover John's stash of porn, this is not an erotic tale.

Nor is *Birthday Girl* an all-out thriller, as it was plugged by the American distributors Miramax. 'I think that it has some of the shape of a thriller,' ponders Butterworth. 'But what I had in mind was sort of genreless in a way, and that can be absolute hemlock at the box office. To sell a film you need to know what its genre is, and I would feel the same if they'd said it was a romantic comedy. I would say, "No, it's not."'

However, the extended delay, the improbable casting, the thin humour and diverging genres hindered the film's success. Critic Karl Williams offered: 'It feels like a heavily edited, chopped-up affair, as if it has been repeatedly mauled by censors, studio executives, or some other authoritative figure lacking confidence in its quirky tone.' He continued: 'Becoming increasingly absurd and pin-wheeling back and forth between a delightfully larcenous loopiness and unwelcome attempts at evoking real menace, the film stumbles badly in its second half until wrapping up with a botch of an act three that moves the characters woodenly and without much purpose from point A to point B.'

Fortunately for Nicole, two other far more successful projects would be released before *Birthday Girl*, and by then any negative criticism of the latter would be unable to harm her career.

22

Holding Hands And Jumping Off The Cliff

After a brief family holiday in America, Nicole returned to Australia in August 1999 and became totally immersed in her next project. Finally, Baz Luhrmann's incredible scrapbook of photos, sketches and ideas had been transformed into a working script and he was ready to commence creating the exciting *Moulin Rouge!*

The Australian director's previous films are deliberately non-naturalistic. Luhrmann wants the audience to know they're watching a movie and be convincingly caught up in a fantasy world. To this end, each project has its own dramatic device. *Moulin Rouge!* is a musical which combines traditional 'burst into song' moments with well-known lyrics being spoken instead of sung, and challenging new conceptions of classic pop songs ranging from the Police's 'Roxanne' to Madonna's 'Like A Virgin'.

Luhrmann reinvented the myth of Orpheus in the underworld, basing the story in the titular Parisian nightclub at the start of the twentieth century. 'It's a bohemian underworld that really isn't hell, but is where disconnected spirits live,' he explains. 'The Moulin Rouge we've created is not the Moulin Rouge of 1899. It's the Moulin Rouge of our last ten years.'

Nicole plays Satine, the club's all-singing, all-dancing courtesan. 'The Moulin Rouge represents a world which Christian [the protagonist] comes to discover,' she says. 'He wants to be a bohemian; he wants to discover life. So he comes into this world and gets absorbed into this crazy, wild, fantastical atmosphere. And he meets Satine and falls in love with her, and convinces her that it's all right to fall in love with him.

'It's a musical and a love story. The film is comedic, and then it's tragic. It mixes all the different eras. But somehow, because of Baz's sense of humour, he is able to balance it all.'

One of the reasons the film appealed to Nicole was its romance. But who was to play Christian, the confused poet smitten with Satine? Luhrmann chose Scottish actor Ewan McGregor (*Shallow Grave*, *Trainspotting*), fresh from the West End stage where he had recently starred in *Little Malcolm*. 'As far as I was concerned they were both stage actors,' says the director, 'so I was feeling very secure about these two people doing a musical.'

Even though she had sung before in *Wills & Burke* and *Windrider*, not to mention her teenage band, Divine Madness, Nicole was less sure of her ability. 'What Baz wanted was for people to *sing*, and obviously I wasn't going to do the film unless I felt I could sing well enough,' says Nicole. 'I auditioned for him twice, for us to be sure I would be able to do it. The last thing I wanted to do was embarrass myself.'

As with *The Blue Room*, the actress suffered from last-minute nerves. 'I called up Baz before we started and said, "I think you're going to have to recast it because there's no way my voice is going to be good enough, I can't do the role and you've made a big mistake." Luckily, he didn't believe me and he pushed me forward.'

Rehearsals started simply with Nicole and McGregor learning to relax and perform together. 'The first day I met Nicole,' recalls her leading man, 'we were introduced to each other, had a little chat over lunch with Baz, and then did a couple of hours' singing.

'That's a hell of a way to meet someone! But we agreed to allow each other to be as embarrassing as we had to be. We agreed to lose our inhibitions because it's quite an exposing thing to sing when there's two of you and a director in the room.' In Luhrmann's rambling Victorian house in Sydney, he asked Nicole and McGregor to cover Carly Simon's 'Nobody Does It Better' and Cat Stevens's 'Father And Son' respectively. He then requested a duet and as McGregor recalls, 'We realized, that very day, that we sounded nice together. Singing together is a lovely, connecting thing, an emotional thing.'

For the next four months they worked hard on their vocal performances, with the help of voice coach Andrew Ross. 'I had sung at different
times in my life, but I had never tackled it the way we did in this film,'
marvels Nicole. When they felt ready, they went into the recording studio
with Marius de Vries, an experienced producer of Madonna and Tina
Turner, who had collaborated with Luhrmann on *Romeo + Juliet*.

'We made a rule from the beginning,' states de Vries, '[that] Ewan and
Nicole should be singing with their own voices. We didn't want to turn
Nicole into an opera singer; even though some of the cues she sings are
essentially operatic cues, it's still Nicole Kidman's voice, but musicalized.'

'They both had to fight with the challenge of hitting those big notes.
It's a Baz Luhrmann movie, after all, and it wouldn't be complete without at least twenty climaxes of earth-shattering dimensions.' In the same
way that Luhrmann had relaxed the actors during rehearsals, de Vries
approached his brief tentatively. 'I had a piano and a tape recorder, and
it really was like starting from square one. We chose a couple of songs
that had nothing to do with the movie – that old musical standard
"Birds Got To Fly, Fish Got To Swim" from *Showboat* and 10CC's "I'm
Not In Love" – then spent two or three hours working our way through
those.' As Nicole's confidence grew, they started recording the film's
songs, and she actually contributed a couple of tracks to the two ensuing soundtrack albums: a duet with McGregor on 'Come What May' and
a solo number, 'One Day I'll Fly Away', both released as modestly successful singles.

While Nicole was timid, de Vries describes McGregor's enthusiasm as
being like 'a rocket out of a bottle – he was more interested in singing
than he was in acting!' Nicole was also impressed with her co-star and
complimented him frequently. 'He has the most beautiful voice,' she
says, 'it has so much compassion. Every time he sings I fall in love with
him.'

Both Ross and de Vries were pleased with Nicole's singing style.
'Generally, it's very light and pure, but she can also really growl it out,' says
her coach. The producer comments, 'I noticed she had a lovely tone to her
voice. It's a nice voice to listen to, an expressive voice. She can communicate emotion.'

But Nicole lacked the unshakeable confidence she had possessed as a
teenager and was happier incognito. 'I feel really exposed and vulnerable
when I sing,' she admits. 'I find it much easier to sing in character than I
do as myself.

'I found it much easier to play the love story onscreen through song,
because it extends the emotions. It lets you get lost in it – when Ewan was

singing to me, it was like magic. When he sings Elton John's "Your Song", although I've heard him sing it at least 600 times, it evokes an immediate emotional adoration.'

Following an intensive four months of rehearsals, Nicole and McGregor were ready to start filming. 'After a lot of giggling and being embarrassed, we were sucked up into the world of *Moulin Rouge!* where everything is possible,' recalls McGregor. 'By doing all that rehearsing, singing had become second nature. The next thing we knew, we were in tights and dance shoes and it was like being at drama school all over again!'

'Only certain roles require *this* much preparation,' said Nicole a little wearily; she and McGregor also worked intensively with a dance tutor: 'Mr Cha-Cha', she called him. 'I did ballet as a kid, so I had that under my belt. But this was different stuff that I had to learn. It was a lot of work, but a lot of fun.'

After such exhaustive groundwork, spirits were high when filming finally commenced in Sydney's brand-new, state-of-the-art Fox Studio. The first tragedy struck immediately, an ominous portent for a film that was to be plagued with problems.

'My father died on the very first day of shooting,' Luhrmann recalls. 'Dad was sick, and we knew he was going to die at some point, but I was having this out-of-body experience setting up the very first shot. Each of us had some realization that no matter who you are, no matter how many gifts you have, how lucky you are, there are things greater than yourself. And they change.' The timing of Leonard Luhrmann's death from skin cancer hit his son hard.

'I was not in it for the first couple of weeks, but as the film went on, I became more and more alive,' says Luhrmann, who dedicated *Moulin Rouge!* to his father. 'As the film became more intense it brought me back to life.'

So the pressure was on the cast to inject enthusiasm into the movie, and by default, the director. Nicole and McGregor were joined by British actor Jim Broadbent (*Little Voice, Topsy-Turvy*) *Romeo + Juliet* veteran John Leguizamo, Australian actors Richard Roxburgh (*Mission: Impossible II*) and Garry McDonald (*Wills & Burke*), and a large male chorus.

Nicole initially looked to her heroine, Katharine Hepburn, for inspiration to bring the sultry Satine to life, but soon found she had to search elsewhere. 'I had to study Rita Hayworth, Cyd Charisse, Ginger Rogers and Marlene Dietrich,' she says. 'I think those women were just extraordinary.'

The director had previously observed this 'old Hollywood showbiz quality' in the actress during the *Vogue* shoot years earlier. 'She embodies a lot of those classical, iconic Hollywood movie stars of the 1940s and 1950s,' he says, 'and that was a crucial element in making this film because we wanted to reference that. We made the decision that Satine should have the iconic maturity of a Lady Di. That she was a woman at her absolute sexual prime.'

While the leading lady was trying to conjure up her own sophisticated aura, co-star McGregor uncovered the true Nicole. 'She's one of those actresses whom you're slightly in awe of,' he says. 'You imagine her as the movie star from the front covers of magazines, that she's untouchable and that somehow gets in the way of her being human and funny.

'But she really is good fun. You meet her and discover she's just funny and girly. She's really giggly and you can make her laugh – a lot! I'd be very rude in front of her, swear and belch, and she'd say, "Ew-*an!*" – like a big sister with her younger brother.'

Luhrmann too was enchanted by Nicole's humour and noted how she had always tried to incorporate this virtue in her public image. He now recalls how astute she was, almost a decade earlier, choosing to be pictured as Lucille Ball for *Vogue*. 'I remember my first impression was how Australian she was. She has this really, really loud, hacking laugh. She was like so many of the girls I knew growing up – so crazy, so noisy. I say noisy because I remember she was eating and suddenly, "Yaaa!" She let out a big scream. I thought, "My God, one day someone's got to release that incredible vitality and that crazy comic energy of hers into a film."'

Unlike previous roles where she would not allow herself to step out of character, Nicole obviously enjoyed the merriment in between takes. 'We had so much fun,' she recalls of McGregor. 'From the minute we met we just hit it off. He is so genuine; he's Scottish, a no-bullshit guy. It was very easy to work with someone like that. He's got one of the best laughs.' The ability to tickle her funny bone was something she always looked for in her friends. As Luhrmann became more involved in directing, Nicole remembers that he would jokingly taunt her, 'Come on, you old hoofer! Show us what you're made of!'

Of course, there was a serious side to proceedings: after all, they were there to work. 'Emotionally, I was always fighting for the love story, to keep it real,' stresses Nicole. 'I kept saying that the simplicity of the love story, the belief that these two people love each other in an extreme way – if you don't have that, then it becomes a spectacle with no heart.'

But her co-star was always on hand to put Nicole in her place.

'At one point, we were discussing the romance and the script and I said, "What you've got to remember, always, is that she is just a skanky old whore,"' reveals McGregor. 'That was an interesting moment, because I didn't know how that would go down . . . But it went down very funnily, so I would remind her about being a skanky old whore constantly.'

As the film is a deliberate mish-mash of the last century, Luhrmann was liberal with the cultural references. 'We were never told, "You can't move that way, you can't say that,"' recalls Nicole. 'We used things from all different periods. We were taking all sorts of things and playing with them and twisting them.' The film drew from all aspects of twentieth-century culture and the soundtrack incorporated Marilyn Monroe, Nirvana, David Bowie, Fatboy Slim and Elton John.

After all her concerns about the prospect of singing, Nicole would claim surprisingly that she found it easier than acting, which had been like second nature to her for some eighteen years. It wasn't all plain sailing though, as the enormity of the project dawned on them all. 'Unlike me, Ewan is an easy, natural singer, and so is Nicole, although she wasn't as confident,' says Jim Broadbent. 'From time to time we'd worry and fret over what we'd let ourselves in for, because it was clear from the start that this was going to be no ordinary film.'

Back in the restrictive bodices last worn in *The Portrait of A Lady*, this time Nicole was expected to be active. 'I was doing things in a corset that no woman would ever have done in the 1890s,' she grimaces. 'You are not meant to dance in corsets. All the dancers were complaining about how you couldn't move in them, but Baz would want you crawling on the floor, throwing yourself on the ground.

'Baz wanted some of my gawkiness to come through a little, in terms of the physical comedy. He just liked the juxtaposition of these long arms and legs that I have, which sometimes I'm a bit awkward and clumsy with. He would just draw this gawkiness out of me, even though I was in 4-inch heels and corsets.'

Always in pursuit of physical extremes, Nicole had been thwarted by the insurance-wary businessmen at Fox Studios – they vetoed her request to go skydiving during filming breaks. Instead, the actress took it upon herself to perform her own daredevil stunts. 'I did all the trapeze work myself,' she says proudly. 'I didn't want anyone else doing my stunts and I loved the trapeze. I was 70 feet up in the air, with men in top hats down below, for two days. It was such fun!'

'She is so blasé,' retorts Luhrmann of Nicole's bravado. 'She didn't mention the fact that she had to be trained by circus people to get up there. I said, "No, I'll have the body double," and she said, "I don't think so."' Swinging freely at the top of the set, Nicole's penchant for aerobatics undoubtedly helped.

Her feet were barely back on firm ground when she suffered not one, but two major accidents. 'It was a shock because I got it from doing a lot of ballet lifts,' she says of the rib she snapped. 'I was taking all the pressure on my ribs and I was being thrown and caught over and over again, over a period of a couple of months. I kept dancing – I didn't know I had broken it for five days, I thought I'd pulled a muscle. I went to the doctor and he said women have a higher tolerance for pain. It wasn't really a break – a small crack is the way they described it.'

Luhrmann wasn't taking anything lightly, no matter how small the crack. 'We shut down for two weeks,' says the director. 'The expert said, "It's really good to put her in a corset, to strap a broken rib." So we put her in a corset and then – Boom! Click! – we broke her rib the second time. So we lost another two weeks.'

'I had never broken a bone before so it was a bit of a shock,' says the actress. 'I'm physically more fragile than I thought. I often think I am a lot stronger than I really am.' With the schedule now running four weeks late, the intensity increased.

Nicole describes her daily routine: 'I'd get up at five and do a little yoga, and then a twenty-minute dance warm-up. Then, at about six, I'd go into the make-up chair for an hour and a half, then the hair chair for another hour and a half. So you're looking at three hours before you've even got to the set. Then you go into the trailer and get harnessed into this corset, which takes twenty minutes.' This is all before acting, singing and dancing for a full day.

'I've never been so exhausted, yet so satiated at the same time,' she continues. 'We were working really long hours to get the film made in the amount of time and with the amount of money that we had to do it. I was pushing myself beyond what I would probably be willing to ever do again because it was so much fun and because we believed in it.'

When she wasn't working, Nicole spent much of her time looking after her children, who often accompanied her on the set. 'I would go back to the trailer still in costume to make sure the homework was being done,' she says. 'Then I'd be doing grade-one reading for twenty minutes, and then back on the set.' Nicole jokes that Isabella and Conor improved their maths by betting and playing poker with the crew.

'My dad said one of the best images he had was when he came to visit on the set and I was in the van, cooking dinner for the kids in 4-inch stilettos, a corset, fishnet stockings, long red hair and a top hat. And the kids didn't seem to think there was anything strange about it.' The trailer was littered with dozens of family photographs and drawings from the children so that Nicole wouldn't feel lonely when Isabella and Conor were away.

As the crew were happy to entertain the children (albeit by engaging dubiously in gambling), it reinforces the feeling that despite, or even because of, all the problems, Luhrmann created one big happy family. 'We had a real ball making this film,' confirms McGregor, 'and being stranded in Australia for a year was great, especially with a Harley Davidson and a tent and a few days to disappear into the outback.'

Nicole agrees, 'On the weekends we'd still hang out together. We formed really solid, lifetime friendships.' There were reports of at least two weekend-long parties, inspired by the bohemian decadence and potent absinthe. McGregor says that, ever the perfectionist, Luhrmann designed these gatherings 'like effing big production numbers'. After one such party, Nicole could just about remember having danced on tables, while McGregor reportedly suffered blurred vision for much of the next day!

'Nicole, Ewan and I made a good team and we spent a lot of time socializing,' recalls Broadbent. One particular festivity stands out in his mind. 'The studio threw a Christmas party while we were making *Moulin Rouge!* and they put together a fifteen-minute trailer for us to see how it was turning out. That was when it really hit us how unconventional it was going to be.'

If the cast were surprised by the direction of the film, what on earth would an outsider make of it? Luhrmann recalls Tom Cruise's first re-action to seeing early footage. 'He said, "My God, the ambition in this film." And what he was really saying was, "The *risk* in this film." And you know, no one shied away from that.'

Although the film's actors worked for Equity's minimum wage (presumably in return for a cut of the profits), *Moulin Rouge!* still managed to run up a bill of some $52.5 million. A portion of the budget was lavished on the exquisite diamond necklace worn by Nicole. Believed to be the most valuable piece of jewellery ever commissioned for a film, the necklace, named 'Satine', comprised 1308 diamonds, totalling an impressive 134 carats.

When she fell in love with the one-off design, Luhrmann said Nicole could keep it. The actress decreed this extravagance too much, and suggested auctioning it off at Christie's and donating the money to charity. Expected to raise approximately $1 million, the necklace was withdrawn by its creator, Stefano Cantur, just hours before bidding began. A spokesperson said: 'Stefano realized he didn't want to part with the piece. He loves it so much he's decided to keep it as part of his personal collection.'

Aside from the jewellery, the set and the costumes, it was the delays that caused the budget to reach such a high figure. In the final fortnight of filming, Nicole sustained another injury, one which the production could ill afford.

'We had three days to shoot one particular scene, so we were shooting seventeen hours a day. It was about one in the morning, and we have to get the shot, and I said, "Yeah, yeah, yeah. We can do it,"' she says.

'I was in these huge heels and I fell down the stairs and tore the cartilage behind my kneecap. It was a painful injury.' With time constraints looming, Nicole forced herself to work through the pain. 'I was an idiot,' she admits. 'I danced on it for two weeks after the injury because we had to finish the film. I'm Catholic, but I have this Protestant work ethic where I cannot say no. I hate to chuck a sickie.' Struggling on like a martyr, she was aided by heavy-duty painkillers, a wheelchair, crutches, and as much rest as possible. 'I felt like one of those Olympic athletes, who goes, "Pain doesn't matter, I'm going to push through".'

Despite her best efforts, as the shoot had dragged on almost seven weeks longer than scheduled, Fox Studios were forced to evict the *Moulin Rouge!* team to make way for an important prior booking in June 2000.

'I couldn't finish the film at that time,' explains Luhrmann. 'We shut down as *Star Wars* had to come into Fox Studios. In the film there's a song about how the show must go on; and there certainly was a bit of a "show must go on" mentality with us.'

Not only did the studios have to make way for their pressing project, the actors too were booked up. Nicole was due shortly in Spain to start work on her next film, before which she had to squeeze in a few scenes to complete *Birthday Girl* with the ever-patient Jez Butterworth. Ewan McGregor was distraught: having left the lavish sets of *Moulin Rouge!* unfinished in May, the following month he had to return to the very same studio to start work on *Star Wars: Episode II* in front of a boringly blank, blue screen. 'It was rather a cruel blow,' he says, 'I wasn't really ready to go on to that.'

Although physically and mentally drained, Nicole was pleased to have accomplished such a fabulous film with one of her favourite directors. 'I love working with directors who have a particular style,' she says. 'The more controversial the film, the better it is. You want to be challenged as an actor, and it's so gratifying working on something you believe in. Working with Baz was like holding hands and jumping off the cliff together. He is completely spontaneous.

'I remember finishing the film being more exhausted than I've ever been in my life. Creatively, I didn't want to make a movie again after I'd finished this one.' The final statement proved an impossible one for the ambitious actress to uphold.

23

Reality Is Not Quite What It Seems

Since appearing in *The Blue Room* in 1998, Nicole had worked herself into illness twice, with barely two months' break between three lengthy projects. She had hardly experienced the luxury of a social life during 1999.

The end of the year saw the regular Christmas festivities and the much-anticipated Millennium Eve. Considering Australia to be her real home, Nicole was thrilled to celebrate a poignant time with family and friends in Sydney. Antonia, Angus and Lucia Hawley were naturally involved, as were Antony and Janelle, and the guests were Iain, Susannah and Finlay Glen.

As Glen said, 'There is not a week that goes by when Nic and I aren't on the phone to each other,' so the invitation was not out of the blue. The Glens had already stayed with their friends in America, but he noted, 'Neither Nicole nor Tom operate greatly in Los Angeles – they like to vanish for a lot of time in Australia.'

Making the most of an unusually overcast day, they enjoyed some time on the beach, undisturbed as the weather kept the sun-loving locals at bay. The group then headed off on the Cruises' 50-foot cruiser, armed with a picnic. Tom and Nicole were torn between celebrating the end of the millennium on their yacht and renting out the swanky Café Sydney at Circular Quay. Either way, they were guaranteed prime seats at the spectacular fireworks display over the harbour, and were among the first to see in the new century due to Australia's time zone.

Being so close to the family, Glen witnessed the regular ups and downs they experienced. 'People have this obsession that it can't be that good between Tom and Nicole,' he said. 'Well, they're right – it's not that good. They argue all the time, they have terrible fights. They hate each other, they love each other; they're human beings. At times they've said to one another, "I never want to see you again." But they still adore each other.'

Nicole's circle of friends remained small but diverse. 'I'm still in contact with lots of the people I grew up with,' she said. 'They come from all walks of life and I know them inside out.' This original Aussie set consisted of Naomi Watts, Rebecca Rigg and Russell Crowe, while her American network included Sarah Jessica Parker and her husband Matthew Broderick, and the Europeans were actresses Juliette Binoche, Kate Winslet and Emma Thompson.

'We hang out a lot,' explained Watts, 'going to movies, shopping or gossiping. Nicole might have a fabulous lifestyle – which she's worked for – but she's stayed true to herself. This is why she's so popular. Most important of all, she never forgets her friends.' Nicole added, 'I am pretty emotional. Highly strung but incredibly loyal. I like to have fun: I love to dance, I like to drink, I like to party.'

In 2000, Nicole displayed an active interest in politics. With Tom, she donated funds to Hillary Rodham Clinton's U.S. Senate campaign and used the experience as an opportunity to pay her respects to Eleanor Roosevelt.

'She was extremely dignified,' said Nicole. 'She used her position to help the poor and to pave the way for people like Hillary Clinton, whom I also admire. Another extraordinary, brave woman is Aung San Suu Kyi, the Burmese leader. She is waging a peaceful protest against her government and basically giving up her whole life for what she believes in. Not enough people know about her.'

March 2000 brought a very special occasion for the woman she held in the highest regard: Janelle Kidman celebrated her sixtieth birthday. Accompanied by Peter Crone, as Tom was tied up in America, Nicole joined the family gathering at trendy Prunier's Chiswick Gardens restaurant in the upmarket suburb of Woollahra. 'I gave a speech where I said, "You're the heart and soul of our family,"' remembered Nicole fondly.

Antonia was pregnant for the second time (a son, Hamish, would be born that autumn), but Janelle rightly stole the show, looking every bit the celebrity mum in a floral dress with a hot-pink feather boa.

It was Antony's turn to shine seven months later. The Kidmans brimmed with pride when the 2000 Olympics were held in Sydney, particularly as Nicole had actively supported the campaign. She had been offered the honour of carrying the torch to the celebrations, but sadly was just too busy to accept. Keeping it in the family, her father instead took her place, accepting the torch from Paralympian Louise Sauvage.

When filming finished on *Moulin Rouge!* in May 2000, Nicole returned briefly to work on *Birthday Girl*, before flying to Spain to start her next film at the end of August. In the interim she was supposed to have rested her damaged knee, but despite undergoing physiotherapy, she still required a small operation. On landing in Santander, she hobbled off the plane supported by Tom and a pair of crutches, her knee yet to heal completely.

It was Nicole's insatiable desire to try something new and work with another experimental film-maker that encouraged her to put her career before her health. Curiously, the story starts with her husband and culminates in his next project.

Tom had for some time been a fan of Alejandro Amenábar, the twenty-seven-year-old Chilean director of *Tesis* (*Thesis*) and *Abre Los Ojos* (*Open Your Eyes*). Cruise was so enthusiastic about the latter that he was preparing to star in the American remake. Although he had already booked Cameron Crowe to direct that film, Tom was still keen to work with Amenábar and approached him about his latest work.

Amenábar had originally conceived *The Others* as another film for his native Spain, written in his own language. With pressure from his backers to pander to unexpected Hollywood interest, he hastily retailored the story for the English-speaking market, moving the setting to the Channel Islands at the end of the Second World War. Tom jumped on board as executive producer and Nicole signed up for the powerful leading role of Grace.

So, what was to be Amenábar's first English-language film suddenly acquired the kudos of two A-list celebrities. 'When you shoot a film in English you have a much more open market,' acknowledges the director. 'And when Tom Cruise and Nicole Kidman got involved, I knew that the destiny of the film was changing. It felt very weird.' Amenábar

Tom finds it hard to concentrate at the 1996 Wimbledon Tennis Championships. 'Every day I am with her, I still have this magnetic attraction to her – I can't keep my hands off her,' he said that year.

Visibly shaken, Tom and Nicole attend the funeral of Diana, Princess of Wales at Westminster Abbey on 6 September 1997.

During their extended stay in England filming *Eyes Wide Shut* in 1997, the Cruises became anonymous joggers in their local park.

Left: The Cruises' mansion in Pacific Palisades, Los Angeles. Nicole was overheard describing it as an 'ugly fortress'.

Below left and right: The houses in Sydney, Australia, and Hertford-shire, England.

The mountaintop ranch in Telluride, Colorado.

One of the Cruises' many London residences over the years.

Top: The Cruises lose their inhibitions for Stanley Kubrick's exploratory *Eyes Wide Shut.*

Centre: Relaxing in between takes with Kubrick.

Above: Promoting *Eyes Wide Shut* in Paris, 1999.

Nicole and Iain Glen took *The Blue Room* to Broadway in December 1998.

Top: Nicole as the doomed courtesan Satine in *Moulin Rouge!* 'I didn't want anyone else doing my stunts – I loved the trapeze,' she says.

Above left: With *Moulin Rouge!* director Baz Luhrmann at the 2001 Cannes Film Festival.

Above: Nicole gave a striking performance as Grace in *The Others,* alongside her screen children Alakina Mann (Anne) and James Bentley (Nicholas).

Left: Nicole's date for the Australian premiere of *The Others* was seven-year-old Nicholas Powell.

Opposite: The changing face of Nicole Kidman.

Above: Letting her hair down with Fatboy Slim at the *Moulin Rouge!* party at Cannes, 2001.

Right: After her traumatic separation from Tom Cruise in February 2001, Nicole was supported by her best friends, Rebecca Rigg (*left*) and Naomi Watts (*right*).

Below: Emerging from her lawyer's offices on 8 August 2001 having signed the divorce papers, Nicole let out a piercing scream of relief.

Since her separation from Tom, Nicole has been linked with Ewan McGregor (*top left*), Peter Crone (*top right*), Iain Glen (*above left*), and Russell Crowe (*above right*).

Right: Tom and Penélope Cruz make their first public appearance together at the August 2001 premiere of *Captain Corelli's Mandolin.*

Above left: Proud parents Antony and Janelle Kidman at the Australian premiere of *The Others*.

Above right: Antonia Kidman is a television celebrity in her own right and is married to entrepreneur Angus Hawley.

Left: 'We're almost like twins,' says Nicole of her special relationship with her sister Antonia.

'My mother gave me the inspiration to do what I wanted with my life.'

was clearly trying to reconcile the financial potential of a blockbuster with his roots as an artistic director, and in Nicole he had the perfect star.

'I make a movie because my gut wants me to make that movie,' she says plainly. 'I never make a movie because I think it's going to make money.' This statement can be verified by any of Nicole's career choices since *To Die For* and was certainly the case here. Her motives lay in the fact that she had 'never made a film in this genre before, and I think Alejandro is one of the best directors'.

The Others is essentially a ghost story about a mother and her two children – the father of the family has been missing since the end of the war a few months previously. The children, a boy and a girl of strikingly similar ages to Isabella and Conor, are allergic to sunlight and therefore precautions are taken to maintain total darkness in the house. The little girl, Anne, thinks she can see ghosts, but when Grace hires three housekeepers, the truth about her child's visions slowly unravels.

Nicole was initially attracted to the role because there was a strong religious theme, alongside a mother's potent need to protect her children. But the more she thought about it, the similarities between fact and fiction began to blur. For the third time in recent years, the actress experienced severe cold feet during pre-production.

'Beforehand, I didn't want to do it,' she says. 'I arrived on set in Spain a week early, sat down, re-read the script and realized what I was up against. I really tried to get out of that movie, I even drew up a list of other actresses who could do it. Every part of me, every cell in my body said no. I couldn't sleep. I was terrified, I thought my kids wouldn't forgive me, that it was a sin to be doing it.

'It was the most extreme reaction I've ever had. For *The Blue Room*, I just had a fear of doing theatre and different accents. But this was a physical reaction against the themes of the film.' As with *The Portrait Of A Lady* years earlier, it was Nicole's passion (this time to get out of the film) that persuaded the director that she was the perfect Grace. Nicole had worked herself into the right mental state to play an exhausted mother on the verge of a breakdown.

'I slept very little through the whole film,' she says, 'and it worked because if you deprive yourself of sleep you exist in an altered state where your emotions become more facile, everything is slightly heightened. I existed on four hours' sleep a night. It was good because the mother that I was playing would not have been a big sleeper. She was waking with these nightmares, screaming.

'It's also about Grace's obsessional love for these children and how her life is driven by her desperate need to protect them. I really felt for her, and said to Alejandro, "This mother must not be judged severely. She must not be a shrew." I wanted her to be someone you can feel for, because everything comes from her desire to be a good mother.'

The director elaborates how deeply Nicole became involved: 'She insisted, and I thought she was right, that she performed the character from the inside, from her heart. It must have been hard for her. She has children. When the character went into hell, she also went into hell. Once, she said, "I bled for this film," and I can believe it. As a director, the best I could do was support her. And I tried to give her freedom to create the character, and to make Grace hers.'

While Nicole concerned herself with the development of the main character, Amenábar concentrated on drawing out the tension to create a chilling movie. 'It was truly a pleasure to work with such an imaginative and original talent,' marvels Nicole. 'He has an incredible ability to build true suspense, which comes from the heart and mind, from the inside, rather than the outside. He's not afraid to go to the very darkest places, and he gave me courage to go there with him as Grace slowly begins to accept that reality is not quite what she thinks.' From the opening scene where Nicole lets out a bloodcurdling scream, the audience are left unsettled, unsure when or where the next surprise will occur.

The director credits his leading lady with much of the edginess. 'What captured me completely about Nicole was her stare,' he says. 'Much of the terror created in the film takes place in her eyes. They're better than any special effects money can buy.' Nicole found this pressure a little daunting, but handled it well. 'I had to modulate the whole performance. Playing fear onscreen is actually much harder than people think. To make it believable you have to generate all that energy in your body, and after a while, it's exhausting. I think it also affects you subconsciously in a way. It affects the way you dream – your whole psyche.'

Like many classic thrillers, *The Others* prefers to let the audience do the thinking, rather than create a scary monster that will frighten only a minority. This approach appealed to Nicole, who divulges, 'I love to be scared! I like to have a strong reaction to a movie. I like to go in there and get my money's worth.'

Although far from an erotic movie, when the main actress is as beautiful as Nicole, it seems a shame not to take advantage of her looks. So the director discovered a very subtle way of pleasing the audience. 'We decided to put her hair under a [short] blonde wig, and there was her neck – with her long hair you don't usually see it, but people have found it to be a very sensual neck.'

Accompanied by Isabella and Conor for the duration of her stay in Spain, Nicole uprooted their comparatively stable lives in Australia. 'We always put them in the local schools,' she reiterated, 'and they'll go to a local school in Madrid. They know that their home is wherever we go. Neither of them is really shy, which is lucky, since I get antsy if I'm in one place for too long.'

The actress strove to portray the undeniable connection she shared with her children in front of the camera. 'You really need to see that the film is generated by Grace's love for her children,' she explained. 'I loved working with the child actors – there's something about the energy that kids bring to films, but for the adult actors having youngsters around makes them work harder.

'When you're working with kids, you realize they don't even understand "Action", they don't even understand "Take two". Everything has to be taught to them in the beginning, and you are responsible for that. I enjoyed seeing the whole process of film-making through their eyes.'

Although Isabella and Conor had not previously displayed any interest in becoming actors, when they saw two children of the same age appearing as their mother's offspring, they began to complain. 'My kids are always asking to be in films, especially after I made *The Others* with two child actors,' said Nicole wearily. 'Tom and I agree that it's not beneficial for our kids to be in the movies. At eighteen we'll see, but now they are not getting any help in that respect from us.'

Although it was supposed to be set in Jersey, *The Others* was shot in Madrid and the northern coastal resort of Santander. While filming spanned just ten weeks commencing at the end of September 2000, unlike *Moulin Rouge!*, Nicole found it gruelling rather than enjoyable. Indeed, Nicole's only light relief during these depressing few months was attending a football match with her husband at Madrid's Bernabeu Stadium.

As the golden Hollywood couple approached their tenth wedding anniversary, journalists looked to them for quotes about their hopes and dreams. With several of their contemporaries going through head-line-grabbing break-ups (Dennis Quaid and Meg Ryan, Kim Basinger and Alec Baldwin, Demi Moore and Bruce Willis, Liz Hurley and Hugh Grant, to name but a few), Tom and Nicole's partnership was hailed as 'the Holy Grail of marriages' and Nicole was asked the secret of their success.

In a frank interview with *Woman's Day*, Nicole told the world that her marriage was as strong as ever, but not without effort. 'Living with somebody requires a lot of understanding,' she explained, 'but I love being married. I just feel so fortunate that I have found someone who'll put up with me and stay with me. I believe we've really evolved together as people and we're very secure in our relationship.

'Sometimes we have huge fights because we're both quite volatile and passionate, but ultimately we're incredibly supportive of each other. I find it fantastic to know that whatever happens, I have my friend and lover on this path with me.

'Of course, our relationship isn't perfect. Anyone in a successful marriage understands the necessity of compromise.'

There she wandered off the point somewhat – it was almost as if she was discussing the situation with herself, justifying the occasional small spats. 'Sometimes at night I want the comforter pulled up and Tom wants it off – little things like that. I've heard marriages can break up over whether someone puts the cap back on the toothpaste or not, which seems vaguely ludicrous. But we're really happily married.'

Nicole concluded by stating that her marriage remained the most stable thing in her life. Tom too confirmed that their relationship was unwavering. 'We've been married for ten years now and it just keeps getting better,' he said. 'We talk a lot, we share things – simple as that. I'm looking forward to growing old with her so we can sit on rocking chairs on the porch together, look back over our lives and say, "Wow, we did all that."'

After a hectic couple of years, Nicole appeared more conscious than ever of the effects of excessive dedication to one's career. 'I work now only if I really feel it's worth it,' she said. 'Distance destroys relationships and families. It just does. Even if you have a really strong love, it can be destroyed in time.

'All I can say is that I hope we're together when we're eighty. I can't say we will be, but I will be so devastated if we're not.'

★

While Nicole worked on Amenábar's *The Others*, Tom had pushed ahead with his remake of *Open Your Eyes*. Co-produced by the actor, the psychological thriller acquired the title *Vanilla Sky* – this had been discarded from director Cameron Crowe's previous film, *Almost Famous*, for which he won an Oscar for Best Original Screenplay. In a startling departure from his standard action-hero roles, Tom stars in this confused tale as a womanizing playboy whose life is turned upside down after a horrific car crash. He appears opposite Spanish leading lady Penélope Cruz, who played the same role in both this version and the original, and the comedy actress Cameron Diaz as his suicidal ex-girlfriend.

Spending a short while in Spain with his wife and children, Tom moved to New York to begin filming in November 2000 and stayed there until the following spring. Working closely with two gorgeous pin-ups incited the inevitable 'more than just co-stars' rumours. However, Cruise was never linked to Diaz – only Cruz. It was insinuated that the pair were having an affair, simultaneously falling in love on and offscreen. Although Tom famously described Penélope as 'simply irresistible', official press statements were adamant that the two were merely colleagues.

The foreign actress offered a plausible explanation for the mix-up. 'The actors I work with are great men – very talented, very handsome,' said Penélope. 'Yet it is always reported that I'm involved with them. I say nice things about them and because my English is not as good as it should be, the translation sometimes means that I love them. But they are like my brothers.'

Far away in Spain, Nicole must have been exposed to constant tabloid gossip about the country's top actress and her husband. However reassuring Tom might have been on the phone, things had been strained between them for some time. The various illnesses, enforced separations, invasive media speculation, career rivalry and balancing work with parenthood were a distressing combination at the best of times – and this latest saga wasn't helping matters.

Tom and Nicole tried to make the most of their tenth wedding anniversary on 24 December 2000. They celebrated with a small party for their close friends before heading off to Las Vegas for a Christmas and New Year break. There, the adrenalin fanatics were seen experiencing the rush of the world's highest thrill ride, the Stratosphere Big Shot.

After this brief respite, a weary Nicole limped back on to a film set – this time for *Panic Room*, directed by David Fincher.

Starting out directing music videos and television commercials, Fincher had only a few film credits to his name, including the disappointing *Alien 3*. After impressing critics with his slick crime thriller *Se7en*, he was hailed as one of Hollywood's most compelling new talents. Despite the subsequent lack of interest in *The Game* and polarized opinion on the overly stylized *Fight Club*, expectations remained high for this next release.

Panic Room's innovative plot sees Meg Altman, a divorced mother, trying to protect her daughter, Sarah, from three burglars. Meg and Sarah are sealed in the vault-like 'panic room' – the intruders' target destination. With her diabetic daughter's health her primary concern, Meg plays an intricate battle of wits through to the film's dramatic end. Always interested in attempting new genres, particularly with maverick directors, Nicole jumped at the chance to play Meg in this uneasy suspense flick.

Catastrophically, the combination of the demanding action scenes and the relentless pace at which she had been working for the past two years proved too much. Having not allowed her knee (first injured in *Moulin Rouge!*) to heal properly, disaster struck eighteen days into filming .

'She was running up steps when she screamed: "Ouch!"' recalls Fincher. 'Her doctor said it was a hairline fracture.' Nicole was unable to continue acting through the pain and by the end of January was forced to admit her limitations.

'I was devastated when I had to pull out of *Panic Room*,' says the actress. 'We had talked for months about it, and done three weeks of shooting, but I was a wreck. I always think I can overcome my weaknesses, but physically I'm fragile.'

Nicole was replaced by Jodie Foster, although rumour has it she contributed an uncredited voice-only telephone cameo as Meg's ex-husband's girlfriend. *Panic Room* went on to receive critical acclaim when it was released the following year, consolidating Fincher's reputation and marking Foster's return to the big screen after a few years behind the camera.

Nicole was disheartened at having to sacrifice the role and furious with herself for getting into such a poor physical state. According to some sources, she became quite bitter about the situation and her husband had to deal with that. Reminiscent of the period when she was filming *The Portrait Of A Lady*, it was reported that Tom found it quite difficult to live with the overworked actress.

On 23 January 2001 Nicole was obliged to attend an industry function. She had been invited to present the award for the Best Actor – Comedy Or Musical at the twenty-first Golden Globes, while Tom was asked to announce the winner of the Best Supporting Actress category.

The pair usually presented a united front for the press, so it was surprising to see Nicole sitting with her father instead of her husband during the ceremony. As award presenters they were duly photographed with their respective recipients, rather than each other: Tom accordingly smiled for the cameras alongside Kate Hudson and Nicole was reunited with old pal George Clooney. The Cruises appeared distant throughout the event and seemed to spend much of the evening avoiding each other, whether intentionally or through circumstance. While Nicole was busy catching up with Clooney, Tom left the celebrations alone to party elsewhere.

24

Solitary Hell

On Sunday 4 February 2001, Nicole Kidman's world collapsed. Her husband of ten years and six weeks packed his bags and left. Still filming *Vanilla Sky*, he checked into the nearby Bel-Air Hotel. There was to be no reconciliation, he said.

Shattered by Tom's decision, Nicole instinctively turned to her family for support and spent many hours on the phone to her mother and sister. She was comforted by the presence of Isabella and Conor, but felt trapped in their 'ugly fortress' in Pacific Palisades.

Existing in an altered state for twenty-four hours, she was abruptly forced to accept what was happening when Pat Kingsley sent word to the media first thing on Monday. Newspapers around the world printed the following statement:

> *Tom Cruise and Nicole Kidman announced today that they have regretfully decided to separate. The couple, who married in 1990, stressed their great respect for each other both personally and professionally. Citing the difficulties inherent in divergent careers which constantly keep them apart, they concluded that an amicable separation seemed best for both of them at this time.*

While still coming to terms with her own feelings, Nicole was obliged to turn her thoughts to work and consider the implications her private life had on colleagues. 'One day, during post production, she rang me up,' remembered Baz Luhrmann of the fateful event. 'I get these calls from Nicole, and I know it is an "Oh my God" moment: the rib, the knee. This time she said, "There are helicopters around the house and Tom has left me." It was a big shock.'

Not only was *Moulin Rouge!* nearing completion; so too was *The Others*. As Tom was executive producer in the film starring Nicole, Alejandro Amenábar admitted, 'That put extra pressure on our situation, but it's been a strange year – that was just another part of it.' Both releases were placed on hold until Nicole felt ready to face the world for the requisite publicity tours.

Nicole also discussed her situation with director Stephen Daldry. She had signed up for his next film, *The Hours*, which had already started shooting, but wasn't due to join him until the summer. He was understandably perturbed by the repercussions but was still keen to work with the eminent actress. 'We will all be very protective of her,' he said sympathetically. 'I don't think she will let any furore get in the way of her performance because she is a consummate professional, but maybe this is one headache production might have preferred to avoid – you know, the constant looking over the shoulder to see if any intruders, with nasty lenses, are intruding on our work.'

For the moment, she just had to take it one day at a time. Janelle and Antonia flew into Los Angeles on Friday, with Lucia and five-month-old Hamish in tow. Antonia's working commitments – hosting a new season of *Premiere* with Molly Meldrum – were postponed indefinitely. While the cousins played, the Kidman women tried to piece together the run of events.

Nicole was bewildered. While she had been conscious of their recent problems, she was unaware that they had become so serious. Rumours suggested that the couple had even renewed their marriage vows on their tenth wedding anniversary. She knew it had been a rough start to the year, but believed they had survived worse, and could not see why this should be any different.

'If there is true love in a marriage, any problem can be worked out,' Nicole once said. 'I saw that in my parents' relationship – my mum walked out on the marriage once, but she returned. They worked things out and forty years later, they're still together.' Sadly, for whatever reason, Tom did not seem interested in trying to work it out.

Nicole was shocked by the speed of Tom's actions: she had received a telephone call from one of his attorneys within forty-eight hours of his departure to inform her that he had filed for divorce. His papers simply cited 'irreconcilable differences' as the reason. Tom requested joint custody of their two children, various pieces of jewellery and other personal effects.

It seems that the Cruises had not signed a pre-nuptial agreement and so the subsequent financial arrangements would be based on the presiding law. Tom stated in the divorce papers that the duration of the marriage was nine years and eleven months. He claimed that they had decided to split up some seventy-two hours *before* their tenth wedding anniversary. If there was indeed no pre-nuptial agreement, this date was crucial as, under Californian law, once a couple have been married over a decade, the wealthier of the two parties can be ordered to pay alimony for the rest of the ex-spouse's life, or until he or she remarries.

The older of the two, with more films under his belt, and always the one to land the blockbuster roles, Tom had amassed an estimated £200 million compared to Nicole's £65 million. The actor was seen to be protecting his wealth by claiming they had split prior to Christmas Eve 2000. Also at stake were their joint properties, including homes in Los Angeles, Colorado, London, Sydney and New York, and other assets totalling around £300 million. If Nicole felt so inclined, she could have ensured that Tom's personal accounts were dragged through the courts.

Tough tactics of this kind were far from her mind. On 11 February she issued a brief statement emphasizing that the divorce was not her decision. Other than that, she kept herself to herself.

While further news from the respective Cruise and Kidman camps was unforthcoming, the tabloids had a field day speculating over every aspect of their marriage, trying to establish the cause of the split after so many years together.

The pressures of work had clearly put considerable strain on the relationship. Much was made in the papers of their intense period working with Stanley Kubrick on *Eyes Wide Shut*. More recently, Nicole had repeatedly worked herself into the ground, accepting role after role without taking a break. Was she still so desperate to prove herself as an actress or just unable to resist a challenge?

The rapid downward spiral of Nicole's career after meeting Tom, and her resilience in rectifying this trend in the second half of the 1990s, cannot be overlooked. She has hinted several times that rivalry existed in their marriage, notably on her side as she felt somewhat inadequate.

While Nicole always expected to juggle motherhood with her career, she had never bargained for her husband's status to be added to the equation. Furthermore, his tendency to stick to safe roles, while she consistently tackled diverse characters in more experimental projects, put them at opposite poles within their field.

Family life was also an easy target for outsiders to blame. Nicole had specifically said early on that the time was not right for her to have children, but then along came Isabella. The decision to adopt had always posed the question: did one or both of them have fertility problems? Whatever the truth of the matter, Tom and Nicole were obviously loving parents who treated their adopted children as their own.

However, they did differ on various aspects of their children's upbringing. Perhaps the most serious of these clashes was over religion. Tom's Scientology was intrinsically important to him. Willing to bend her beliefs to appease her husband when they first married, Nicole reverted to her old habits as she reasserted her independence. 'Catholicism will keep me going,' she said. 'I'm a Catholic girl. It will always stay with you.'

While Tom respected her faith, there was always the thorny issue of what Isabella and Conor should be taught. When Nicole started taking the children to the Santa Monica Catholic Church, it must have been a bone of contention. Equally, as marriage is sacred to Scientologists, Tom presumably resisted extreme pressure to resolve their issues.

Perhaps the most widely discussed topic was sex. Not just the never-ending slurs on Tom's sexuality and the insinuation that the couple were locked in a celibate marriage of convenience, but the possibility that one or both of them had been unfaithful.

The most recent report was that Tom had begun a relationship with Penélope Cruz when filming for *Vanilla Sky* commenced in November 2000. The accused parties both maintained their innocence but were not helped by 'leaks' from the crew, who claimed, 'They were all over each other like a rash.' Tom was also spuriously linked to the actress Patricia Arquette.

Nicole had her own allegations to defend. She was supposedly romancing every man with whom she had so much as spoken. Her *Moulin Rouge!* co-star Ewan McGregor was a prime suspect, despite being happily married. 'I can't believe people are saying there was something going on between us,' she said. 'Ewan is a lovely guy and he's a friend. We spent a long time on this film. During all that time Ewan's wife Eve was there and she's a mate of mine. We went out, she and I, and had some fun together. It's absolutely crazy.'

Then there was her long-time Aussie pal Russell Crowe. He had recently been involved in the messy split between Dennis Quaid and Meg

Ryan, and it seemed unlikely that he would jeopardize an enduring friendship with Nicole for a quick fling. 'He has a very, very deep soul,' she said of Crowe, 'and he is truly one of my dearest friends. He is loyal beyond belief and we've spent almost every New Year's Eve together for the past few years – Tom and Russell and me.'

But the papers weren't content to accept that Crowe and Nicole were 'just good friends'. One magazine discovered that one of the songs on *Bastard Life Or Clarity*, the latest album from Crowe's band, 30 Odd Foot Of Grunt, was written shortly after Nicole married Tom. It was called 'Somebody Else's Princess' and the lyrics describe an unattainable woman with red hair and deep-blue eyes. Further aspersions were cast when the pair were spotted hitting several Hollywood bars one night after Tom's departure – as good friends naturally would.

Nicole was also romantically linked to George Clooney, probably as a result of them being observed together at the Golden Globes. Then it was suggested that the man who originally lost out to Tom, Marcus Graham, had caused the marriage to fail. Graham, who was starring in *When We Were Modern*, a Sidney Nolan biopic, and the new David Lynch thriller *Mulholland Drive*, asked his publicist to issue a concise statement: 'Marcus is shocked and saddened by the news. Marcus and Nicole are just friends, and he hopes that she and Tom get back together again.'

Even Nicole's minder, Peter Crone, was implicated, as the actress was often seen on his arm at functions (that being his remit, of course).

With so much potentially explosive material that could be used against each other, it was next rumoured that Tom and Nicole had hired private detectives to dig up ammunition for the divorce case. Cruise was supposed to have employed Anthony Pellicano, Los Angeles's most notorious private eye, nicknamed 'The Big Sleazy'; Kidman apparently opted for Gavin DeBecker.

Ultimately, the tabloids reached no firm conclusions about the cause of the collapse of Hollywood's golden couple. Most probably the Cruises suffered from a lack of stability and time spent together, either as a couple or a family unit.

Fundamentally, as several friends suggest, it would appear that they simply 'fell out of love'.

Whether the cause of the break-up was sinister or not, the result was the same. Normal, everyday life for Nicole suddenly became a dead weight hanging round her neck. She used her loved ones as an emotional prop.

'My family, my friends, my children – they are people who give me strength,' said Nicole during this time. 'My parents are very together, always willing to tell me the truth. Sometimes they're very tough on me but they are always there for me.'

Nicole describes Janelle as 'pragmatic and strong, but still sweet', and she feels equally at ease with Antony: 'He's a great father, I can call him at three in the morning and he's there for me.'

Antonia was sympathetic and supportive of Nicole, but also deeply shocked. 'It's made me realize that divorce is real and it happens to people you don't think it'll ever happen to,' she says. Being a contemporary, Antonia was able to offer more pertinent advice than their parents. This was also true of Nicole's circle of female friends.

'I have about six really close girlfriends I could call on at any time and who could call me, and we'd be there for each other,' explains the actress. 'We've all had a substantial amount of life. Some have never been married, some are desperate to be married, some have been married twice. One is a physical therapist, and one's an acting teacher. Then I have a girlfriend who's a single mother of three, and one who's an accountant.'

This group includes childhood friends and fellow actresses Rebecca Rigg and Naomi Watts. 'We've shared boyfriends, break-ups, bottles of wine when we thought our lives were over – every single thing you can imagine,' says Nicole fondly of Watts, who had just secured her first major break in *Mullholland Drive*, starring alongside Marcus Graham. 'I've seen her struggle for years, knowing she has all this talent, and suddenly David Lynch spots her.

'She moved into my house when I got divorced and took care of me. So did my friend Annette. So there were three women and a lot of children, all living in the house.'

Nicole's male friends also offered their support, although they were careful not to excite the interest of the press and thus cause further strain. Iain Glen proved his loyalty and offered a sturdy shoulder for her to cry on. While the press tried to make more of this development, Glen's wife Susannah stated: 'Nicole's an old friend of mine too. Nothing can be read into Iain speaking to her. It's something I approve of. He's a friend of hers and so it's all positively OK.' Glen, however, was enduring relationship troubles of his own, and Nicole was able to commiserate and return the favour.

Baz Luhrmann had also become intimate with the Cruises. 'I have respect for both of them,' he says, 'Nicole's a great, close friend of mine and I care about her deeply. Tom I really like as well. Relationships are a mystery. I'm surprised it didn't happen earlier really, when you think of it, because they're like a royal couple and they were both going through the most extraordinarily testing times.' It does remain something of a mystery that Tom and Nicole could stay together through such 'testing times', and then now, without any apparent warning, implode.

✻

During February, everyone kept a low profile. Tom calmly continued filming *Vanilla Sky*, Nicole remained holed up in the Pacific Palisades house with her support group, and all would-be third parties kept quiet, except to protest their innocence.

After all the emotional and physical stress of the past few months, it didn't seem strange for Nicole to miss a period. In the present circumstances, the possibility of pregnancy couldn't have been further from her mind.

On 16 March 2001 she experienced heavy bleeding and sharp pains. Fearing the worst, she was swiftly taken to see fertility specialist Dr Alan DeCherney, at the Iris Cantor-UCLA Women's Health Center.

An ultrasound confirmed the devastating news. Nicole had in fact been about three months pregnant, but had suffered a miscarriage. Even more upsettingly, the doctors explained that the foetus had probably died a few weeks earlier, and Nicole had been unaware she was carrying the lifeless child.

Not having known about the pregnancy, Nicole had been unable to tell Tom that he was to be a father. Now, instead, she had to break it to him that she had lost his baby. It was not a phone call she wanted to make.

Nicole insisted that the pregnancy was the result of their final holiday in Las Vegas. But if she thought this tragedy could repair their marriage, she was wrong. Tom did not even visit her in hospital. Instead, it was loyal Peter Crone who was there for her throughout the ordeal.

Returning to the sympathetic women at her home, Nicole was drained of all hope. A week later, she resignedly returned to UCLA for a check-up with Dr DeCherney to ensure there were no complications. A clean bill of health was the only good news he was able to deliver. Deeply saddened by this latest cruel twist of fate, Nicole felt more fragile than ever before.

✻

As if matters couldn't get any worse, during the month of her miscarriage Nicole found herself receiving some unwanted and unnerving attention.

Matthew E. Hooker, a self-styled poet and screenwriter, runs a series of websites, including Artists In Motion, a site for aspiring artists. He began a poetry section on one of his web pages and posted a poem of his own, entitled 'Nicole': 'Lightning strikes twice/I hope/those eyes will sparkle/and shine on me again . . . look into my eyes/Nicole'.

Hooker claimed to have met Nicole at Borders bookstore in Santa Monica on 4 March. He said they talked about his latest screenplay, *The Activist*, and the actress expressed an interest in reading it. According to Hooker, Nicole suggested sending the manuscript to her agent, Rick Nicita at CAA, so he was disappointed when his parcel was returned with a note stating that they did not accept unsolicited material.

In early April he took matters into his own hands. According to Nicole, Hooker wrote directly to her, offering to tutor Isabella and Conor, 'to give us a chance to get to know each other'. He said that he was 'strongly attracted' to her and believed they were 'soulmates'. It seemed that there was more than just his manuscript on offer.

Hooker then turned up at her property a few times: once with flowers; once to ask her and her children out for an ice-cream; and a third time with an invitation to the ballet. While he may have been genuine in his interest, Nicole did not welcome this persistent attention. She was not in the mood for socializing with anyone, let alone a stranger.

On each visit he was told she wasn't in and asked to leave by the security guards. According to Nicole's staff, Hooker then became aggressive and threatened to 'commit acts of violence'. Conversely, he claims that the security guard followed him off the property and assaulted him.

Nicole at this point involved the police, who advised her that Hooker was 'mentally unstable' and recommended obtaining a restraining order against him. She did just that, claiming that Hooker was 'stalking me and my family and I am fearful for our safety and security'.

Following only a handful of visits to the house, was she overreacting? After all, she was in a troubled state emotionally, and Hooker claimed he only wanted to comfort and help her. However, his website gives a good indication of his fanaticism, and his reaction to her rejection suggests that she had taken the appropriate action. Shortly after being accused of stalking Nicole, Hooker claimed *he* had been stalked by the actor Ben Affleck. He had a theory that the big names in Hollywood were stealing his scripts and, feeling threatened by his talent, were preventing him from progressing in the industry. (His thoughts on this conspiracy have since been removed from his website.) Nicole certainly had grounds to be concerned.

The case went to the Santa Monica Superior Court in May. Judge Alan Haber issued an injunction against Hooker: he had to remain at least 250 feet from the actress, her family, her home and the children's school and day-care centre for three years. Haber concluded that there was 'clear and convincing evidence' that Hooker had harassed and 'seriously annoyed' Nicole.

Despite the verdict, Hooker insisted, 'I am not a stalker. I am a non-violent pacifist who was attracted to a beautiful woman. All I simply did was ask Nicole out three times. Some women want you to ask them out more than once and that's what I did, but after the third rejection I gave up . . . Since when is it a crime to ask a woman to the ballet and bring her wild flowers, or to write a lovely poem about her and her beautiful eyes, or to ask to take her and her kids out for ice-cream to cheer them up?'

Defiantly protesting his innocence, he threatened to appeal against the decision. Then, claiming to be the injured party, he considered suing Nicole for slander and said, 'This woman has severely wronged me, I've lost jobs, I've lost work, this is severely damaging to my personal life.' So far he has not pursued his case, although he is hoping to stand in the 2004 presidential elections.

The internet was proving an unlucky medium for Nicole Kidman. Previously, in February, just as she learnt of Tom's decision to leave her, she fought and won a legal battle to prevent her name being used in two websites offering sexual services.

25

The Show Must Go On

Having been through the emotional wringer in just eight weeks, Nicole found herself at a crossroads. She could either sink or swim. With courage, she decided to face the world.

Refusing to cancel a low-key pre-Oscars party, she hosted the event at a Los Angeles restaurant on 22 March 2001. She also found time to pose with Catherine Deneuve, Meryl Streep and Gwyneth Paltrow for an Annie Leibovitz portrait entitled *Legends Of Hollywood*. The striking photograph was augmented with two other panels of diverse actresses (including one Penélope Cruz) and was featured in *Vanity Fair's* seventh annual Hollywood issue in April. Nicole looked ravishing in a gold corset and full skirt and was beautifully made up with her copper hair swept to one side.

A little solitude would be needed if Nicole was going to get through the current ordeal. Escaping intrusion from the press and public alike, she left America and headed for the home comforts of Australia. She made a plea for privacy to the *Sydney Morning Herald*: 'It's been a very painful time. It's very upsetting and it's very invasive. I understand that people are interested but it's *my* life – my personal life.'

Safely ensconced in Sydney, Nicole was grateful to be in the one country where she felt at ease – what she needed was a bit of space. So heaven knows how she must have felt when suddenly her house was besieged.

The local radio station, 2DayFM, heard a false rumour that Nicole's ex was in town and irresponsibly challenged their audience to knock on the door and ask to speak to Tom Cruise. Nicole's bodyguards had their work cut out for them. After one intrepid listener scaled the high-security fence, they eventually called the radio station, begging them to call off the cruel stunt.

Nicole lashed out and condemned the prank. She said it was very difficult 'seeing your life being dragged through the newspapers and the tabloids'. Concentrating on her responsibilities as a mother, she vowed to protect her children and maintained her policy of 'no comment'.

Baz Luhrmann was a great friend of Nicole's and naturally had been very understanding of her need for seclusion. But now the launch of his film could wait no longer and his leading lady was required for its promotion.

Moulin Rouge! had already received a lot of negative attention which urgently needed to be redressed. After the on-set delays, the director ran into various problems, specifically with the special effects. Rumours spread like wildfire as the film's release was continually put back – it had originally been pencilled in for December 2000. Claims were being made that the movie was too confused. When reports suggested that Kylie Minogue was being brought in as an invisible fairy to narrate the story for clarity, critics fell about laughing.

Pint-sized Aussie pop star Kylie Minogue did appear in the film, but not as the press imagined. She played the green absinthe fairy and was perfectly visible, if a little smaller than usual, in her fleeting appearance. The singer had been impressed with Nicole's vocal skills and later commented, 'Nicole and I have done the acting thing together, now it's time to do a song together. She has a fabulous voice. I would love to do a duet with her but I just haven't plucked up the courage to ask her yet.'

Dismissing the film before they had even seen it, reviewers also doubted the ability of Nicole Kidman as a singer and dancer. Perhaps, they pondered, Baz Luhrmann had gone too far this time.

The truth of the matter was that the editing had simply overrun, just as the shooting had beforehand. Luhrmann was also trying to consider Nicole's feelings, as she was understandably less than keen to face the press. Finally, all these concerns were laid to rest.

Making her grandest public appearance since the split and miscarriage, Nicole bravely attended the New York premiere of *Moulin Rouge!* on 18 April 2001. Well versed in premiere protocol, she smiled broadly for the cameras. Although she looked stunning in her strappy white gown, it was hard not to notice that she was a little thinner and, if possible, paler than usual. The audience was equally impressed with both Nicole's resilience and the spectacular movie.

★

One advantage of being separated from Tom Cruise should have been that Nicole no longer had to protest his heterosexuality. However, in May, while still dealing with the Matthew Hooker restraining order, the actress was once again caught up in a rumour that Tom was homosexual.

The French website Actustar published a supposed interview with gay porn star and erotic wrestler Chad Slater (real name Phil Notaro, stage name Kyle Bradford). The article claimed Slater had engaged in a gay relationship with Tom, but when it was translated in the Spanish magazine *TVyNovelas*, it was embellished to insinuate that Nicole walked in while they were engaged in torrid sex.

Cruise launched a lawsuit against Slater, who was criticized for capitalizing on a difficult time for the actor. Initially defending himself, Slater soon changed his mind and admitted the claims were false: he had never met Tom and didn't know from where the story had originated. That he had been unfairly targeted was partially substantiated when Actustar published its own statement: 'We never said we had an interview with Mr Slater. *TVyNovelas* misunderstood our French article and invented we had an interview with Mr Slater.'

Although her name appeared in the accusations, Nicole chose to sit this scandal out and sensibly declined to comment. Her only concern was to protect her children from hearing unpleasant rumours about their father.

Nicole had other matters on her mind. In the first week of May, she responded to Tom's original divorce petition, filing her twelve-page document at the Los Angeles Superior Court three months after he started proceedings.

There were several issues she needed to address, but the main financial arrangements boiled down to their break-up date: was it before or after their tenth wedding anniversary? On this point her papers were adamant: 'During the balance of December and thereafter the parties were intimate; in fact respondent [Kidman] became pregnant by petitioner [Cruise] but lost the baby through a miscarriage.'

She said she had photos to prove they had enjoyed romantic evenings together in Las Vegas and outings with their children. Her response also revealed that she had urged Tom to consider counselling, or other steps, to reconcile their differences, rather than seek an immediate divorce.

The other issues raised mainly concerned the children. She was prepared to share custody of Isabella and Conor, but expected Tom to pay maintenance for the next twelve years, until Conor became an adult. She made it clear that she would prefer to live with the children in her native Australia, or 'elsewhere in the United States', but realized it was in their best interests to remain in Los Angeles for the immediate future. Her demands seemed reasonable, but there was bound to be contention over exactly when they split up.

Rather than being a bolt out of the blue, as Nicole claimed, a statement from Tom's lawyers replied, '[Nicole] has always known exactly why the parties are divorcing.' This suggested that there was a specific reason that she was carefully omitting in her statement. The tabloids were quick to pick up on this and claimed that the dispute was over the paternity of the miscarried child.

Ignoring this latest speculation, Nicole was pleased to have put her version of events down in writing. She finally felt able to get on with life, and this included opening up a little to the public about her miscarriage and the way forward.

'It was a big shock for me,' she said the following week. 'It's surreal. I did have a miscarriage, and I'm still coping with that.

'At this time, all I'm doing is adjusting to a new way of life. I don't have an overall plan. I just do the best I can, take each day as it comes and hope that it is going to be enough, and that I'll be good enough.'

Nicole spoke widely of settling down and taking off the rest of the year to be with Isabella and Conor. While this contradicted her publicity commitments and her upcoming project with Stephen Daldry, she did confess that her plans tended to shift from week to week. 'I want to have two kids who grow up and say, "We are happy and we are healthy and we love you, mum." I want to know them well and have them know me well, and to accomplish that I'm willing to give up everything. I would love to be able to balance career and family, but if that doesn't work out my choice is an easy one.'

Both parents understood the importance of their joint involvement in the children's upbringing, regardless of the living arrangements – Tom's major concern being not to repeat events from his own troubled childhood. 'We have always been a family,' he said. 'Even though the parents are no longer together, we still care about each other. We are going to raise these kids together, Nic and I.'

✻

'My kids and the film, *Moulin Rouge!*, are the two things that are my shining lights,' said Nicole. Indeed, now was the time to take Tom up on his offer of looking after the children while she did the rounds of promotion for her latest movie.

After the success of the New York premiere, *Moulin Rouge!* was chosen for the prestigious opening slot of the fifty-fourth Cannes Film Festival on 6 May 2001. Nicole again called upon Antonia for support, who duly left her children with Angus in Australia and flew to Cannes.

At the gala evening Nicole wore a dramatic black silk crêpe georgette bustier and taffeta skirt, which had been specially designed for her by Tom Ford for Yves Saint Laurent Rive Gauche. The heaving crowd outside the Palais des Festivals were thrilled when she stopped to greet them. With big smiles all round, no one could imagine the terror racing through Nicole's mind.

'I panic in front of all the cameras,' she later told *Vogue* in an in-depth interview. 'My hands start shaking and I have trouble breathing. Tom would always whisper to me that everything was all right.

'I came out of the cinema and I was wearing this Yves Saint Laurent corset dress. Suddenly there were all these people bearing down on me and lots of lights. I was so panicked I just couldn't breathe. I heard myself say, "I need my sister, I need my sister . . ."

'Suddenly, there she was – right in front of me, looking into my eyes. She took my hand, turned me around and led me back inside to the ladies' loo. There she undid my corset, took off my shoes, held me in her arms and told me that everything was going to be OK. So I got up, got dressed and got out there.' Although Nicole had previously relied on her husband to help her through such situations, with a little support the actress was proving that she could cope alone.

The immediate panic over and with a little Dutch courage from a few cocktails, Nicole mingled with the public, blew kisses to her fans, signed autographs and danced the night away at the party afterwards. She had a ball with the DJ, Norman Cook, aka Fatboy Slim. He misheard when the audience screamed 'Give her a disc': thinking they had said, 'Give her a kiss', he blushed, muttered, 'I'm a married man', and then obliged with a modest peck on the cheek. Nicole giggled before dragging Baz Luhrmann up to the decks to try his hand as DJ, then hit the dance floor with Ewan McGregor.

She looked fabulous and laughed freely, seeming as though she hadn't a care in the world. This was the kind of behaviour that only those close to Nicole had ever witnessed, and the public merely read about in interviews. During her years as Mrs Tom Cruise, she'd remained poised and reserved in public. She wasn't out of control now, but she was able to let her guard down and genuinely enjoy herself.

The extraordinary, daring and decadent *Moulin Rouge!* received rave reviews, and one critic described the pairing of Nicole and McGregor as 'the sweetest musical duo since Gene Kelly and Cyd Charisse'.

With the first night out of the way, Nicole was able to relax during the endless interviews over the following week. She was pleasantly surprised by the sensitivity of the journalists. 'I could have said, "I'm not doing any press for this film. I'm not coming out until I am completely healed," but I don't know if that will ever happen,' she said. 'Obviously it would not be my choice to be here in very difficult circumstances and to sit in front of everyone and answer questions about my personal life. But I feel proud of this work and it is important to promote it because it is something that the public would not obviously want to see – it's a musical and the kind of film which is very hard to describe in a few sentences.'

She seemed to have forgotten the physical toll the filming had taken on her, as she offered, 'I would love to do another musical. Vocally, a Broadway show is very tough on your voice. But I'm up for any challenge.'

During her stay in France, Nicole was flattered by the attentions of thirty-seven-year-old Italian director Fabrizio Mosca. The actress had known the head of Miramax's Italian arm for years, and they became re-acquainted when he attended the festival to show his acclaimed debut film, *I Cento Passi* (*The Hundred Steps*). Together they appreciated Rodin's famous sculptures, *The Thinker* and *The Kiss*, at the artist's museum and toured the area in a limousine. They dined out often and were seen together on the French Riviera. Nicole was said to have found the handsome and single film-maker 'charming company', but, despite his reported lavish gift of a £20,000 white-gold, topaz and diamond choker, a romance did not ensue.

At the end of the week, Nicole was pleased to rejoin her children. 'I miss them,' she confessed to one journalist. 'We speak on the telephone constantly and we send faxes backwards and forwards. They do little drawings and there was one waiting for me when I woke up. I can't wait to give them a hug and kiss and a big lick.'

Upon her return to America, Nicole was obliged to continue the promotional rounds for *Moulin Rouge!* Along with Ewan McGregor, she attended various junkets and a question-and-answer session with film fans in California.

'What I loved is that it's a love story, and its message is that, no matter what goes on in your life or what experiences you've had in the past, you can always fall in love,' she said, somewhat poignantly. The film's premise, that it is better to have loved and lost than never to have loved at all, became Nicole's mantra. 'It's a very brave thing to fall in love. You have to be willing to trust somebody else with your whole being and that's very difficult, really difficult, and very brave.'

Although Nicole often professes that she is unable to watch herself in a film, this fantasy love story proved the exception to the rule. 'Usually I have trouble with that, but I can watch this one. I saw it with my mum and my sister first, and my mum cried. People cry when they watch the movie, which is a good thing. We want people to cry.' She confessed that Janelle had always wanted her to appear in a musical: 'Now that I have, she is proud of me.'

Having spent some time with her children while in America, Nicole was due in London at the end of May to start filming with Stephen Daldry. Isabella and Conor accompanied her initially, as they were both so fond of English life.

Director Stephen Daldry, Oscar-nominated for *Billy Elliott*, had been working on *The Hours* in America since Nicole and Tom split earlier in the year. Although the actress had a key role in the story, she had not been required previously as the shoot was divided into three sections. It was only when filming moved from Miami to Pinewood Studios and Richmond-on-Thames during the summer of 2001 that she was called upon.

The Hours is based on Michael Cunningham's Pulitzer Prize-winning novel of the same title. Published in 1988, Cunningham's book pays homage to Virginia Woolf and her tome *Mrs Dalloway*, which was itself turned into a movie in 1997 starring Vanessa Redgrave. *The Blue Room*'s David Hare wrote the screenplay for Daldry.

The story revolves around three female characters from the twentieth century. The first is Virginia Woolf herself, seen working on the novel *Mrs Dalloway* in 1923 while struggling with depression and suicide. The next is Laura Brown, a pregnant housewife in 1949, who is planning a party for her husband, pondering her own existence and avidly reading Woolf's novel. The last is Clarissa Vaughn, a woman in contemporary New York throwing a farewell bash for Richard, a former lover and famous author dying of AIDS, who nicknames her 'Mrs Dalloway'.

It is no wonder that Nicole would be eager to get involved in such a highbrow project: she would be co-starring with acclaimed actresses Meryl Streep and Julianne Moore, and the rest of the cast was no less impressive, including Ed Harris, Miranda Richardson, Claire Danes, Toni Collette and Eileen Atkins.

While Nicole had at last earned her place among the finest actresses of the day, she was in awe of Streep, particularly in light of her own recent experiences. 'I think she's the greatest actress of her generation, if not the greatest of all time,' she says. 'She's conducted her life with such aplomb. She's managed to raise lovely children and sustain her marriage and had an extraordinary career as well.'

Streep took the part of modern-day Clarissa Vaughn and Moore the post-war housewife, which left the unglamorous role of feminist and novelist Virginia Woolf for Nicole. Without a scrap of make-up, she wore a faded auburn wig scraped back into a bun and an aquiline pros- thetic nose. 'I sat in the make-up chair for two hours every morning, which I hate,' she says, reminiscent of her gruelling routine for *Moulin Rouge!*

As with all her films, Nicole took time and care to fully immerse her- self in her roles. 'I've really had to throw myself into this, which may be no bad thing,' she reflects. Most importantly, she read up on Woolf's life, including her highly charged bisexual flings. 'That's one of the first things you deal with in preparing a character, because sex is such a driving force beneath us all.'

Daldry wanted to portray Woolf's antics in glorious technicolor, which would, of course, require steamy sex scenes. Without a prudish husband to complain, it was Nicole who drew the line at appearing naked in an outrageous orgy.

Instead, she agreed to wear a made-to-measure flesh-coloured wetsuit. The outfit was designed by a Devon company specializing in watersports clothing, in order to make her appear completely nude. 'We received a call from Pinewood Studios inquiring about a wetsuit for Nicole and we realized we had made our name in the film industry,' laughs owner Chris Reed. 'We were given Nicole's measurements and all I shall say is that she is a very tall and shapely lady with a very small waist!'

Despite her misgivings about the nudity requirement – a rare protest from Miss Kidman – she obviously found it a great privilege to work on such a project. 'Playing Virginia was incredible,' she says, 'and I loved working with Stephen Daldry. When I first met him, I was so shy I could barely talk to him and he would call me and say, "I'm coming over." Now, I lie curled up all over him, with my head in his lap!'

The feeling was reciprocated. 'I think she's great to hang out with,' says Daldry, delighted with both her performance and her attitude. 'She is happy just to relax, and she's happy to work hard. She is shrewd about people – you don't have to find the language with her just because she is the star.' Like her relationship with Sam Neill fourteen years earlier on *Dead Calm*, Nicole took pleasure in showing her colleague how to have a good time. 'She likes to have fun!' exclaims Daldry. 'She took me dancing at Attica and gambling at Aspinalls. She knows how to enjoy herself.'

When all was said and done, Hare, too, was pleased with the casting. 'She has a natural kindness,' he explains. 'A lot of agents thought she was a strange choice for playing Virginia Woolf in *The Hours*. She's not the stereotype feminist, but what she has done with the part is amazing.' With the film due to premiere at the end of 2002 and general release set for January and February the following year, it will be interesting to see what the public make of this return to highbrow work.

This latest outing would be the last for some time. Nicole was long overdue some quality rest and relaxation. 'After filming I'm taking some time for myself to be with the children,' she said in the summer of 2001. 'It's an important time for them. I don't know whether we'll be in Los Angeles or at our home in Sydney. I'd love to be in Sydney again. I miss being there.'

26

The Scream

While Nicole was quietly celebrating her thirty-fourth birthday in June 2001, Tom was embroiled in yet another lawsuit. It stemmed from an advert published by Michael Davis in *Bold Magazine*, offering $500,000 for visual proof of a gay affair involving the actor. When Davis told major newspapers he *might* have a video, Tom sued on the basis that it was impossible for such a tape to exist. Davis apologized and the case was dropped. Thankfully, this time Nicole was not implicated, other than by former association; but, more to the point, someone else had to deal with Tom's bruised ego.

It seemed that despite his adamant protestations to the contrary, Cruise had been secretly seeing Cruz. The cat was let out of the bag when Penélope showed up, among 200 other celebrity guests, at Tom's thirty-ninth birthday bash in July. Although arriving separately, they ended the night cheek to cheek on the dance floor.

A week later they were spotted dining privately at Spago in Los Angeles. This time the paparazzi were on hand and the couple awkwardly kissed for the cameras. Three days later Tom relented and authorized Pat Kingsley to confirm that 'Tom and Penélope have had a few dates'. When pushed, she said they had been together for the last two weeks, shrugging, 'He's allowed, she's allowed.'

It was true: they were both single, so why keep it quiet? The actress's personal assistant Kira Sanchez revealed, 'Penélope has told her friends she's mighty relieved it's all out in the open. She told Tom she didn't like skulking around.' But how long, exactly, had they been 'skulking around'?

Cameron Crowe, director of *Vanilla Sky*, apparently witnessed their progression from friends to lovers. 'They fell in love onscreen,' he said. 'You watch them actually go through that hideous, great, awful, intoxicating moment. Without it, we wouldn't have a movie.' Since filming had ended in March, the pair lacked an obvious excuse to see each other, but had maintained discreet contact. Until now, that is.

The circumstances surrounding his current marriage break-up and the new relationship with his leading lady were strikingly similar to Tom's divorce from Mimi and public outings with Nicole eleven years earlier. Even Tom's protestation that 'It just keeps getting better' at the end of 2000, referring to his second wife, harked back to his 'I just really enjoy our marriage' in January 1990, referring to his first.

While his first marriage may have already been on the rocks during *Days Of Thunder*, it soon became clear how significant a role Nicole had played as both parties later acknowledged their instant mutual attraction. Now the director of *Vanilla Sky*, who had worked so closely with both Tom and Penélope, suggested there had been a similar chain of events.

This was not only how it appeared to the public, but also to those close to Nicole. 'It's fair to say Nic is seething,' good friend Amy Gill told the press when Tom and Penélope went public. 'What she wants to know is why Tom didn't come clean with her in the first place. During shooting of that movie there was a lot of speculation about Tom and Penélope. Nicole says she even called him one day and asked, "What is this with you and that woman – are you guys having an affair?" She said Tom bristled with indignation and told her, "Absolutely not."

'Nic asked him again and again. She said, "Each time he flat out swore to me there was nothing going on." All this time she's been wondering why he wanted out of the marriage.' Gill was not convinced enough to claim that an affair between Tom and Penélope was the direct reason for the split, but she believed that Nicole was still unaware of the cause and deserved an explanation.

As Nicole was obliged to give numerous interviews promoting *Moulin Rouge!*, she was exposed to endless prying. She endeared herself to fans around the world through her refusal to crawl away and hide. But as *Vanilla Sky* wasn't due out until December 2001, Tom was let off the hook. This meant that he seemed to remain gallantly quiet about matters by default, again reminiscent of his previous divorce. With his latest leading lady suddenly on his arm, Tom was unanimously perceived as the bad guy – guilty until proven innocent. So who was his new lover?

Penélope Cruz Sánchez was born on 28 April 1974 in Madrid. After years of intensive training in ballet and jazz, the young dancer broke into acting in the early 1990s. Her third film, *Belle Epoque* in 1992, gained her international recognition and she went on to appear in several native films, including Alejandro Amenábar's 1997 Sundance entry *Abre Los Ojos* (*Open Your Eyes*). The subsequent acclaim helped her break into mainstream English-language movies, and she gained praise for her roles in *All The Pretty Horses* in 2000, and *Blow* and *Captain Corelli's Mandolin* the following year. In less than a decade she had made a name for herself as 'the Madonna of Madrid'. Her dark Mediterranean good looks also secured her a contract to promote Ralph Lauren's new perfume, Glamorous.

With popular opinion putting her at 5 feet 6 inches, Penélope was perhaps better suited to Tom in height, but the age gap stood at some twelve years. As a Buddhist, she also might have experienced a clash with his strong belief in Scientology.

The actress has said that as she's the shy type, she let Tom make the first move and he was clearly hooked by her seductive charms from an early stage. 'As a person, and on film, she invites you in, and she's incredibly romantic, and yet real, you know?' he gushed. 'She's beautiful. She's a very skilled actress, but has an effortless quality about her. You look at Audrey Hepburn. She has that kind of elegance and yet is accessible.' In response to such overwhelming praise, Penélope could not resist repaying the compliments. 'He's so smart, his energy is so amazing and he's so generous,' she said, reiterating the words of many of Tom's close friends.

By December 2001, the affair had grown into something more serious and both Tom and Penélope spoke openly about their relationship. 'We don't hide that we are together and we are very, very happy together,' said Penélope. 'All I want to say is that we're having a lot of fun together.' By then, she had moved into his Beverly Hills home and the pair were quite inseparable.

Evidently, she would always be compared to Tom's second wife now that she was openly dating him, but Penélope's only comment was: 'I have huge respect for Nicole Kidman and I think she is one of the best actresses working right now.'

★

'I think that divorce is hard for anyone. It's a nightmare. You can pretend you're fine and some days, you're great – and some days, you're not,' admitted Nicole on Oprah Winfrey's chat show in July 2001.

In the wake of recent revelations, Nicole was glad of a break. As a family, the Cruises had planned to escape to Wakaya, Fiji, in July. With the reservations already made, the exes agreed to split the two weeks – Nicole and the children took the first half, and when they left, Tom, along with Penélope, moved in.

They had rented all nine of the beach-front villas on the 2200-acre island in the South Pacific, in order to ensure maximum privacy. Nicole arrived with Isabella and Conor and was joined four days later by Russell Crowe. The media were delighted, thinking that they had finally exposed the 'secret lovers', but as Crowe was accompanied by a tall blonde, the rumours fell flat.

'Yes, I was in Fiji and, yes, I did see my good friend Nicole Kidman,' he reported, teasing the journalists. 'It was a refuelling stop for the plane and I am not implying anything by using the phrase "refuelling stop" – I want to absolutely clarify that. Nicole's a really good friend of mine, has been for ten years and I hope will be for the next hundred, or however long we last. There you go. Sorry, mate.'

Just forty-eight hours after Nicole departed, Tom, his sister Lee Anne, Penélope Cruz and some friends from the set of *Vanilla Sky* arrived. After their brief sojourn in paradise, Tom and Penélope flew to the Telluride ranch in his private jet, now stripped of the name 'Sweet Nic'. The couple took Isabella and Conor with them, and looked after the children for much of August.

Nicole was busy once again with promotion, this time for *The Others*, and very quickly had to get used to the idea of her children having a much younger stepmother figure. Tom and Penélope made their first public appearance together at the August premiere of Cruz's latest film, *Captain Corelli's Mandolin*. Although glad that the children would spend time with their father, Nicole was anxious to restake her claim and hoped to take them back to Sydney once her current commitments were out of the way.

The American premiere of *The Others* was in New York on 2 August. Nicole arrived alone in a revealing black chiffon dress with her hair swept up. As executive producer, Tom was noticeably absent, again allowing Nicole the limelight.

The next function for *The Others* was the Los Angeles premiere five days later on 7 August. Belying the fact that their divorce was imminent, this time both Nicole and Tom attended – separately, of course – the screening at the Directors' Guild on Sunset Boulevard. Nicole arrived first, again in black: this time, a stunning corset and knee-length skirt by Frédéric Molénac. Striking one for womankind, she partied with Naomi Watts and Rebecca Rigg until the early hours at the Mondrian Hotel. In contrast, Tom turned up twenty-five minutes later and left before the after-show party.

Although they did not obviously cross paths at the event, both were continually obliged to comment on the other's presence. Nicole kept her views to a minimum, offering only: 'I am glad Tom is here to support the movie.' Tom was a little more outspoken, and chivalrous with it. 'I'm here supporting this picture,' he said. 'I believe in the film and I'm proud of it. The performance that Nic has given is flawless. You can see it in the rushes and I knew when I read the script that she would be great.'

Next, the journalists' questions turned to a potentially thorny topic. Would the soon-to-be ex-husband and wife ever work together again?

While Nicole diplomatically replied, 'I can't say it's going to happen but I would hope to,' again, Tom offered a little more detail. 'We definitely will,' he said confidently. 'I have another picture in development for her that I'm going to produce.' It is possible he was referring to *The General's Woman*, a Micaela Gilchrist novel optioned by his production company for Nicole back in May 2000, but only time will tell.

The Others received great critical acclaim, with the Los Angeles *Daily Variety* astutely observing: 'As exec producer of *The Others*, Tom Cruise has handed Kidman the most generous divorce settlement any wife could ask for. *The Others* is a luxuriously old-fashioned vehicle custom-fit to its star's strengths, which come across to sensational effect.'

As the supernatural drama went on general release, it proved a popular slow-burner across the world. With a distinctly intimate feel even on the big screen, *The Others* somehow seems more like a theatrical production than a movie. Nicole's performance is indeed faultless and she was soon being compared to her character's namesake, Grace Kelly.

But some audiences found fault with the film itself. Billing it as 'a spooky thriller which the producers hope will repeat the success of Bruce Willis's *The Sixth Sense*' not only gave the game away, but suggested that Amenábar had fallen foul of jumping on the bandwagon a little too late. The Spanish director fully exploits all the potentially nail-biting scenes, but unfortunately his direction somehow came across as a bit hammy, and the more cynical English audiences could be observed sniggering at some of the supposedly scarier parts.

Across the Atlantic, responses were less restrained. The *Daily Star* reported that American audiences fell about laughing during the movie's more poignant moments. For example, raucous outbursts occurred when

Anne asks her mother when her father will return and Nicole as Grace grimly replies, 'Daddy isn't coming home. You'll find out soon enough that this place isn't always a happy home.' It seems that crueller viewers found the uncanny similarity to Nicole's real-life situation too funny to bear.

Fortunately, such unkind responses were in the minority. *The Others* was hailed as a 'breakthrough hit' for Nicole in many countries, including America, as the buzz intensified via word of mouth. Having only had a budget of $20 million with which to make the film, as the box-office takings edged towards $100 million Miramax made noises about procuring an Oscar nomination for Nicole. Flattered, the actress remained realistic: 'I've had situations like that before, and it hasn't eventuated into anything so I feel that whatever happens, happens. The work is the thing that speaks for you.

'*The Others* feels like forbidden fruit for me in a way. I was in *Batman Forever*, but I've never had *my* movie be a hit movie. It gives me power now to do something else a little bit offbeat, and they'll finance it. I'm surprised at its success. I just thought I was making this strange atmospheric little thriller with dark undertones.'

In the meantime, the separation had been finalized. Superior Court Judge Lee Smalley Edmon granted Tom Cruise and Nicole Kidman an accelerated bifurcation request on 31 July. They were officially divorced as of 8 August, with the contested issues to be thrashed out at a later date.

Neither party was in court, but Tom later explained why they opted for a 'quickie divorce' after months of wrangling. 'I feel it will assist Nicole and me in moving on with our lives emotionally,' he said. In fact, under Californian law, it is impossible to obtain a divorce in anything less than six months, and by achieving a conclusion six months and one day after first filing for divorce, Tom was sending Nicole a clear message that there would be no reconciliation.

While Tom had already moved on, Nicole unforgettably displayed her relief that the ordeal was over: emerging from her lawyer's offices on 8 August having signed the divorce papers, she threw her arms out, her head back and let out a piercing scream, releasing months of pent-up tension.

All was not quite over, however, as they still had to settle the specifics of the financial agreement. A hearing was initially scheduled for 4 October, but the press speculated that discussions had run into difficulties. All kinds of wild rumours ensued. Tom was allegedly fighting to retain most of his fortune and trying to prevent his ex-wife's lawyers from speaking to his business managers, essentially hiding the full extent of his assets. Things took a turn for the worse when Tom was reported as mysteriously threatening to 'tell all' in court. The papers claimed that Nicole's *pièce de résistance* was threatening to produce DNA evidence from her miscarriage to prove Tom was the father.

Spurred on by Nicole's desire to spend the end of the year in Australia, the couple finally met in Los Angeles on 12 November 2001 and agreed the monetary settlement amicably. The deal avoided prolonging the proceedings or any courtroom showdown, and the negotiations were said to have ended with an affectionate embrace.

The exact details about the carving-up of such an extensive estate remain private, but the most significant items are thought to be known. Nicole naturally kept their home in Sydney, but also retained the Los Angeles property of which she was less fond. Tom kept his apartment in New York and the ranch in Telluride, along with his beloved planes. The claim on their London property is unknown, as is the exact nature of the alimony payments, although one source suggests that Nicole received a substantial lump sum of £20 million, followed by regular sizeable contributions. Nicole requested 'specific items of jewellery' in her petition, believed to include her wedding ring, a matching pair of earrings and thirtieth-birthday necklace.

'I'm actually really surprised by how little – and I'm really grateful about how little – I have been asked about the divorce,' she said after signing the papers in August. 'I have declined to answer a lot of stuff. I just don't want to get into it, the legalities of it and the privacy issue. I've not made any sort of comment publicly; I've just not gone into it. I don't think it's the right place to be talking about it. It's between me and Tom.'

27

Got Up, Got Dressed And Got Out There

A single working mother in her mid-thirties, Nicole Kidman could now either slip into career apathy or forge ahead stubbornly. It will surprise no one that she opted for the latter, and quite spectacularly so. As she carved out a new persona complete with both feminist and romantic overtones, not to mention a major image overhaul, the world took the courageous actress to its heart.

Almost by default, the divorcée became an inspirational role model for women everywhere. Setting out to prove the point that she could get along just fine without her husband, yet admitting on occasion that she was struggling to cope, Nicole's frankness was refreshing and appealing in equal measure. She never stopped giving interviews and her gradual acceptance of her new life could be clearly traced as the year progressed.

'It's both the best and the worst time of my life,' she said in May. 'I'm still in a daze and I'm not sure what the future holds. All I do know is that I intend to be positive and not wake up feeling desperate. I owe that to my children.' Several months later, she had gained valuable perspective on being suddenly alone, and on life in general.

'What has happened to me in the last few months has been very difficult. People say I have been strong about it, but I must say that I don't feel strong at all! What I've been trying to do is move forward one day at a time, keep smiling and remember that tomorrow is another day.'

Nicole readily admitted that the split, no matter how distressing it had been, had taught her many things.

'It gave me wisdom,' she said. 'Anything that involves suffering or pain makes you a wiser person. You acquire compassion, understanding.

'In the weirdest way it's opened me up. I'll look back on this time as surreal. I've had the most intimate details of my life exposed in the media in a way I never thought would happen. It's been horrible. It's been strange, but at the same time it's allowed me freedom. I've thought, "OK, I get looked at and talked about. That's humiliating," but you also think, "Well, it doesn't get much worse than this."'

The closest Nicole came to maligning her ex-husband in public was positively negligible. 'The divorce has been the biggest blow of my life and I was totally unaware and unprepared when it happened. I was terribly wounded by it all because it came from someone I had loved and trusted with all my heart.' Her very public 'coping' with it all finally got the better of Tom, who up until January 2002 remained remarkably silent, gallantly stepping back to allow his ex-wife her say.

The actor, who had endured much criticism for stepping out with Penélope Cruz 'too soon', briefly broke his silence in an interview with *Vanity Fair*. Accompanied by photos of the thirty-nine-year-old stripped to the waist in poses squarely aimed at his female fans, he said of the reasons behind the divorce: 'She knows why, and I know why.' When it was suggested to him that the intriguing statement might invite further speculation, he retorted, 'I don't care if it piques people's interest. Honestly, people should mind their own damn business.'

Nicole was clearly strong enough to survive such insinuations. In contrast to her previous incarnations as an actress, wife then mother, now the media witnessed the compelling emergence of Nicole Kidman Mark Four: tough yet vulnerable, a woman's woman who loved life and wasn't prepared to waste any more time mourning what might have been. The front-page pictures of her demonstrative cry of relief as she exited her lawyers' offices provided the first step. The fearsome female battalion that literally moved in to support her after the split was the next.

While Tom attended premieres with his Spanish lover, Nicole defiantly showed up with her closest girlfriends, proud to be photographed holding hands with Naomi Watts and Rebecca Rigg (even though she towered over them in her rediscovered high heels).

'Thankfully, I've got great girlfriends,' she said. 'If you have sisters, you're pretty much set up that way. When you are in your thirties and on this journey, you really need those women who know you to see you through.'

Nicole's comparably radical upbringing now came into effect as she reconciled herself to life as a single mother who also needed to work.

'I was raised by a feminist, and I grew up reading Germaine Greer,' she said. 'She provoked a reaction and she was important. So were Gloria Steinem and Betty Friedan. If you believe in equality, you recognize that the feminists fought a hard battle. It's great to be able to say, "I want to be a mother, but I would like to work as well." Still, there's no such thing as having it all . . .

'I used to say, "Well, my hat is off to a woman who has to do it by herself," and now I'm a single mother. Obviously my kids have a father who's going to be completely involved, but in terms of doing it alone, that's scary. It's a whole new path to walk. And it's daunting.

'I am my own worst critic — especially now. If I'm working too much, I worry that I'm a bad mother and when I'm with my kids I feel like I'm doing everything wrong. Motherhood is riddled with guilt. You've got to go easy on yourself, I guess.'

Nicole next tugged on the public's heartstrings by reinventing herself as a romantic heroine. Having enthused about the love story in *Moulin Rouge!*, months later the actress remained open to amorous possibilities.

'I am still a romantic. One must never lose hope of falling in love. No matter what goes on in your life, I believe that you can still fall in love. I believe in destiny, in a soulmate out there for every one of us. I'm determined to keep believing that.

'I'd love to be in love again for the tingles. It's silly to talk of marriage again, but you can just be in love. I don't know if I believe in forever — for obvious reasons . . .'

After eleven years of wearing flat shoes to avoid towering over Tom Cruise, the statuesque star famously charmed her public by gleefully giggling, 'I can wear heels now!' when quizzed by David Letterman on the benefits of being single. Nicole's unquenchable spirit was only one side of her transformation. Suddenly she became a style icon for the new millennium.

Clothes shopping with girlfriends was now one of her favourite pursuits. But Nicole's sartorial tastes hadn't actually changed all that much from the days she used to spend trawling around flea markets. 'I think clothes are creative. It's wonderful when someone like John Galliano has the ability to change the way people think of clothes or how they dress on a global level. Fashion is incredibly relevant. There's something admirable about boldness, because with boldness comes the opportunity to fail. But it's becoming harder now, because when you fail, people judge it so severely.'

A practical mum, Nicole is a 'bike shorts and sloppy joe' person around the house. 'It's like leading two different lives,' she jokes. 'I have my life, then I have this sort of fantasy life – going to premieres and putting on make-up and beautiful dresses.' Given the choice, the 'fantasy' Nicole favours Prada, Dolce & Gabbana, Nicholas Ghesquiere and Frédéric Molénac. Her most prized possessions are a loose-fitting vintage embroidered Mexican dress and all the Ossie Clark dresses her mother has given her over the years. Her underwear comes from La Perla, and her favourite shops are 'Virginia in London. In Paris, Didier Ludot for vintage, and Colette'.

For footwear, Nicole prefers Michel Perry, Ann Demeulemeester and Manolo Blahnik, and she has a veritable treasure trove of antique accessories. A lover of unusual jewellery, Nicole's all-time favourite piece is an expanding eighteenth-century gold snake, which she wears variously as a choker, armband or ankle bracelet.

Thanks to all the extra exposure with *Moulin Rouge!*, *The Others* and also her very public divorce, Nicole's eclectic taste in clothes, her paleness and her long-legged figure have become fashionable, something which she finds most amusing. 'Believe me, my body is only OK,' she laughs. 'I get by, but it's not great. I have a boy's body, and I would rather look like a girl. *Moulin Rouge!* was all about corsets and padding.'

Nicole had never obviously been very interested in pampering, preferring to jump out of a plane than laze around getting a manicure, so it surprised her fans when in August 2001 she opened a chain of nail salons called Nail Bar Generation. Having launched the business with six others, including her sister Antonia and cosmetics publicist Anna Marchant, she announced: 'Nail Bar Generation and [its own product range] Regeneration is a direct result of a small group of family and friends working to create something original and fresh. After months of testing and ideas, Anna, Antonia and I have created a range of products which are high quality and beautiful to use – we hope they will appeal to everyone.'

Added Antonia, 'Nicole is our eyes on the world. Because she travels so much and sees all the new trends, she can make sure we are doing the right thing.' With the first outlet established in Grace Bros, one of Sydney's larger department stores, Nicole and her business partners eventually hope to 'go global' with their venture.

★

And so, equipped with a new, more accessible personality and style to match, Nicole spent the latter half of 2001 out and about, enjoying herself. In September she was spotted cheering on Russell Crowe's band, 30 Odd Foot Of Grunt, at the House of Blues on Sunset Boulevard. 'It would be easy for me right now to become cloistered, to say I don't want to go out because I'm embarrassed or because I don't like being looked at,' she said. 'I could say, "I'm not going to go to a shopping mall or see a movie." But I'm determined to go on enjoying my life. I love to meet people, I love to talk to people, I love to be around people and I love to be part of the world.'

Nicole then greeted her fans at the London premiere of *Moulin Rouge!*, accompanied by what the papers dubbed a 'mystery man' – it turned out to be Stephen Daldry. She spent at least fifteen minutes signing autographs for fans who had queued for hours in Leicester Square and later reappeared to wave from the balcony with Ewan McGregor. Again, it was noted how long she stayed at the after-show party held at Tobacco Dock, something of a rarity for a star of her rank. She mingled both with celebrities and the public, surprisingly ignoring normal security measures by ditching any bodyguards and socializing outside the cordoned-off VIP area.

'My feet are killing me in these high heels – I can't wait to take them off,' she gushed. 'I'm surrounded by all these tall men but I can't dance as I've got the wrong shoes on!' Nicole warmed to the overly demonstrative fans, who abandoned their British reserve on meeting such a famous woman. 'I don't think I've ever been kissed so much in my life, it's amazing,' she said. 'Wherever I go, people come up to me and kiss me – you Brits are certainly friendly. I've had enough kisses to last me a lifetime!'

Baz Luhrmann was one who noted Nicole's method of throwing herself into the public eye at this event. 'There are others who would rather hide, but she ran out towards it,' he observed. 'When the crowd outside the cinema were yelling her name last night, that was a revelation to me. If people bother to turn up, then she bothers to acknowledge them. She scares me when she goes belting up into those crowds to sign autographs, it absolutely freaks me out. But she was so excited.'

Meanwhile, the incredible runaway success that was *Moulin Rouge!* shot to number one at the U.K. box office, taking £2.5 million in its first weekend. During the equivalent period in Nicole's native Australia, it had taken £1.3 million. Nicole and her handsome co-star celebrated by dining at Vong, a trendy but low-profile Knightsbridge restaurant, the night after the London premiere. Presumably McGregor refrained from his trademark belching in the elegant surroundings.

No sooner did Nicole take a breather from promoting one of her movies than another claimed her attention. Once again she was spotted in the company of Fabrizio Mosca when *The Others* was shown at the Venice Film Festival (*Birthday Girl* finally made its first appearance there). Keeping a low profile, the pair relaxed on a boat ride along the Venice canals, dined out and attended a private party. But still it seemed that a serious romance with the director was not on the cards. 'I'll take a tall man,' she declared coquettishly to hundreds of reporters at the festival.

Perhaps the most touching appearance Nicole would make in 2001 was when she arrived with seven-year-old Nicholas Powell at the Hallowe'en opening of *The Others* in Australia. The little boy had been diagnosed with cancer at the age of sixteen months and continued to fight the disease. When he presented the actress with a bouquet of flowers at the entrance to Fox Studios, she took him under her wing. 'Little Nicholas is my date tonight,' she told reporters. 'He's very brave and he's taking care of me and I'm taking care of him.' Proceeds from that particular event were donated to the Children's Hospital in Randwick, and Nicole generously gave $100,000 towards the night's total of $280,000.

The last few months had been a whirlwind of premieres, parties and promotion, and, in late September 2001, Nicole decided it was high time to try her hand at something completely different. No one could have predicted her next move, even following the extraordinary success of *Moulin Rouge!*

One morning when Nicole was checking her mail, she spied a note from a man she had never met. It said: 'Will you be Nancy to my Frank?'

The writer was one Robbie Williams, the outspoken pop star and arguably Britain's most eligible bachelor. Following his smash hit 'Kids', a duet with Kylie Minogue released the previous October, he now wanted to record a duet with the taller, equally famous Aussie. While compiling an album of swing covers entitled *Swing When You're Winning*, he had fallen in love with the track 'Somethin' Stupid', first made famous by the father-and-daughter team of Frank and Nancy Sinatra. The song had been a number one in 1968 and he wanted to update it – with Nicole's assistance.

'I got an advance CD of the *Moulin Rouge!* album,' Williams recalls. 'And she sings a gorgeous song on that. She's got an amazing voice. I asked if she would be interested, fully expecting to be knocked back – she's a proper Hollywood star. But she said yes. I was thrilled.'

'We didn't negotiate – he asked, I said yes. I'm a terrible business-woman!' laughs Nicole. Shortly afterwards they arranged to meet in secret at a Los Angeles recording studio. This is where Williams's true cheeky-chappie persona predictably made an appearance.

'When I was told I had a meeting with Nicole Kidman the arse fell out of my world,' he says. 'I was like, "How am I going to get through this and not look like an idiot or try to lick her face?"'

'She came into the studio and she was really shy. And I was dead shy anyway, because she was coming to the studio. When she arrived I just took all her shyness and all her nerves as well and it was like a double whammy. I was falling asleep, I was that nervous!

'But she was wonderful. We got on really well and we chatted and I just had a real blast with her. Nicole has a beautiful voice and I was amazed how well we worked together. I think it really helped that we are the same height!'

'It was fun,' Nicole agrees. 'We did it very quickly one afternoon. We did the song at the same studio Sinatra recorded at, so I hope some of his aura has rubbed off on us.

'I usually get frightened when I'm singing because I'm worried about my voice. I always feel like it's going to let me down, but Robbie just threw away my fears with his enthusiasm and encouragement. I had a giggle . . .'

The recording was a great success and Williams decided almost immediately that he wanted to release it as a Christmas single. The next step was filming the accompanying video, and this time the newspapers got wind of events. The press took great pleasure in tirelessly reporting the pair's movements as they met up in London in the second week of October, worked out a story for the promo and rehearsed. They were spotted together at Ronnie Scott's, Acton's Black Island Studios, The Royal Albert Hall and, rather more suggestively, Nicole's hotel room at the Dorchester and Williams's Notting Hill home.

No stranger to manipulating the media in order to sell records, Williams (who had previously been romantically linked with Kylie Minogue during the publicity for 'Kids', and Geri Halliwell when they both had singles to promote) was all too happy to tease the press. The singer was quoted as saying: 'I love being around Nicole. If I'm perfectly frank, I am having the time of my life. I can't remember being happier.' When he was asked what they had got up to behind the doors of his home, he relayed that they had tried – and failed – to watch a DVD, as 'we couldn't concentrate on the storyline . . .' Apparently, he had even written a song about the new woman in his life, whom he described as 'cool, dead, dead genuine . . . and tremendously charismatic'.

And what was Nicole's reaction to all this feverish speculation? When the first reports surfaced, she thought it was hysterical. 'Me and Robbie? My God, are you mad? He's so funny, we wouldn't be able to stop giggling long enough to have sex!' All the same, the supposed 'relationship' certainly wasn't doing her status as an unattached *femme fatale* any harm. And as for the video clip, well: 'Robbie And Nicole Enjoy Seven Hour Session!' screamed one headline. 'Nicole and Robbie Williams have fuelled speculation amid rumours of a saucy affair. During filming their Christmas video, the two joked and messed around, turning the session into a marathon! Workers were forced to stay late, due to the delay caused by the excitable pair. Onlookers reported major chemistry between Robbie and Nicole, claiming they couldn't keep away from each other . . .'

The video for 'Somethin' Stupid' follows the fictional romance of two lovers, who meet up on a series of cosy dates and eventually liaise together in a ski lodge. Snuggling close together, they gaze adoringly into each other's eyes before stripping down to, in Nicole's case, a £5 million diamond necklace, and in Robbie's, a diamond-encrusted watch. Nicole is also seen brandishing a whip and French-kissing her man. In stark contrast to the saccharine sweetness of the single, the video was one of the raunchiest ever released.

While the rumours were enough to kickstart Nicole's latest reincarnation as a pop singer, she did her best to halt them before they got too much.

'Robbie and I have become great friends, that's all,' she insisted. 'He is talented and driven. But most of all, he's respectful of my situation as a single woman. It is hard to make friends when you can't just do anything or go anywhere because people are constantly watching you. When you try to be private, people assume you have something to hide and jump to conclusions . . . those conclusions are not always accurate.'

The new friends were to meet up several more times before the release of their duet. Williams' tour of Australia corresponded with Nicole's promotion of *The Others* in Sydney, and she attended his concert there, dancing happily in the aisles along with 12,000 other fans, and joining him for the after-show party. They were also to indulge in a Cruise-esque go-carting expedition, culminating in a race in which Williams came second and Nicole third. When 'Somethin' Stupid' reached the coveted Christmas number-one position in the U.K. charts on 17 December, all the rumours had done the trick.

'Robbie is a sweet soul and a great singer,' Nicole concludes. 'He also gives me amazing confidence. I've been breaking through my fears a lot this year and Robbie has helped me do that.'

And as for Mr Williams, he sums up: 'I know it might sound trite, but I am honoured to have Nicole on the album. She's wonderful, she's a great person. I know it sounds slushy, but she really does have the most beautiful soul of anyone I've met.'

28

I Don't Want To Conform

Some of the biggest waves made by Nicole in the U.K. were the result of her appearance on Michael Parkinson's chat show on 13 October 2001. Appearing alongside Ewan McGregor, she was her usual perky self, looking elegant in a black suit and tie with her long hair scraped off her face. Thanks to the success of her two films and tabloid stories of romps with Robbie Williams, fans could be forgiven for thinking the actress was having the time of her life, but Parkinson's gentle questions revealed a different story. Nicole was still balancing the good with the bad.

'Everyone keeps asking me all the time, "How are you?"' she said. 'Divorce is divorce and it's a really tough thing to go through. It leaves you shaken and your whole foundation is sort of a mess. And then you have to pick yourself up and move forward and that's what I'm doing. It's my journey. I didn't expect it to happen to me and it has happened. That's it.'

Obviously that wasn't quite 'it', as there were two young children to consider.

'You have those times when you say, "I just want to curl up in a ball and never get out of bed," and then you have a six-year-old coming in and going, "Where's breakfast?"' The harsh reality could sometimes prove an unexpected comfort.

Nicole was also remarkably charming in her reminiscences about her ex-husband.

'I spent eleven years with him and there's something strangely romantic about being very well known and being together which people don't understand, because you're in a fish bowl. You only have each other because nobody else really understands. So you have this bubble that you exist in together and that's quite romantic.'

Coming across very much as a modest, down-to-earth Aussie girl, Nicole was a big hit with Parkinson and everyone who tuned in to watch the show that night. The mood was further lightened when she braved the wrath of the other guest, Anne Robinson, host of *The Weakest Link*. When Nicole attempted an imitation of Robinson's trademark wink, the formidable presenter responded sternly in her best schoolmarm manner: 'That looks like a twitch.' The audience lapped it up. Notably, Nicole then slipped quietly and courteously out of her high heels to be photographed in an after-show line-up with the shorter guests.

As she was proving so popular in Britain, it came as no real surprise when Nicole announced later in the year that she was considering moving to London on a semi-permanent basis.

'I've had some good times here and the kids love being in London,' she said. 'We'll spend time in Sydney as well, but I want London to be our main home.' In happier times, the Cruises had spent some four years in England, and as a single woman Nicole relished the social aspect of the capital – the restaurants, the people and the more relaxed ambience. She even adopted the nation's fascination with football, cheering on David Beckham at the England–Greece match early in the season.

'I was envious of all that running around the pitch he did, because I'll never run again,' she said sadly. 'Once upon a time I'd run 8 miles a day and play tennis, but since I damaged my knee, I don't run.'

Nicole was also very impressed by the reputation of British schools. All this was enough to prompt her to start house-hunting, beginning in Notting Hill, Robbie Williams's stamping ground. Additionally, there was much talk of Nicole being reunited with Sam Mendes (now renowned for the award-winning film *American Beauty*) for a return to the London stage and the Donmar Warehouse. Plays bandied about as possible vehicles included Shakespeare's *Twelfth Night* and Chekhov's *Uncle Vanya* or *Three Sisters*. She also hoped to work with Trevor Nunn at the National Theatre in 2003.

★

Ironically, Nicole's social life towards the end of 2001 had never been so active. Alongside cavorting in London with Robbie Williams, Sam Mendes and his new girlfriend Kate Winslet, she was proud to present Naomi Watts with a *Movieline* Magazine Award for Breakthrough Of The Year on 27 November, following her friend's appearance in *Mulholland Drive*. Around the same time, Rebecca Rigg had her baby, having spent her final month of pregnancy *chez* Kidman, and Russell Crowe invested in a £5 million property near her Sydney home, so there was plenty going on.

Nicole was also romantically linked to Counting Crows frontman Adam Duritz, but, as they had never actually been introduced, it seemed unlikely. 'I'm supposedly dating the singer with Counting Crows and I can't even pronounce his surname,' she laughed cheerfully. 'Well, we've never met but I can tell you we're having great sex!'

The umpteen films, pop singles and public appearances began to pay off. On 13 December Nicole was named the E! Entertainment Celebrity Of The Year. This was swiftly followed by two Golden Globe nominations for Best Actress – Drama for *The Others* and Best Actress – Comedy Or Musical for *Moulin Rouge!* There were also whispers, not for the first time, of potential Oscar nominations.

But for once, Nicole was content to leave behind the starrier aspect of celebrity life and return to Australia to be with her family over Christmas. 'There's something about the place,' she says happily. 'It's the smell of the gum leaves. Australia's in my blood, it's in my humour.'

Nicole was overjoyed to be reunited with her parents. In addition, Tom had generously allowed her custody of Isabella and Conor over the holiday period, so her little world was complete.

'At the Spanish press conference for *The Others*, I was asked what my biggest fear is – I suppose it would be losing my parents,' Nicole had admitted a few weeks before her trip. 'That frightens me because they really are my force. I have very pragmatic, realistic parents who can put a whole perspective on my life and my world because they have lived. They are now sixty-two and sixty-three years old and they have that wisdom of age and have helped me.

'I think they are proud of me, I think at times they're worried. They're just very real in their reactions. Their whole thing is that I'm their daughter and they want to protect their daughter and not have her hurt. My father just kept saying, "Come home now!"'

On Nicole's return to the modest house in Longueville where her parents still live, she was comforted to find nothing had changed. 'I have always looked to my parents for inspiration,' she says. 'Their love is realistic, not the sort of kissing around ridiculously and pretending everything's great kind of relationship – that just doesn't deal with all the ups and downs of a forty-year marriage. I cherish that and I'm so glad I have that to hold up. Hopefully, one day, that might be me.'

Nicole was also delighted to catch up with her beloved eighty-six-year-old grandmother Joyce, who lives just fifteen minutes away from her famous granddaughter. 'She is amazing!' Nicole enthuses. 'She drinks Scotch, doesn't wear glasses and proudly says that she has all her own teeth. We're very close. I adore her. She took care of me when I was little and she always believed in me.'

Christmas was also a time to catch up with her children. Nicole indulged in spoiling Isabella. 'I dressed her in knee-length black dresses and chunky shoes. And her hair in braids – adorable,' says the actress. 'I admire her purity. And she's so funny. It's exciting raising her, thinking about her future and giving her wings . . . I don't know if she admires me at the moment. I think she sees me as uncool.' Maybe it was the braids.

'You do live through your children. You rediscover everything. Through the hard times, they can make you laugh – and cry. And, no matter what else is going on, they need you and keep you emotionally true.' Nicole's love of domesticity even prompted her to discuss the possibility of moving into a huge house with Antonia, Angus and their children at this time. 'I like lots of people in the house,' Nicole explains. 'I just like that feeling of family.'

By pure coincidence, Tom Cruise and Penélope Cruz flew into Sydney at the end of a promotional tour for *Vanilla Sky* on 19 December. Much was made in the press of the clash of festive plans, but Tom patiently explained that he was in fact very excited to be seeing his family again. 'I certainly don't feel any trepidation about going to Sydney,' he said. 'I love Australia. My kids are half-Australian and nothing has changed in my feelings for that country.

'What happened between Nic and me is very personal. Anyone who's ever gone through anything like that knows you're the only people who know what really happened. It's no one's business and it's time to move on.

'I'm very happy right now for Nicole and myself and for our kids. I've had some beautiful times with Nic. I'll always love her and we'll always have this family together.' Nicole's gracious response was to invite Tom to spend the Christmas period with her and their children. Penélope, who was presumably not invited, flew back to Los Angeles a couple of days later.

The erstwhile couple stayed in regular contact over the next week, and after Nicole's low-key Christmas Day excursion to Palm Beach with Isabella, Conor, and her niece Lucia, Tom took the children out on a trip around the nearby bay.

Of course, the press couldn't accept the possibility that the 'warring exes' might actually have reached a comfortable reconciliation, and immediately proposed an alternative view on why Tom might be socializing with Nicole over Christmas: obviously he was breaking it to her gently that he was about to marry Cruz. According to the *Sun*, for example, he had made the special trip to Australia to tell her the news personally – it had nothing to do with the promotional tour for *Vanilla Sky*.

This was complete nonsense. Said Tom: 'I'm enjoying myself. You don't have to get married to enjoy a relationship. I'm not ruling out marriage – in fact I think that, yeah, maybe I will get married again. But right now I have no plans for it.'

As for Penélope, she made it quite clear that, at twenty-seven, she was nowhere near being ready for the responsibilities of marriage and perhaps children. 'I'm not in that moment yet, although I love children and I come from a very close family,' she stated.*

Nicole had weathered worse storms than this, and, at the end of the year, she ably kept it all in perspective.

'This Christmas was fantastic – we were all in the house together,' she said. 'After the break-up with Tom, being with my family was the most important thing. I had been hurt and humiliated and I needed to spend time with people who loved me.

'Two thousand and one has been a horrible year for me personally and now for the world; the events that happened in America [the atrocities of 11 September] and the way in which times have changed.

'But the thing I've taken out of it all is that it's a very long life and it needs to be filled with many things besides work.' Fully restored to her old daredevil outlook, she revealed that her challenge for 2002 was to learn how to fly a helicopter. 'I'm thinking about getting my chopper licence . . . I've put it off and off . . . well, I'm just going to do it!

'The thing for this year is live for the moment, live for the day.'

The new year began with a flurry of awards and nominations for Nicole, now one of the most popular and accomplished actresses of her generation. Her hard work and vibrant performances were rewarded with a Golden Globe for Best Actress – Comedy Or Musical for her portrayal of Satine in *Moulin Rouge!* This was no mean feat against stiff competition from

* At the time of going to press, the couple have yet to prove otherwise, and in fact rumours began to circulate that they were splitting up in early April 2002.

Renée Zellweger (*Bridget Jones's Diary*) and Reese Witherspoon (*Legally Blonde*).

Show-stopping in a strapless, partially see-through, black Yves Saint Laurent dress with a daringly high split, Nicole was visibly nervous as she tearfully accepted her trophy.

'My hands are shaking,' she confessed. 'I never thought I would be in a musical, let alone win an award for one!' In her acceptance speech she thanked Ewan McGregor and Baz Luhrmann, 'the two men in my life', her parents, who had accompanied her to the ceremony, and revealed she had promised Russell Crowe he would win the Best Actor award for *A Beautiful Mind* – which he did just moments later. Presumably McGregor forgave her her lack of loyalty!

Her co-star didn't miss out, however. On 5 February he and Nicole were named Best British Actor and Best Actress respectively at the *Empire* Awards in London. The following week the pair were crowned Actor and Actress Of The Year at the London Film Critics' Circle Awards. Nicole then went on to collect a Distinguished Decade award at the ShoWest 2002 Gala Awards, held in Las Vegas in March. Sadly, she lost out on an Oscar four days later.

This was a great shame, as she had been hotly tipped for the Best Actress Award. Nicole had eventually been nominated for *Moulin Rouge!* rather than *The Others*, but she was prepared for disappointment before the event, saying, 'I remember with *To Die For*, everyone said to me, "You'll be nominated" and I kind of invested emotionally in it, and thought, "Oh cool," and then I got the phone call saying, "Sorry, it didn't happen," so I am trying not to think about that because I've never been nominated before and who knows? It may not happen. For me, it's about having a good night, I'm not obsessed with "I've got to win" – I'm just going to have a laugh.'

Unfortunately for Nicole, who had the pleasure of sporting a Bulgari choker of raw 200-carat diamonds valued at $4 million, Halle Berry won the top award. Satine was instead honoured in spirit by presenter Whoopi Goldberg, who initiated proceedings by descending from the roof on a trapeze in an outrageous *Moulin Rouge!*-style corset.

After taking six months off to recover from the tumultuous events of 2001, Nicole returned to a film set to begin work on *Dogville* in early January 2002. The beginnings of the actress's involvement in this latest project were shrouded in scandal and misinformation, somewhat typical of the controversial Danish director, Lars von Trier.

Von Trier's films had always fallen under the category of unconventional rather than mainstream. After graduating from the National Film School in the early 1980s, he went on to make such cult classics as *Element Of Crime*, *Epidemic* and *Europa*, and won the Grand Prix at Cannes in 1996 for *Breaking The Waves*. *The Idiots* notably experienced censorship problems on its release in 1998 due to a hardcore orgy sequence, which was solved by superimposing black bars over the offending body parts. The same year, von Trier's production company, Zentropa, launched a new division called Pussy Power, producing erotic films.

The director himself was notorious for being difficult. His most infamous experience had been working on *Dancer In The Dark* with Icelandic singer Björk. Their noisy on-set quarrels – during which the singer had broken down several times, once allegedly attempting to eat her costume in frustration – had spilled over into the 2000 Cannes festival, at which the film scooped the coveted Palme d'Or. Although Hollywood beckoned, sporadic attacks of agoraphobia and an intense fear of flying ensured that von Trier remained in Scandinavia, forcing actors to travel to him. To Nicole, the unusual director must have been strikingly reminiscent of one Stanley Kubrick.

Much to the actress's disbelief, von Trier had written *Dogville* specifically with her in mind. Perhaps inspired by her performance in *The Others*, her character's name was Grace.

'I'm a big fan,' she said, immensely flattered. 'I loved *Breaking The Waves* and thought *Dancer In The Dark* was magnificent. There are certain directors in your lifetime that you know you're a good match with. This is a good match.'

However, Nicole took her time signing on the dotted line. The offer to star in *Dogville* suffered from atrocious timing, as it arrived during the aftermath of the break-up with Tom. Nicole's delay prompted much controversy within the Scandinavian film industry, which was reported with relish in the Swedish newspapers. Apparently, producer Peter Aalbaek Jensen was so fed up with the lengthy negotiations that he fumed, 'It may be commonplace in major movies that stars play the diva, but we can't handle that either psychologically or financially.' After 'revelations' that Zentropa had shelved the possibility of working with Nicole, her co-star Stellan Skarsgård reportedly told *Expressen*: 'It feels nice to be rid of her. Nicole's behaviour in this case hasn't been particularly loyal to her co-workers.'

But Nicole did eventually sign up for the film in July 2001, blaming a 'miscommunication' for the setback. Then it was all smiles at the Zentropa office, with another producer, Vibeke Vindelv, commenting, 'Our lawyers in New York just told me that Nicole Kidman has signed the contract. I just talked to Lars and obviously we are both very happy.' Still, Nicole faced the embarrassment of working alongside Jensen and Skarsgård after all the spiteful tittle-tattle.

A co-production between Denmark, Norway, Finland, Sweden, Germany, Holland, Italy and France, *Dogville* had a meagre £5 million budget, yet in addition to Nicole and Skarsgård, von Trier had secured an impressive cast including Lauren Bacall, Chloë Sevigny, Katrin Cartlidge, James Caan and Ben Gazzara.

A psychological drama set in the 1930s, *Dogville* tells the tale of Grace, who arrives to the sound of gunshots in the small woodland town of the title in America's Rocky Mountains. The citizens of Dogville are pleasant, law-abiding citizens, but Grace is about to change all that through her relationship with Tom, an eccentric philosopher and author. Details of the full story have remained vague so far, but it is said to comprise disturbing undertones with an unpleasant conclusion. Said Nicole at the outset: 'It's about faith. But it's hard to define before we've shot it.'

Taking up residence in a rather basic hotel near Trollhättan, just outside Gothenburg, Nicole's first overwhelming experience of Sweden was the freezing fog. Surrounding herself with a handful of books and her trusty Nina Simone CDs, she felt very much alone and looked forward to the arrival of Isabella and Conor a few weeks later. 'I like to shut down when I do a film, so this place is perfect because it is so remote,' she said.

Shooting took place between 7 January and 1 March in a recently refurbished sixty-room studio in Trollhättan. Filmed exclusively indoors (which at least insured insulation from the bitterly low temperatures outside), the intense drama apparently only used very few props as von Trier experimented with heightening the atmosphere via a variety of other artistic means.

Bearing in mind von Trier's unpredictable temperament, Nicole must have felt some trepidation when he began to invite her on long secret walks in the fog. 'I'm not quite sure what he's up to, but I know I'm embarking on a real adventure,' she said in an interview conducted during filming. 'It's terrifying and fascinating. We just talk and talk. He's very intense. He likes to hold my hands between his . . .

'I go into everything open. Any director is manipulative and you have to accept that.' Those long walks were given a bizarre twist by the *Daily Mail*, who reported that the director was taking advantage of the location's isolation. An 'insider' allegedly told the paper that von Trier took Nicole into the woods early on and told her, 'I don't like you. The reason I don't like you is that you are richer than me and I want to fuck you.' Obviously the problem would be solved if Nicole would kindly part with her earnings and sleep with him. One can only imagine what the no-nonsense Australian thought upon reading that story.

As news continued to filter out about *Dogville*'s progress, the world also learned that Nicole had apparently fought back so violently during the filming of an unpleasant rape scene that the 'rapist' was covered in bruises. Some might query why Nicole would take on such an unpalatable and low-paid role when she could easily make a fortune headlining a mainstream blockbuster, but the actress's worthy motivations, formed when she was a teenage television star, remained unchanged.

'I don't want to be normal, I *want* to do strange and experimental things,' she stressed. 'I could do huge commercial things like *Men In Black II*. Studios think I'm out of my mind. I think I'm out of my mind. And I want to stay out of my mind. I don't want to conform.'

Indeed, the world can rest assured that Nicole Kidman will never conform. Shortly after the American premiere of another unconventional Kidman movie, *Birthday Girl*, at the Sundance Film Festival in Utah, she embarked on another project, *The Human Stain*, on 23 March.

Based on the novel of the same name by Pulitzer Prize-winner Philip Roth, the film is set in 1998, in the wake of the Clinton impeachment scandal. In a small New England town, a seventy-one-year-old college professor (played by sixty-three-year-old Anthony Hopkins) is forced into retirement when his colleagues wrongfully accuse him of being a racist. In a further twist, the professor himself is in fact a very pale black man, but has spent his entire life passing himself off as Jewish. The allegation leads to other revelations about his past, including an adulterous love affair with Faunia Farley (Nicole), a ferociously independent young caretaker. As the movie supposedly includes nude love scenes, much hype ensued about the twenty-nine-year age gap between the leading actors.

For Nicole, it was a welcome opportunity to reconvene with the director Robert Benton, who had been so encouraging back in the days of *Billy Bathgate*, welcoming her into the crazy world of American movies. With two such dynamic actors in the lead roles and a script adapted by Nicholas Meyer, who had written the similarly intriguing *Sommersby*, *The Human Stain* is set to be a guaranteed ratings-grabber.

The final word therefore goes to Nicole's most recent director. Says Benton: 'She is truly one of the most amazing actors I've ever worked with.'

EPILOGUE

A Fun-Loving Aussie Girl Who Just Happens To Be Famous

Incredibly for such an accomplished actress, Nicole Kidman only celebrated her thirty-fifth birthday in June 2002. The youthful, glamorous, award-winning star has the world at her feet and plans to exploit her new-found freedom to pick and choose her next screen role.

'Most of my choices were based around somebody else's schedule,' she says pointedly of her lesser decisions. 'Now that I've got to support myself? I love theatre. I love art films. Different things are available to me. I've got a very different life now.'

In fact, the artiste has many ideas about projects she would like to tackle and people with whom she would like to work.

'In the future what I would really love to do is an epic love story. It's fun doing love stories. But I've got to get offered it first!

'I love passion and dedication. I love people like David O'Russell and Spike Jonze. I'd love to work with Angelina Jolie – we've talked about it. And Russell Crowe and I will do something eventually.' Nicole continues to cite Katharine Hepburn as her role model. 'I'd love to make a movie as an ode to her. I just need to find someone good enough to write it.'

Despite Nicole's pleas for assistance in this direction, evidently a lack of potential parts is no longer a problem. These days, the actress wades through a veritable sea of scripts and the roll call of titles she has recently turned down is almost longer than her considerable CV.

Over the last year or so, it has been reported she has turned down Alan Parker's *Life Of David Gale* and George Clooney's directorial debut, *Confessions Of A Dangerous Mind*. It is also unlikely she will play Eleanor of Aquitaine in *Court And Spark*, or appear in *The Painted Veil*, which will be directed by Gillian Armstrong – who made the 'Bop Girl' video that Nicole graced with her fifteen-year-old presence back in 1983. Another picture tenuously linked with the Kidman name was Columbia Pictures' *Other Powers*, in which she would have played the turn-of-the-century suffragette and free-love advocate Victoria Woodhull.

While Nicole has been in discussions with Sam Mendes and Trevor Nunn about a possible return to the London stage since 2001, Baz Luhrmann is reportedly very keen to take *Moulin Rouge!* to Broadway, preferably starring his original leading lady.

One concrete project is Anthony Minghella's forthcoming *Cold Mountain*, a drama set in the American Civil War in which she will star with Renée Zellweger and Jude Law; Minghella and Law have previously won awards for their work together on *The Talented Mr Ripley*. All three actors signed up for *Cold Mountain* in early April 2002.

Throughout her career, Nicole has repeatedly suffered panic attacks prior to her more demanding roles, and to this day admits she has never been completely satisfied with her performance – *Moulin Rouge!* being the one exception.

'I think it looks like I'm acting and it's a bad thing,' she says of *The Others*. 'I can only see my films once, and then I never see them again. I usually sit next to somebody and talk through the whole movie to distract them – especially when I know a big scene is coming up.' Considering that the actress now commands more than $10 million per film, it's surprising that she cannot recognize her own extraordinary ability.

In spite of her much-praised bravery, Nicole admits there is a downside to forever being in the public eye.

'You wonder if becoming dinner-party fodder is worth the joy you receive from acting,' she says. 'At times it isn't and at times it is. I still say that my love for what I do outweighs all the other things.

'There may come a time when I say, "This isn't working anymore – I don't want to do it." It can be hard, but I believe if you stay true to the reason you went into the industry and be pure to the choices you make, then that *will* outweigh all the other things. Sometimes I wish I had chosen to be a director because you stay anonymous but can still be very creative and do something you really enjoy.'

With this in mind, and following in the footsteps of many Hollywood greats before her, Nicole is increasingly interested in working behind the camera. After acquiring the screen rights to *In The Cut* with Jane Campion back in 1996, heavyweights Miramax and Universal initially agreed to co-finance the movie with a $20 million budget, but this changed when the project was picked up by Pathé International. Campion plans to start filming in New York as soon as the screenplay is finished, with Nicole acting as executive producer. Meg Ryan's is the name most frequently suggested as the film's heroine.

But acting, movies and production make up only one side of the multi-faceted Australian, and Nicole has much more to achieve than just gaining her helicopter pilot's licence.

'I still dabble in everything,' she says. 'I believe the experiences of life are more important than any film you make. I'd love to get a degree in philosophy and I'm adapting a book into a screenplay. I'm exploring other things.

'When I was married and living in L.A., I was *married* – that was my commitment. Primarily I was a wife and mother. Tom's career came first.

'Then, when we split up, everything changed. Now I don't have the kids all the time. So I have to think, OK, I'm going to delve into all the ideas and literature and things that I put on hold, because now I have the chance to explore them.'

Motherhood, naturally, remains her top priority. 'It takes a lot of understanding and a lot of work,' she smiles, 'but it's one of the most fascinating things to do: to raise children and give them experiences, love, encouragement – basically to teach them to go out into the world.

'They are still my driving force.'

Looking back, one of Nicole's greatest achievements has been overcoming being physically 'different' and continually propelling herself forward in her quest for approval. From her daringly upfront performance in *Spring Awakening* at just fourteen, to laying her career on the line in *The Portrait Of A Lady*, to her string of avant-garde ventures, to speaking so candidly of her misery in 2001 – underneath, she still sees herself as the gangly girl with freckles and frizzy hair, abandoned on the dance floor.

'My whole life I've tried to push through fear,' she says. 'It's strange. I've chosen the worst career. I was the kid who didn't want to get on the school bus and walk down it, carrying my school bag, and having boys look at me. But I'd do it. That's the weird part of my personality. I don't run away from things. I push myself into them.'

As a green twenty-one-year-old, eight months before this very desire turned her whole life upside down, she made a startlingly mature observation.

'Do you know, I'm always scared that one day I'll look back and say, "God, they were the best years of my life and now what?" There are moments when you feel as if you have been blessed for a while, moments when you think this is perfect, moments when you start to believe that – even for an hour, even for a year – it might all happen . . . So I'm determined to keep making it get better and better.'

The young actress went on to watch her world 'get better' beyond her wildest dreams, but one of the most outstanding things about Nicole Kidman is that success has never changed her.

Says Denny Lawrence, one of her many directors: 'A final comment from me is that, in later years, when I was Chairman of the Australian Film Institute, and asked Nicole to come back and present an award for us, she was only too pleased. She remains the same straightforward, unspoiled and most professional person she always was – never forgetting old friends and colleagues.'

Baz Luhrmann continues to marvel at her sheer strength and endurance. 'You never know what's going to happen with Nicole,' he says. 'That's why, within a year, she's gone from being the "king's wife" to one of the most interesting actors on the planet. Everyone wants her. She's so damned magnetic and great to be around.'

David Hare agrees: 'She has a quality of seeming intimate which makes audiences want to know her.'

Nicole has never been afraid to show her vulnerability, something which has endeared her to fans and critics alike. Despite the string of awards she won for *Moulin Rouge!*, she recently divulged, 'At the moment, I don't feel that admirable. It's a really tough world. But I don't like to hide away. To live a really full life, you must stay open.

'In the end, I hope I've done some unusual films and kept my very public life private, quiet and dignified.' Certainly she has always championed challenging work and, while she hasn't always succeeded on the counts of privacy and prudence, there is no question that Nicole Kidman's dignity remains fully intact.

'I can tell you, this woman has guts, as we say in Australia,' Luhrmann concludes. 'She has guts.'

Curriculum Vitae

Films are listed in the order of shooting; the date is of release.

Spring Awakening	Theatre	1981
Bush Christmas		
aka *Prince And The Great Race*	TV film	1983
BMX Bandits aka *Shortwave*	TV film	1983
Chase Through The Night	TV mini-series	1984
'Bop Girl'	Music video	1983
Winners (episode: 'Room To Move')	TV mini-series	1985
Matthew & Son	TV film	1984
A Country Practice		
(episode: 'Repairing The Damage')	TV series	1984
Wills & Burke	Film	1985
Five Mile Creek (episodes 28–39)	TV series	1984
Archer's Adventure (aka *Archer*)	Film	1985
Windrider	Film	1986
Vietnam	TV mini-series	1986
Nightmaster (aka *Watch The Shadows Dance*)	Film	1987
Un'Australiana A Roma		
(aka *An Australian In Rome*)	Film	1987

Dead Calm	Film	1989
The Bit Part	TV film	1989
Emerald City	Film	1989
Steel Magnolias	Theatre	1988
Bangkok Hilton	TV mini-series	1989
Flirting	Film	1991
Days Of Thunder	Film	1990
Billy Bathgate	Film	1991
Far And Away	Film	1992
Malice	Film	1993
My Life	Film	1993
Batman Forever	Film	1995
To Die For	Film	1995
The Portrait Of A Lady	Film	1996
The Leading Man	Film	1996
The Peacemaker	Film	1997
Eyes Wide Shut	Film	1999
Practical Magic	Film	1998
The Blue Room	Theatre	1998–9
Birthday Girl	Film	2002
Moulin Rouge!	Film	2001
The Others	Film	2001
The Hours	Film	2003
Dogville	Film	2003
The Human Stain	Film	2003
Cold Mountain	Film	2003

Index